IMAGES
of America

TACOMA

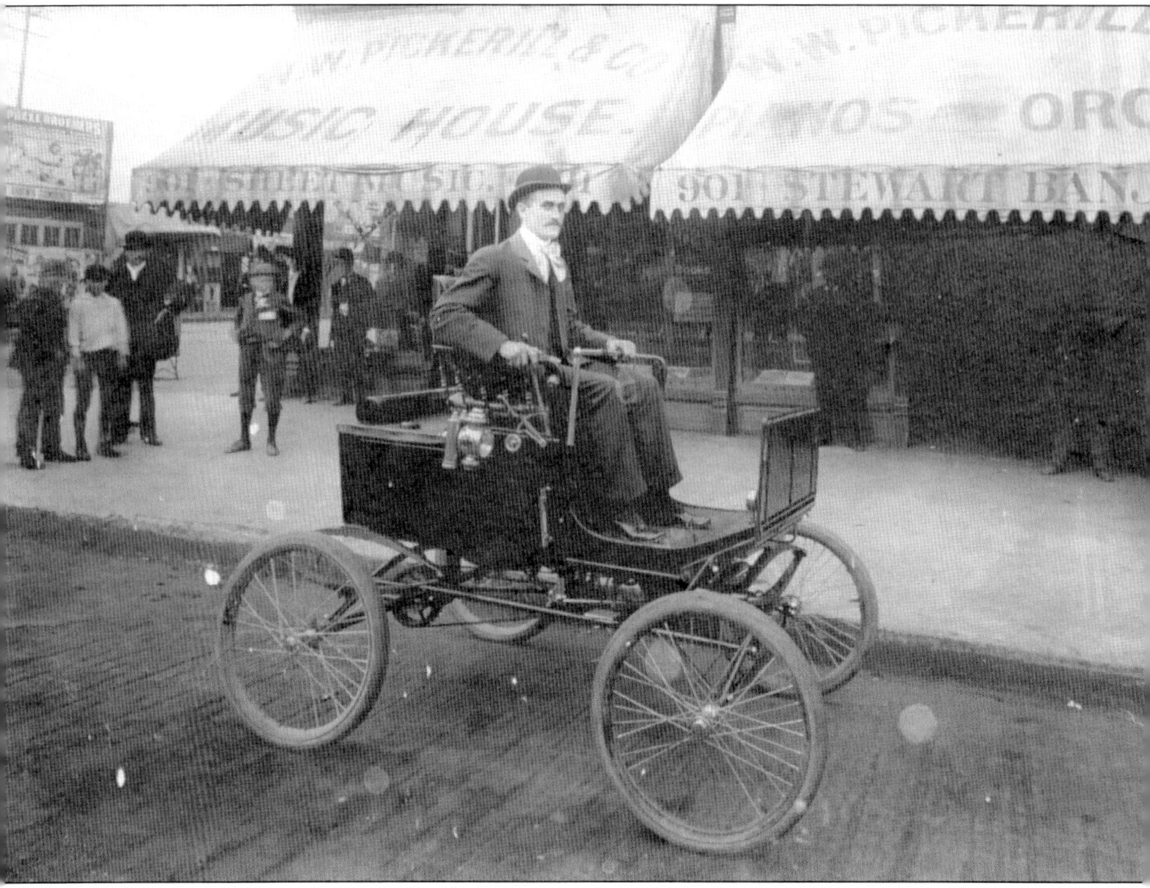

W.W. Pickerill is shown with the first automobile in Tacoma, which he purchased for $750. It was the summer of 1899 when this four-horsepower Locomobile made its appearance in front of the W.W. Pickerill & Co. Music House. Crowds gathered to see the wagon that ran without horses. (Courtesy Tacoma Public Library.)

On the Cover: These construction crew members atop the first Narrows Bridge across Puget Sound are very proud of their progress. This photograph was taken on March 21, 1940, and the bridge opened for traffic on July 1. It collapsed due to high winds and design flaws on November 7. The replacement bridge was not opened until October 14, 1950. (Courtesy Tacoma Public Library.)

IMAGES
of America

TACOMA

Donald R. Tjossem

ARCADIA
PUBLISHING

ISBN 978-1-4671-0312-1

Published by Arcadia Publishing
Charleston, South Carolina

Printed in the United States of America

Library of Congress Control Number: 2018961607

For all general information, please contact Arcadia Publishing:
Telephone 843-853-2070
Fax 843-853-0044
E-mail sales@arcadiapublishing.com
For customer service and orders:
Toll-Free 1-888-313-2665

Visit us on the Internet at www.arcadiapublishing.com

This book is dedicated to the early Tacoma photographers, whose efforts, dedication, tenacity, and pioneering spirit made this book possible. Their works are held by the Tacoma Public Library and are available for public viewing. The staff of the Northwest Room has always been helpful to any inquiries from the public and authors during their research. To these people, who preserve Tacoma's history, this publication is dedicated.

Contents

Acknowledgments

I would like to acknowledge the Northwest Room of the Tacoma Public Library for opening their digital files for public download and use in a publication such as this. Especially, I would like to thank Brian Kamens and Ilona Perry of the Tacoma Public Library Northwest Room for their help in this project. My wife, Becky Alexander, also deserves special mention as she reviewed my writings and made the flow better than my rough draft. Erin Vosgien, Caroline Anderson, and Jim Kempert, editors at Arcadia Publishing, have both been of great help in guiding me from the conception of this book to its final publication. It would not have happened without them.

All images are courtesy of Tacoma Public Library unless otherwise noted.

INTRODUCTION

Native Americans were well established in the Puget Sound and Tacoma area long before "first contact," as historians like to say. Without their initial acceptance of and help to the first Europeans exploring the area, Tacoma may not exist. They taught early settlers how to catch salmon, irrigate the land, protect themselves from animals, and wear the right clothing for the climate. The environment was much different than what early settlers came from, and the indigenous peoples had been living there successfully for thousands of years.

It was in 1792 that Capt. George Vancouver of the British Navy visited Tacoma from a camp near Dash Point. In 1824, the Hudson's Bay Company explored the area, and later, in 1833, the company established Nisqually House near what is presently called DuPont for trading purposes. This was reported to be the first European trading post on Puget Sound. Nisqually House was closed in 1869. In 1930, the trading post was rebuilt at Point Defiance Park, where two of its original buildings have been restored and are now National Historic Landmark buildings.

Capt. Charles Wilkes of the US Navy visited what is now Tacoma and named Commencement Bay in 1841. Job Carr made his initial claim on what is now called Old Tacoma in 1868. At that time, Old Tacoma was called Commencement City but was changed to Tacoma shortly after.

As early as 1834, Dr. Samuel Bancroft Barlow, a physician from Granville, Massachusetts, wrote about the government building a railroad from New York to the mouth of the Columbia River. This idea eventually was realized when the Northern Pacific Railroad determined that its transcontinental terminus would be Tacoma in 1873. This quickly led to the incorporation of Tacoma on November 12, 1875. The names of Tacoma City, Tacoma, and New Tacoma had been variously used to describe the new settlement before the formalization of its name.

By 1880, the population of Tacoma was 1,098, and Thomas Theodore Hosmer was named its first mayor in 1882. Incorporation and the fact that the Northern Pacific Railway was building a new headquarters building caused an increase in the population to 36,006 by 1890, as indicated by the first census after Washington became a state in 1889.

With the turn of the century in 1900, much activity was taking place in Tacoma when the population stood at 37,714. This was the year Weyerhaeuser was founded in a small office with three employees. In 1905, the Northern Pacific Hospital was built, and Stadium High School was founded in 1906. By 1910, Tacoma's population had increased to 83,743.

Construction on Union Station was started in 1909 and completed in 1911. The year 1916 brought the citizen approval of a military base near American Lake, which has now evolved to Joint Base Lewis McChord (JBLM). By 1917, World War I brought many new residents to Tacoma, as the industrial boom came to the region's lumber mills and shipyards on the tide flats. The Port of Tacoma was created in 1918, and by 1920, the population had increased to 96,985.

The time between World War I and World War II was a quiet time that included the Great Depression starting in 1929. In 1940, the buildup for World War II helped the economy with the building of the Narrows Bridge and the development of the shipyards.

Tacoma agreed to join Seattle financially in establishing an airport between the two cities. The result was Sea-Tac airport, which opened in 1944 and is presently owned by the Port of Seattle. By 2017, it was the 31st busiest airport in the world and 9th busiest in the United States, serving over 46 million passengers that year. By 1950, Tacoma's population had increased to 143,673.

The years following World War II saw urban renewal in Tacoma that included new schools, port development, parking garages, the second Narrows Bridge, and Interstate 5. This activity took place while the pace of shipbuilding and other military activity slowed down in peacetime. By 1970, the population of Tacoma had increased to 154,407.

The Tacoma Dome opened in 1983 and started the serious renovation of cultural structures for Tacoma. The University of Washington opened its Tacoma branch in 1990, the Museum of Glass opened in 2002, the Tacoma Art Museum opened in 2003, and the new convention center opened in 2004. Along with a renovation of many downtown buildings and improvements to the Port of Tacoma, the LeMay–America's Car Museum was opened in 2012. The Foss Waterway Museum and the Children's Museum of Tacoma are also in the central downtown area.

Today, the population of Tacoma is over 210,000, and future growth and development appears certain. The old "aroma of Tacoma" is long gone and only remembered by seasoned residents or visitors to the area. The smelter is gone, and fine condominiums, restaurants, and other facilities line Commencement Bay on Ruston Way in Old Town.

This book shows only a fraction of the diverse, interesting history of Tacoma. The purpose is to show the variety of activity, culture, diversity, and development of the city. There is no attempt to make this a chronological history, only an effort to share interesting images from the past.

One

Indigenous Peoples

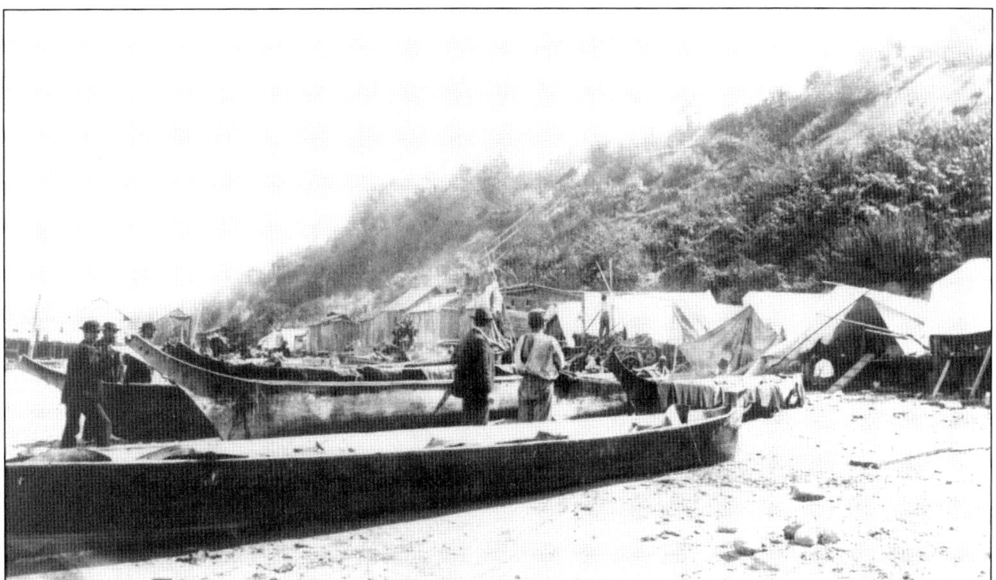

This image documents the early blending of the newer Americans with the indigenous peoples of Tacoma. Suited men in derby hats are going ashore at a village, believed to be south of the James Williams cannery in Old Tacoma. It is estimated this photograph was taken in 1885.

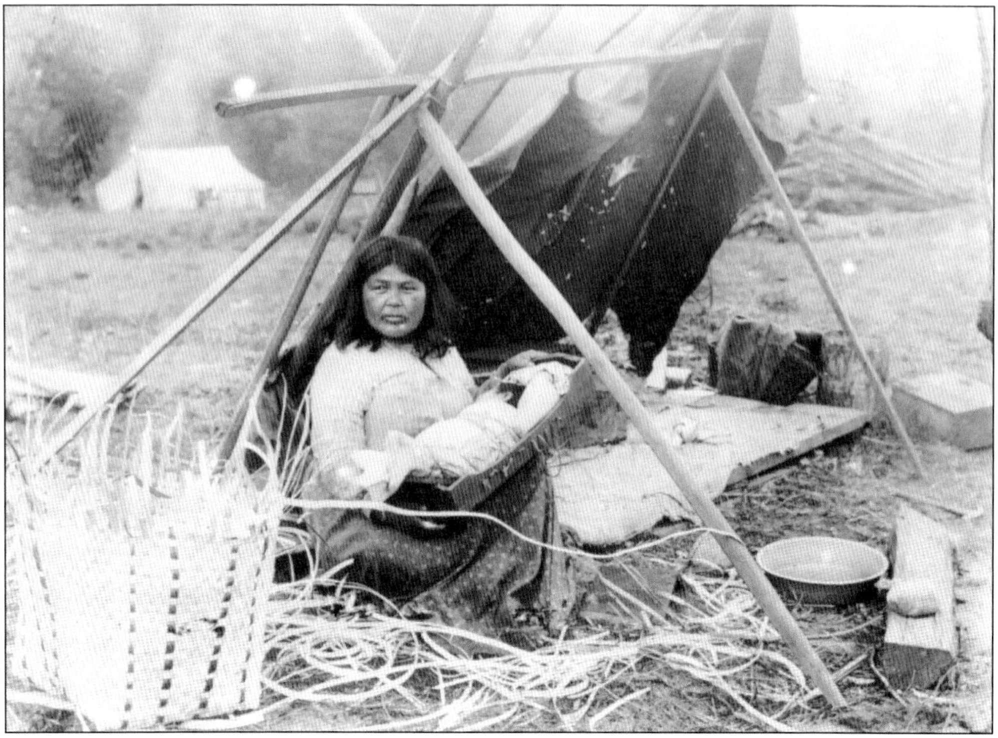

This Native American hop picker and child were photographed shortly after the turn of the 20th century. The baby is held in a wooden cradle. The shelter shown was typical of what was used in the fields while hops were being harvested. The Tacoma area and Puyallup Valley had many hop fields before weather and disease eliminated the industry.

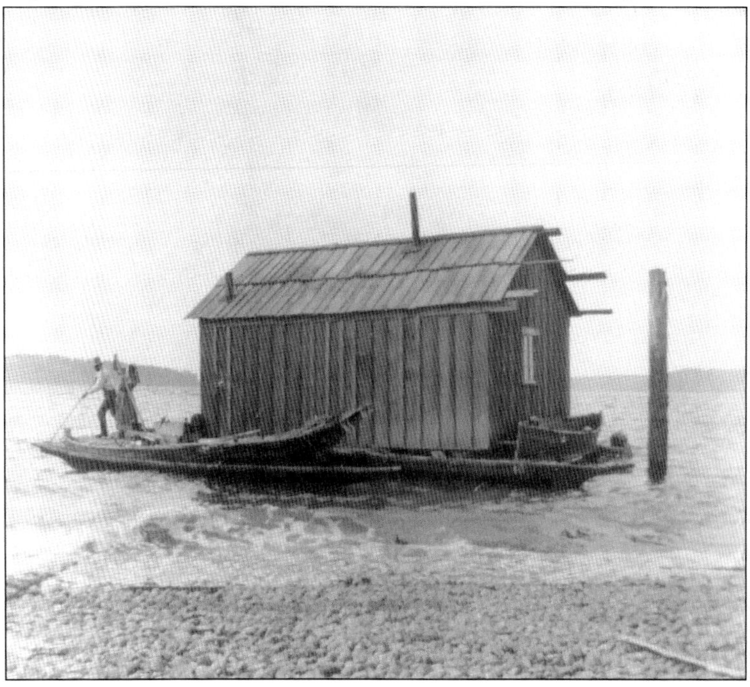

"Indian Annie" and her son John are shown aboard their new houseboat, which was a Christmas gift from friends around 1906. This house was gifted to them after their previous home had been destroyed by fire and they lived in a tepee on a Puget Sound beach. They were descendants of Chief Steilacoom.

Jerry Meeker of the Puyallup Tribe is shown cooking salmon in the Native American style for 1,500 Masons in Tacoma for their 1930 national convention. Meeker originated the Brown's Point clambake (later salmon bake) in 1912, which became a longtime tradition in the Tacoma area. Meeker Middle School in northeast Tacoma was named for him in 1958.

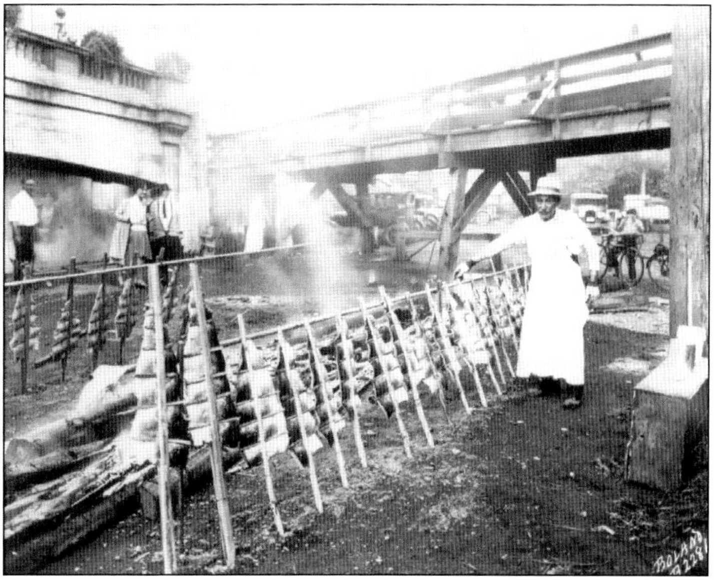

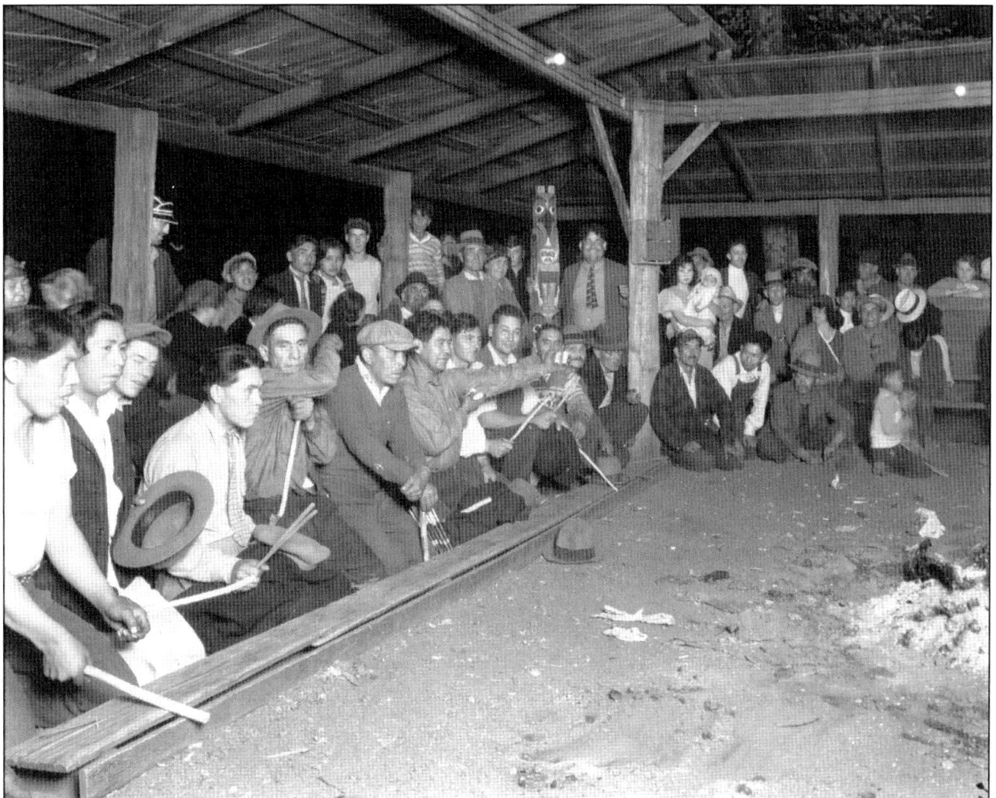

Northwest Native American tribes gathered annually near Puyallup for the harvest of hops, and this would normally include rounds of the Indian bone game. The game is played with four small white bones, which are passed rapidly from player to player, accompanied by pounding of sticks and tom-toms along with the chanting of ancient songs. These games would often go on for hours.

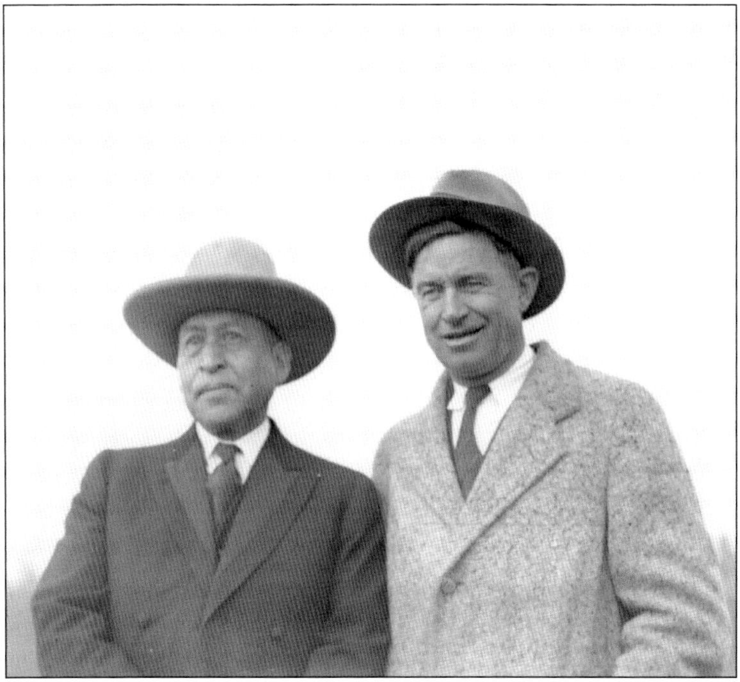

Puyallup Indian leader Henry Sicade (left) is shown with Will Rogers, an Oklahoma native who was part Cherokee. Sicade was a life member of the Puyallup Council and served on the board of state education for Indian scholarships. He was a chief of the Puyallup Tribe, served as president of the Pierce County Pioneers, and was a member of the Fife School District Board for more than 25 years.

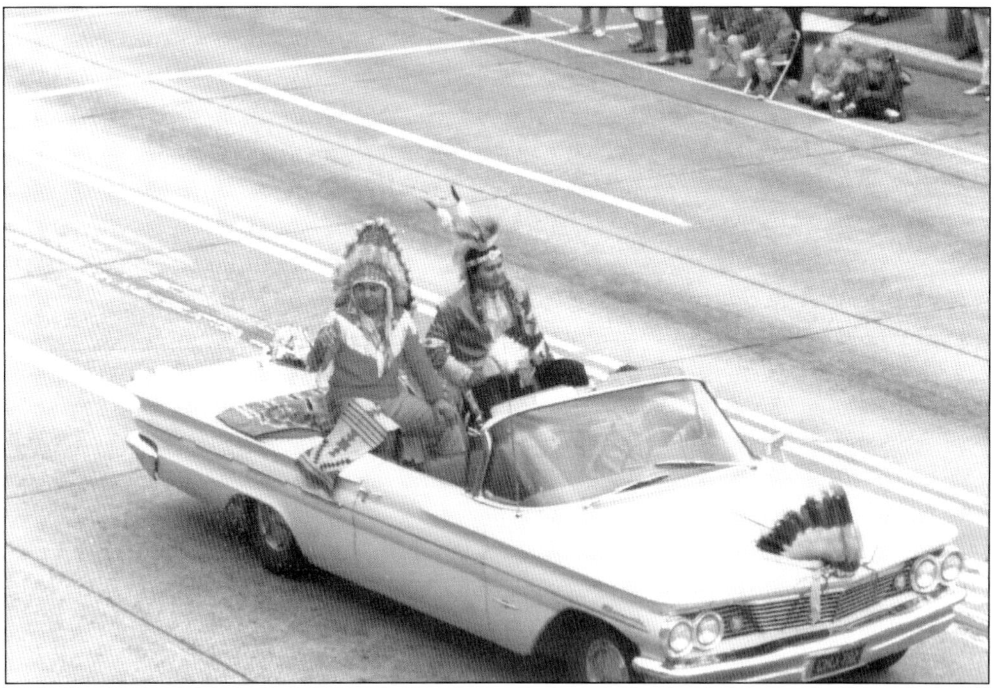

In 1969, when Tacoma had its 100th-anniversary celebration, which lasted eight days, there was a grand parade down Pacific Avenue in June. Shown here is Chief Robert "Bob" Satiacum of the Puyallup Tribe of Indians, waving to the crowds during the centennial parade. Satiacum is seated on the left, wearing a full headdress. Chief Satiacum was well known as an Indian rights activist and an advocate for fishing rights of the Native Americans. He passed away in British Columbia in 1991 at the age of 62.

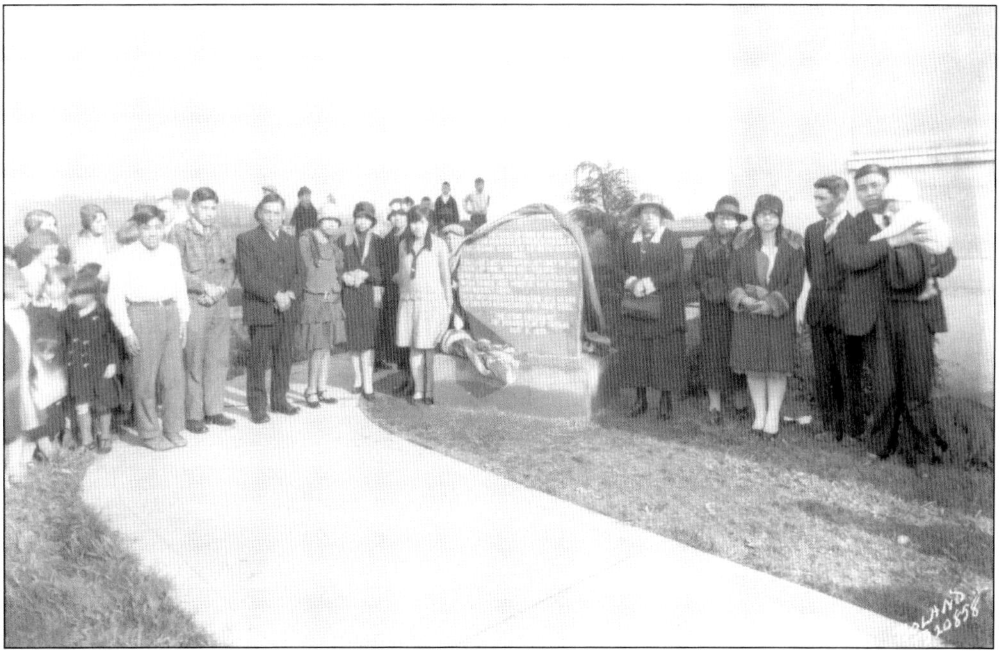

This marker on the grounds of Fife High School honors the Puyallup Tribe and Thomas Lane, their last chief, along with tribal member Henry Sicade. This presentation was made by the Women's Study Club of Tacoma on May 9, 1929, and was attended by several hundred people. Lane (1852–1905) was also known as Chief Inoyoupkin. Henry Sicade (1866–1938) was recognized for his promotion of education and tribal advancement.

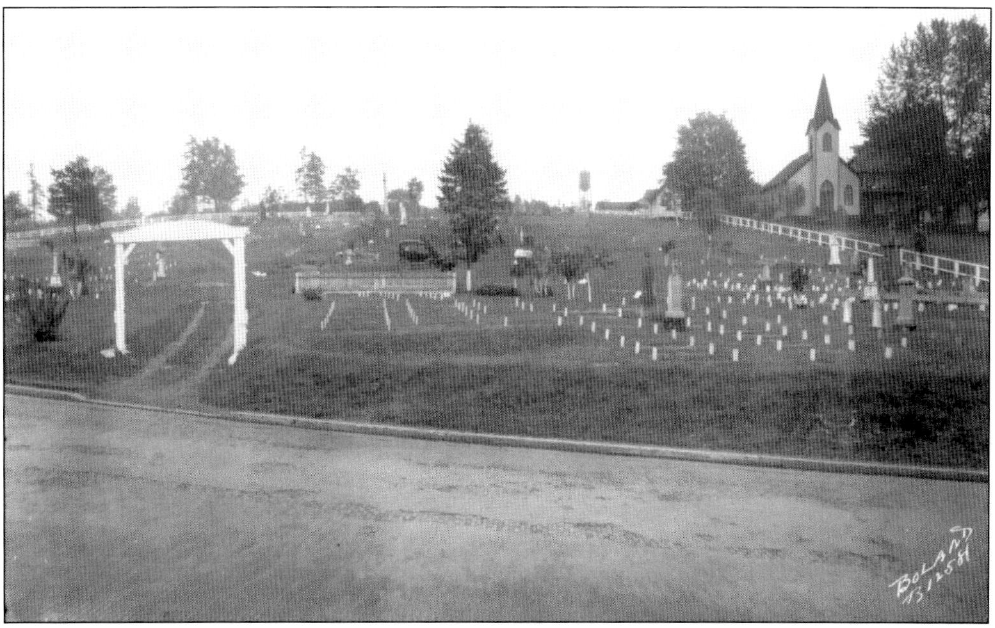

This is the Puyallup Indian cemetery located at 2002 E. Twenty-Eighth Street near what was the Cushman Veterans Hospital in May 1925. There were about 2,000 graves at that time, with many that had been obliterated. Presently, high stone walls of river rock surround the cemetery rather than the low white fences seen here.

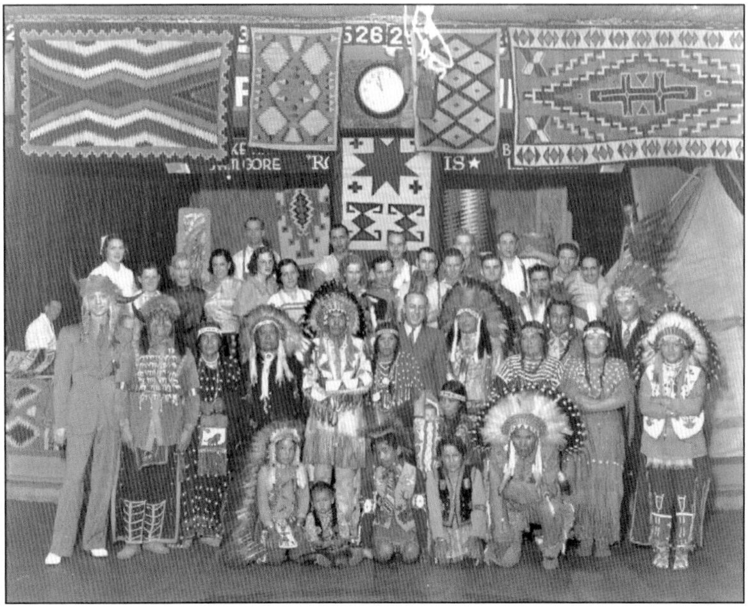

Chief White Eagle conducted a Native American wedding for So-To-Le-O and groom Que-Le-Ales at the Century Ballroom in Fife in 1936. Five different tribes participated in this wedding, which was held in conjunction with a walkathon that was heavily attended by citizens of Tacoma and Seattle. The backdrop is made up of tribal blankets.

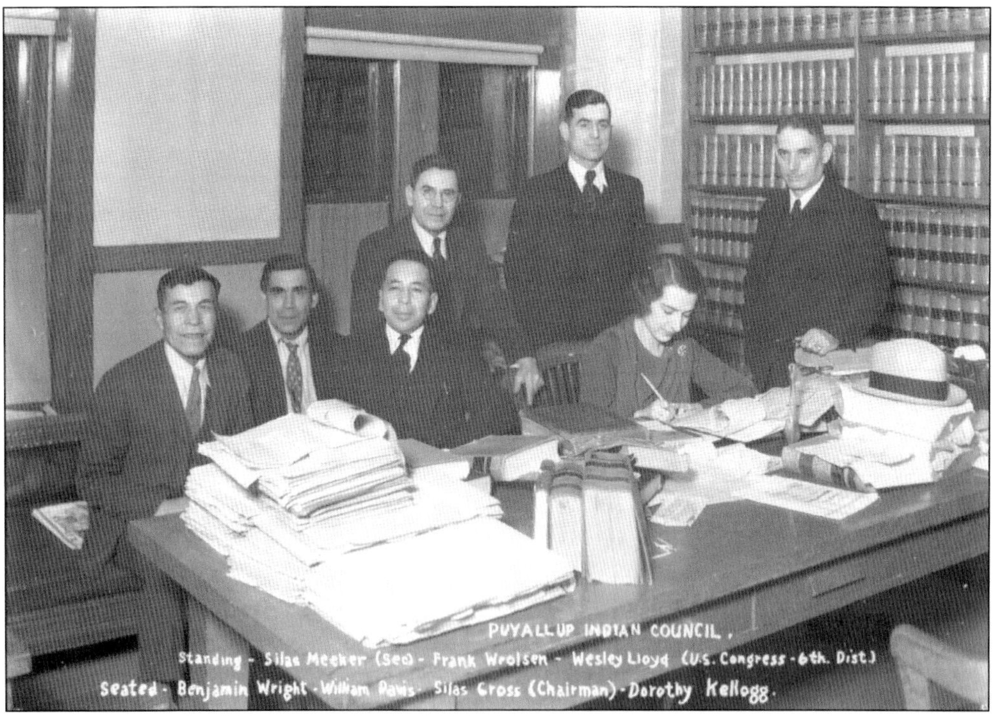

In February 1933, US representative Wesley Lloyd met with the Puyallup Tribal Council when it was urging the federal government to purchase the Tacoma Indian Hospital and build a new facility. The new hospital was finally completed in 1943. From left to right are (first row, seated) Benjamin Wright, William Davis, Silas Cross (tribal chairman), and Dorothy Kellogg (assistant to Representative Lloyd); (second row, standing) Silas Meeker (tribal secretary), Frank Wrolson, and Representative Lloyd.

Two

The Early Years

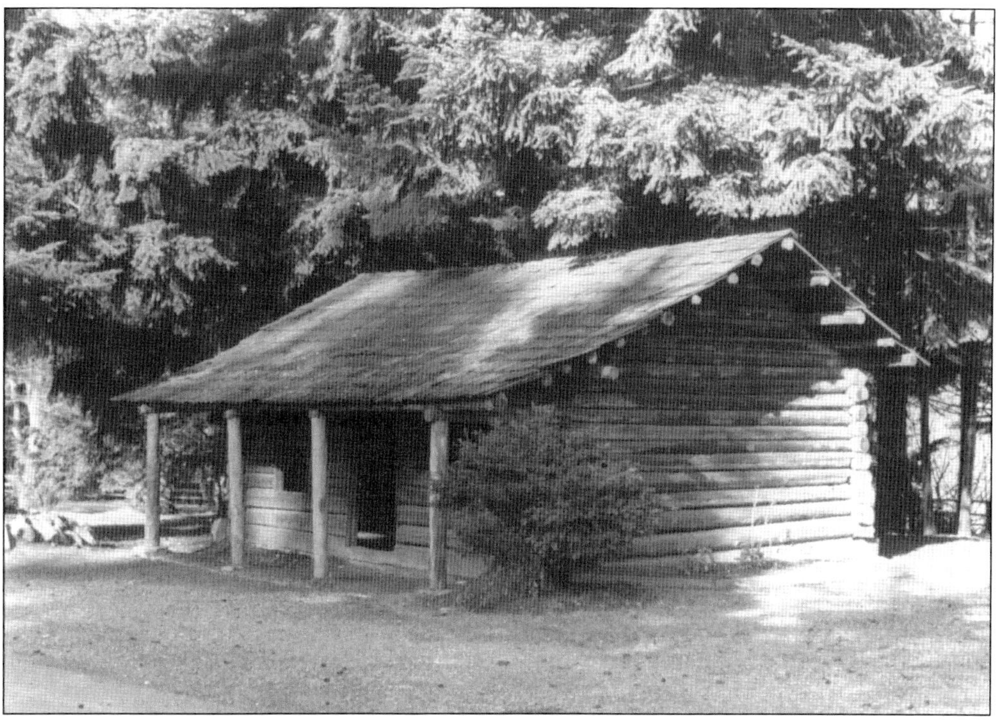

Job Carr was Tacoma's first permanent settler and lived in this cabin near the beach between what was then Carr and McCarver Streets. Carr's son Anthony assisted him in building the cabin in 1865. In 1900, the actual cabin was moved to Point Defiance Park, until it had to be destroyed due to deterioration in the 1980s. A replica of the cabin was built in 2000 within a few yards of where it was originally built, at 2350 North Thirtieth Street in Old Town, and is now a museum.

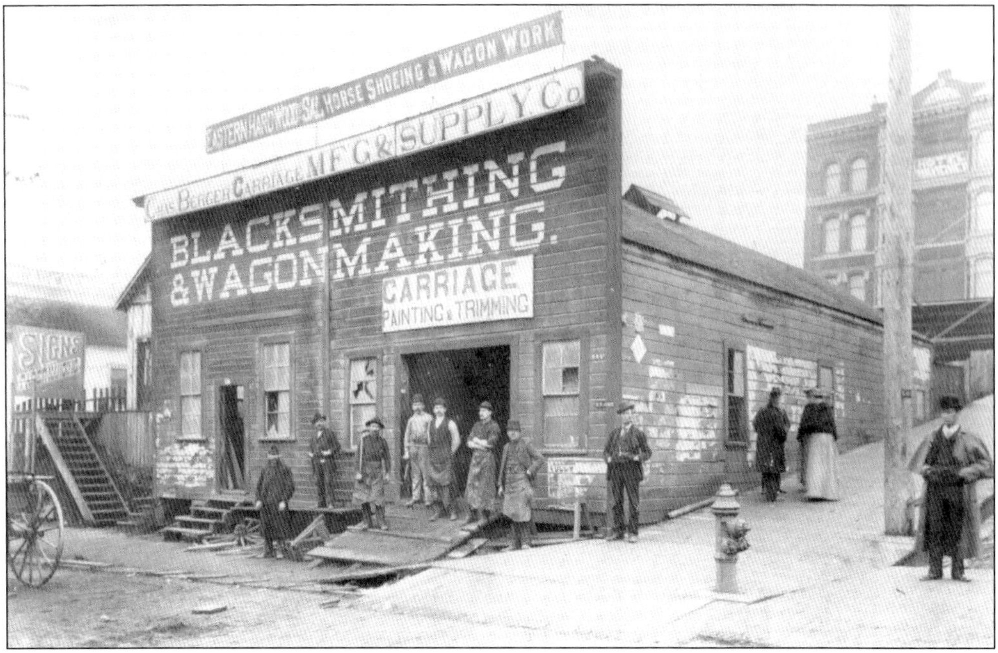

The Charles Berger Carriage Manufacturing & Supply Company conducted business at Fifteenth and Commerce Streets in the 1890s. Sidewalks made of boards can be seen running down the hill with the Waverley Hotel visible in the background to the right. Besides blacksmithing, these employees, some in leather aprons, made and repaired wagons.

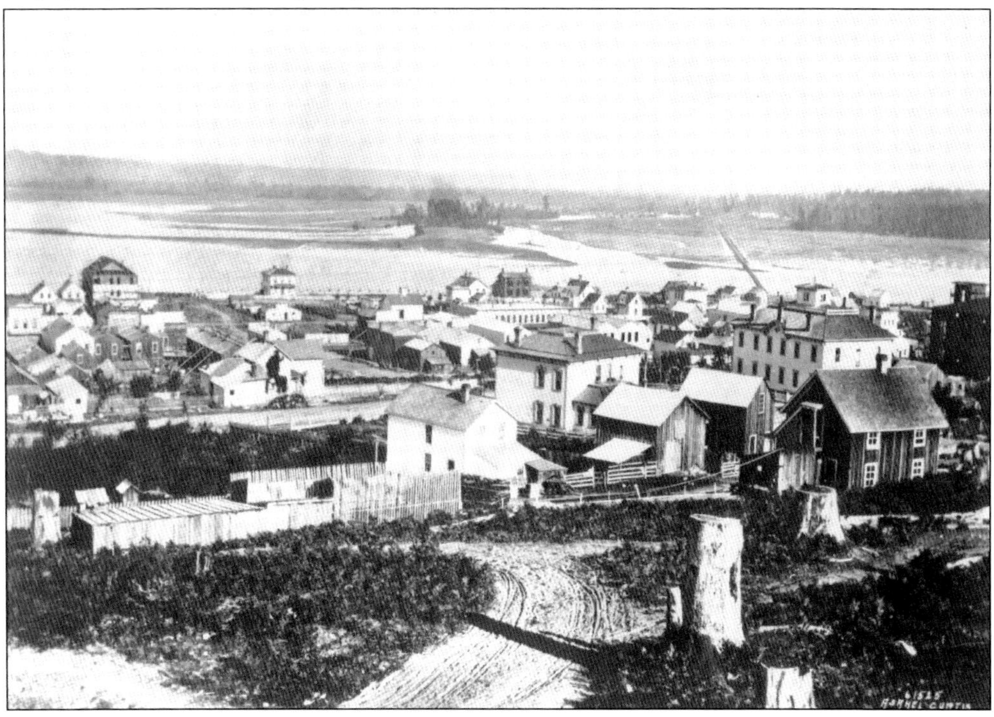
This photograph from 1881 was taken from what is now the 800 block of Fawcett Avenue, the dirt road in front of the two-story white house in the foreground.

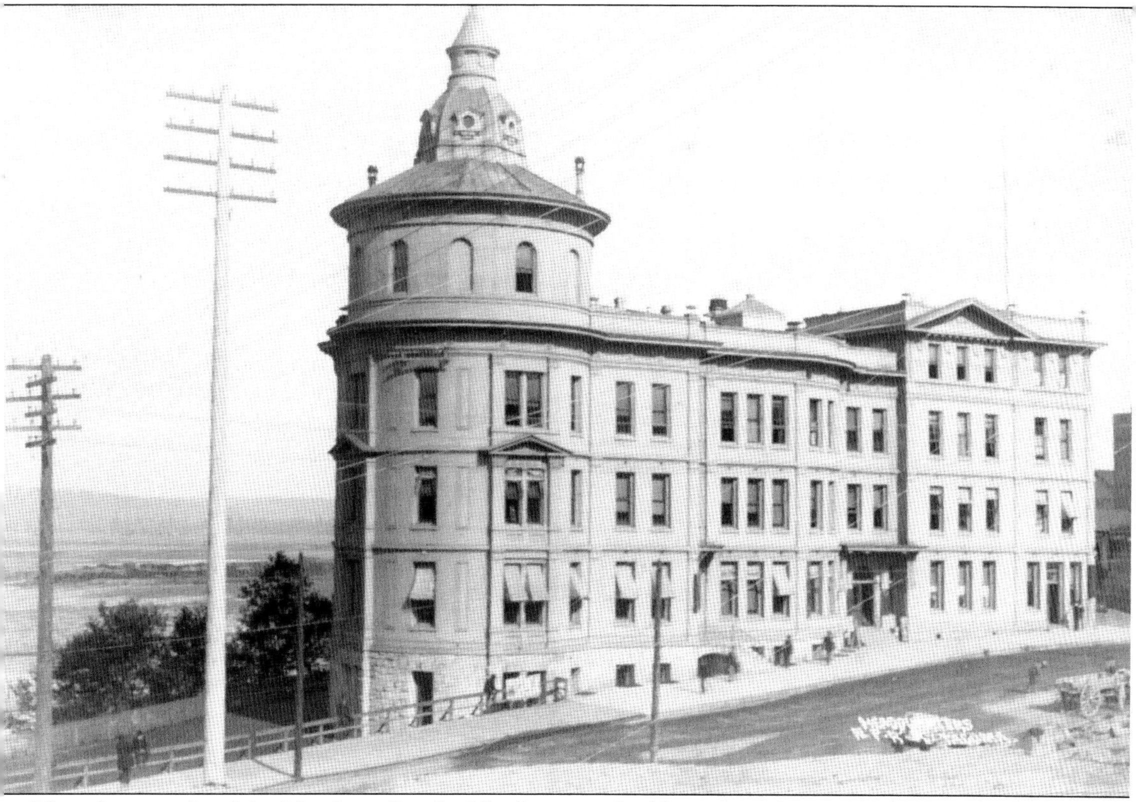

This photograph of the Northern Pacific Headquarters building was taken around 1889 at 621 Pacific Avenue, where it stands to this day. It originally had 53 office and storerooms and 19 vaults that were used by the Tacoma Land Company, Weyerhaeuser Company, and the Northern Pacific. This building was eventually sold to the City of Tacoma in 1922. It is listed in the National Register of Historic Places and is part of the Old City Hall Historic District. It is presently being leased out for office spaces.

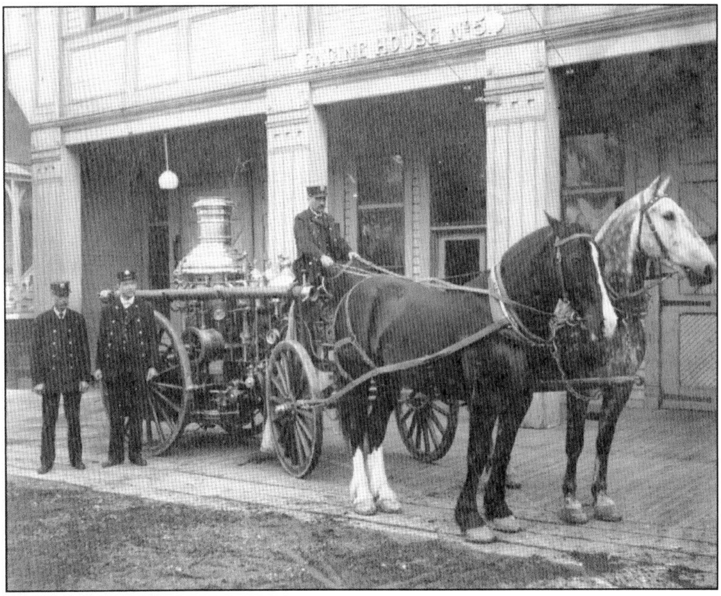

In the early 1900s, horses played a very important role in fighting fires, by getting the equipment to the scene. This firefighting team is shown in front of Engine House No. 5, which was built in 1890 at 1215 South I Street. At the turn of the 20th century, the department had 33 horses working alongside firefighters on their calls. The equipment seen here is a 1910 Metropolitan double pump.

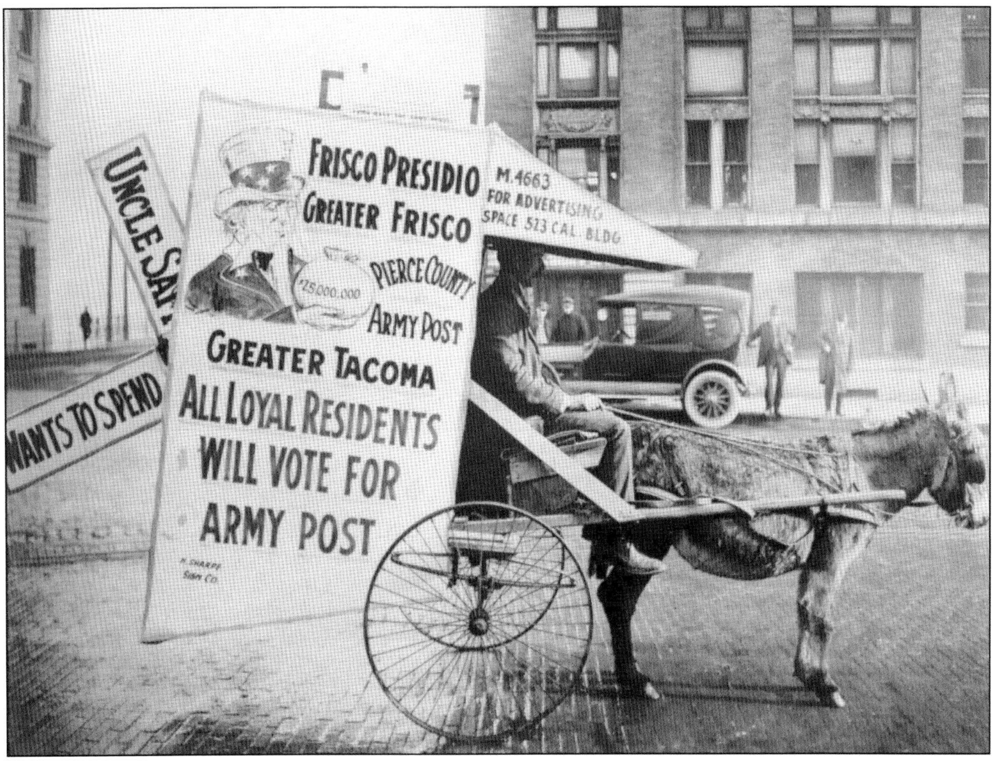

In 1917, prior to the United States' entry into World War I, the Army needed a northwest location for a staging camp in case the country got involved. H.B. Blitz was an advocate for selling $2 million in bonds to purchase 20,000 acres south of Tacoma for a military site. Blitz hired a man to drive this two-wheeled cart, towed by a burro, around town to promote the fund drive for Camp Lewis. The proposal carried six to one and what is now known as Joint Base Lewis McChord (JBLM) was born.

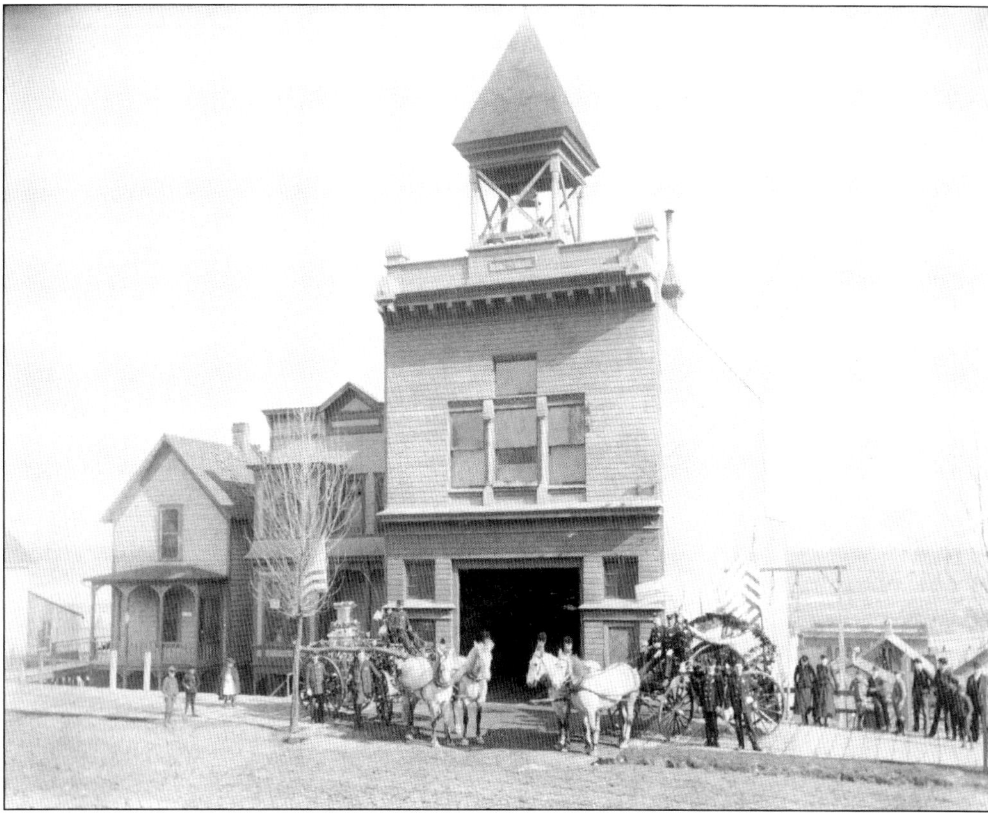

From 1889 until 1911, Tacoma's Fire Station No. 4 was located at 407 E. Twenty-Sixth Street. This photograph shows a Silsby rotary pump drawn by three horses. The hose wagon is shown on the left; it is a T.T.Y. Schneck drawn by two horses. At this time, Henry L. Knoell was listed as captain in charge of this company. Station 4 is now at 224 E. Twenty-Sixth Street.

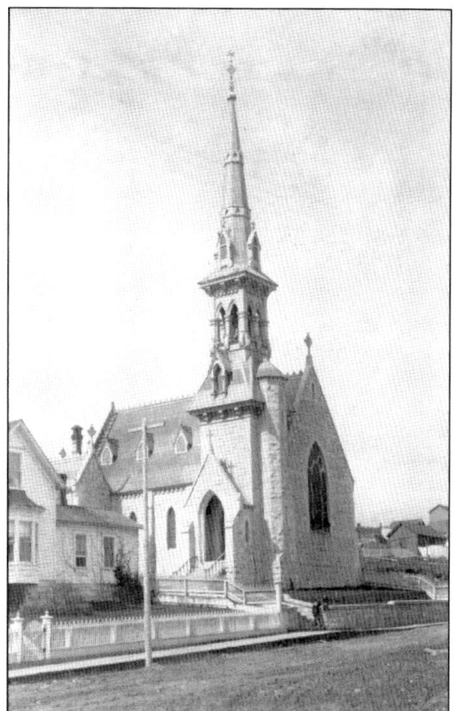

This is St. Luke's Episcopal Church as it appeared at its original location at 602 Broadway in 1885, two years after it was built. In 1934, the church was carefully dismantled and reconstructed at its present site at 3601 North Gove Street. This process took over 12 years to complete and was finished in 1947. The church is still in use today.

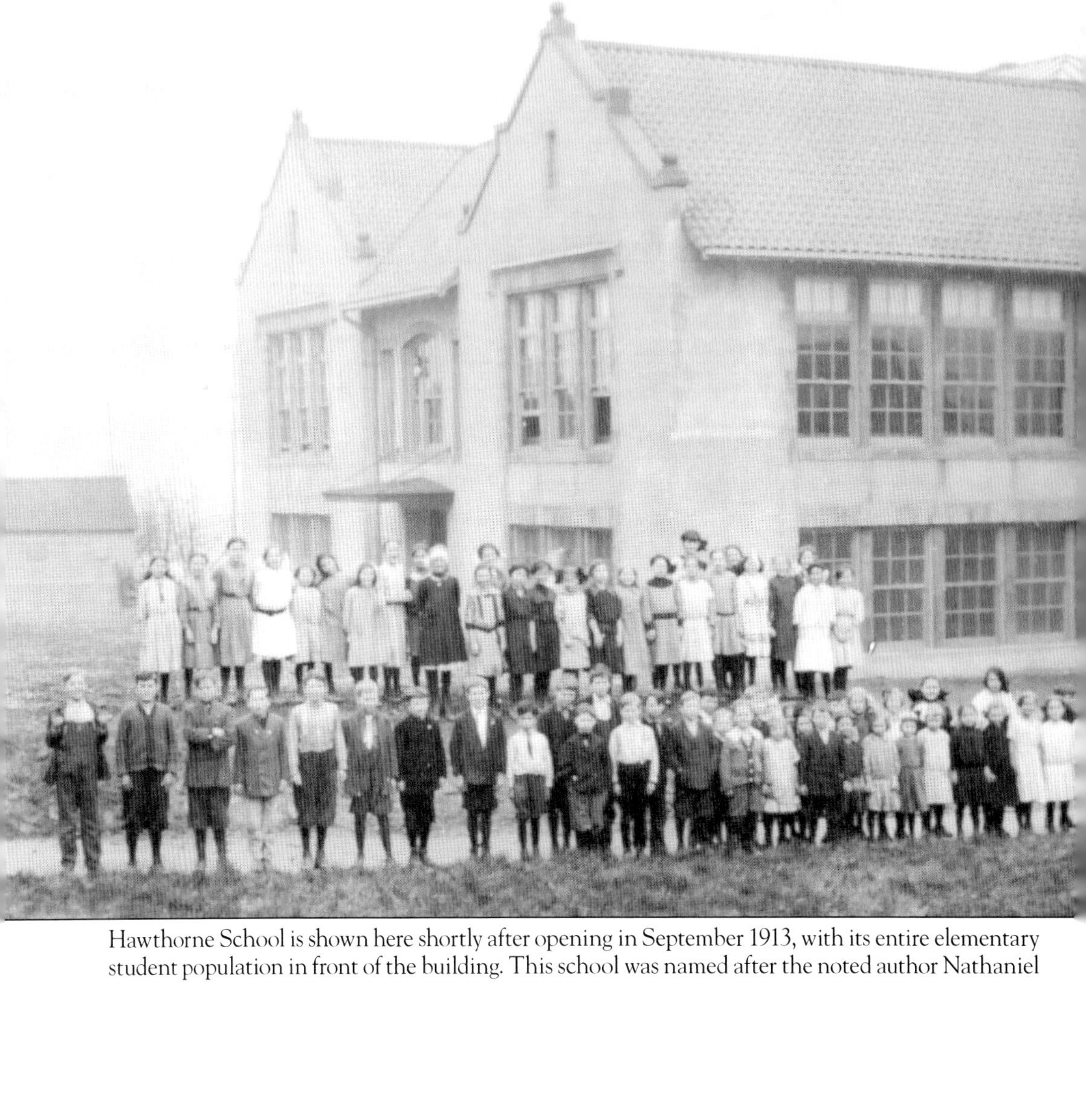

Hawthorne School is shown here shortly after opening in September 1913, with its entire elementary student population in front of the building. This school was named after the noted author Nathaniel

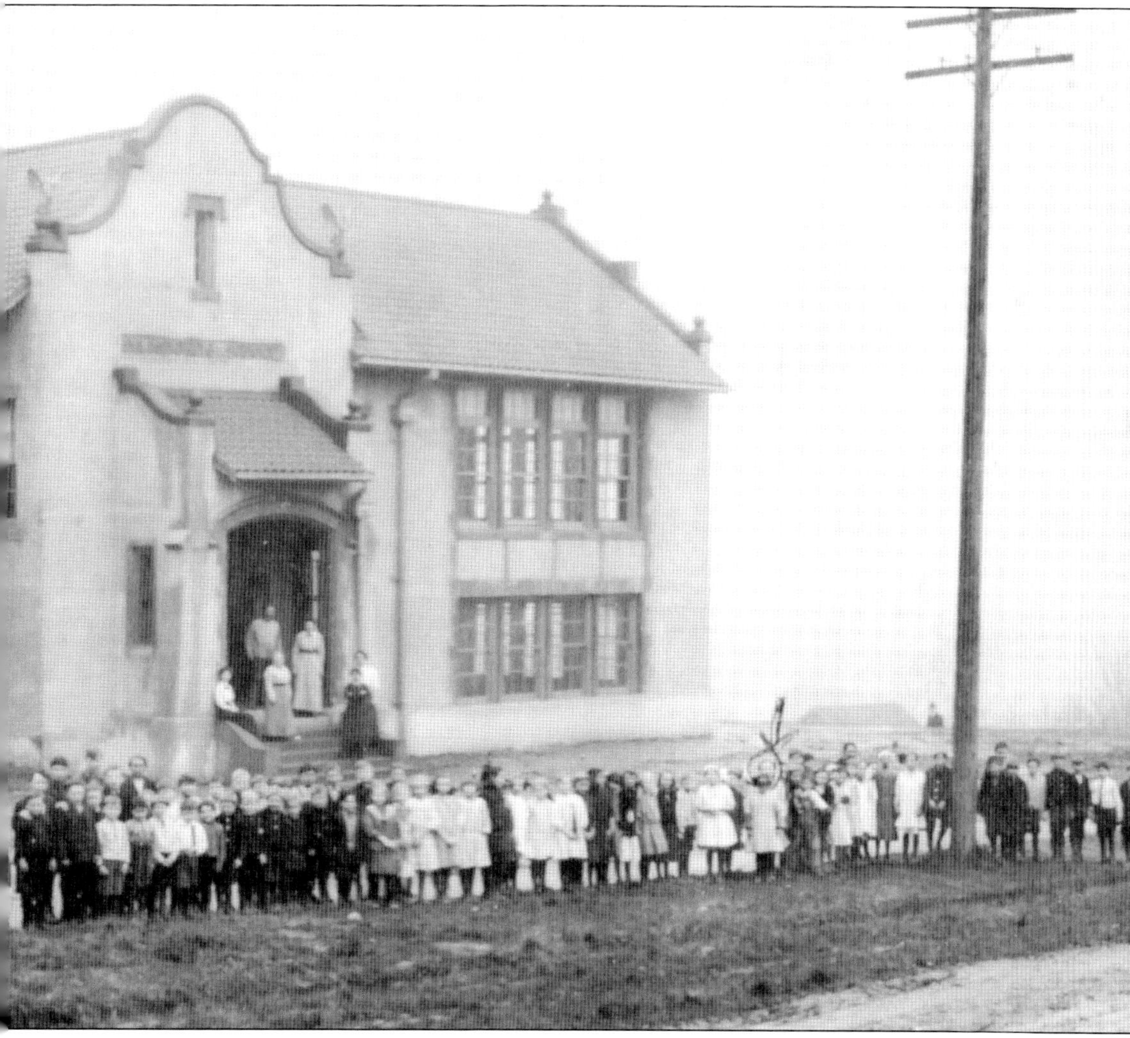

Hawthorne. After a few years, it became the Puyallup Tribe's Chief Leschi School before being closed in 1963 and demolished in 1981 to make way for the Tacoma Dome.

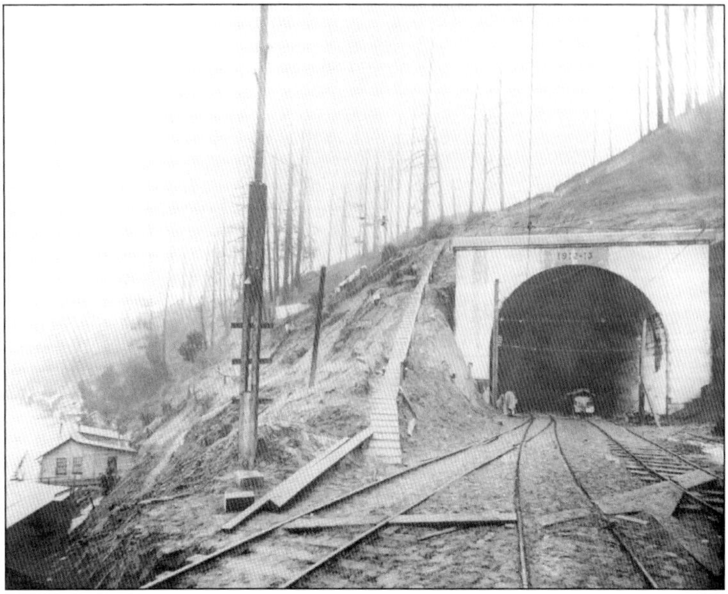

This Northern Pacific train tunnel, built in 1912–1913, is just south of Point Defiance Park. To the left, some of the early houses of Salmon Beach can be seen. Nelson Bennett, the contractor for whom this tunnel is named, died in July 1913, the eve of its completion.

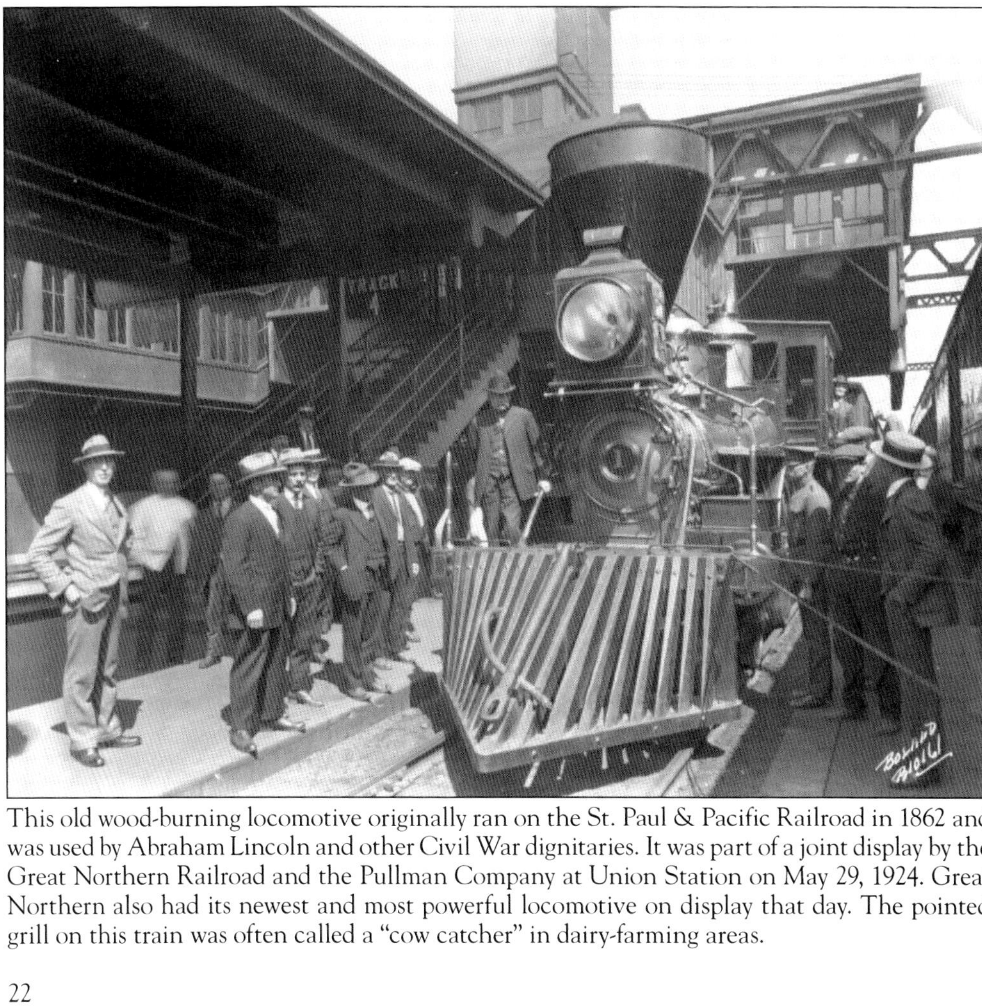

This old wood-burning locomotive originally ran on the St. Paul & Pacific Railroad in 1862 and was used by Abraham Lincoln and other Civil War dignitaries. It was part of a joint display by the Great Northern Railroad and the Pullman Company at Union Station on May 29, 1924. Great Northern also had its newest and most powerful locomotive on display that day. The pointed grill on this train was often called a "cow catcher" in dairy-farming areas.

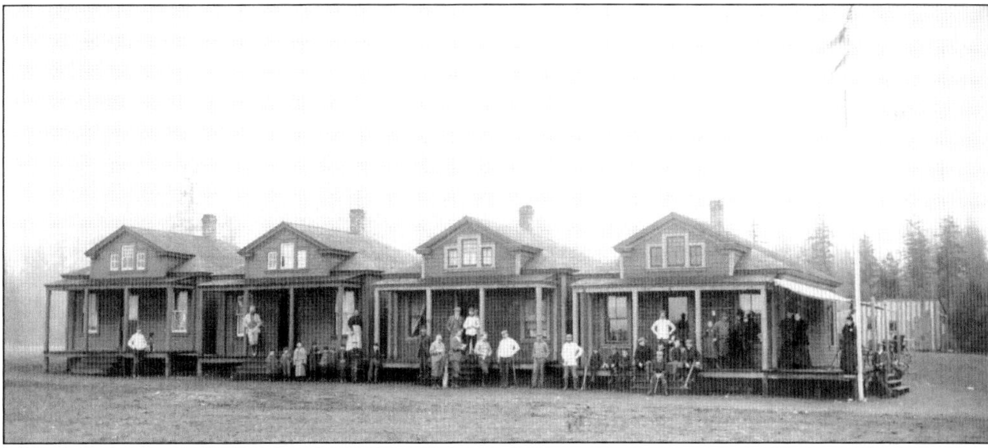

In 1885, these four wooden houses were the early beginnings of the Tacoma Golf & Country Club, located in the Edison area of Tacoma on 280 acres of land. One served as the club room, another as the caretaker's home, and the other two as locker rooms for men and women. The club eventually relocated to the American Lake area in 1904.

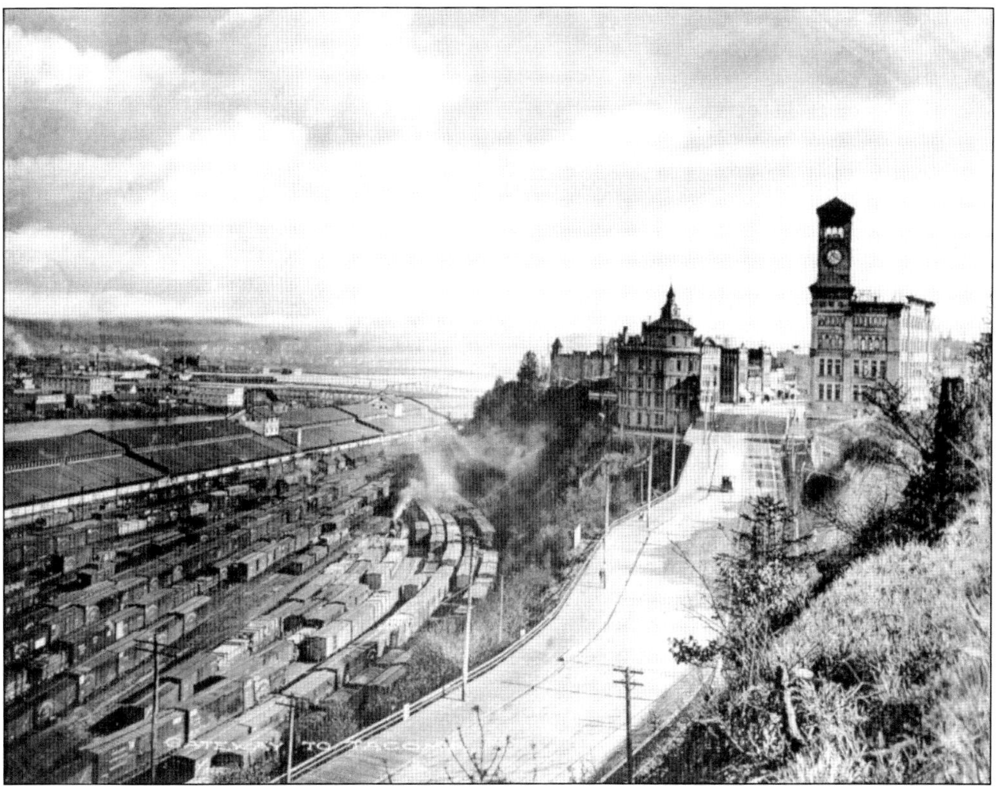

At the time this photograph was taken, Tacoma's population was estimated at 55,000, about half of what Seattle's was at the time. Shown is the Northern Pacific Railroad headquarters building to the left of Pacific Avenue, along with city hall, which was built in 1982, on the right. Both buildings are in the city, state, and national historic registries. Presently, city hall is for sale.

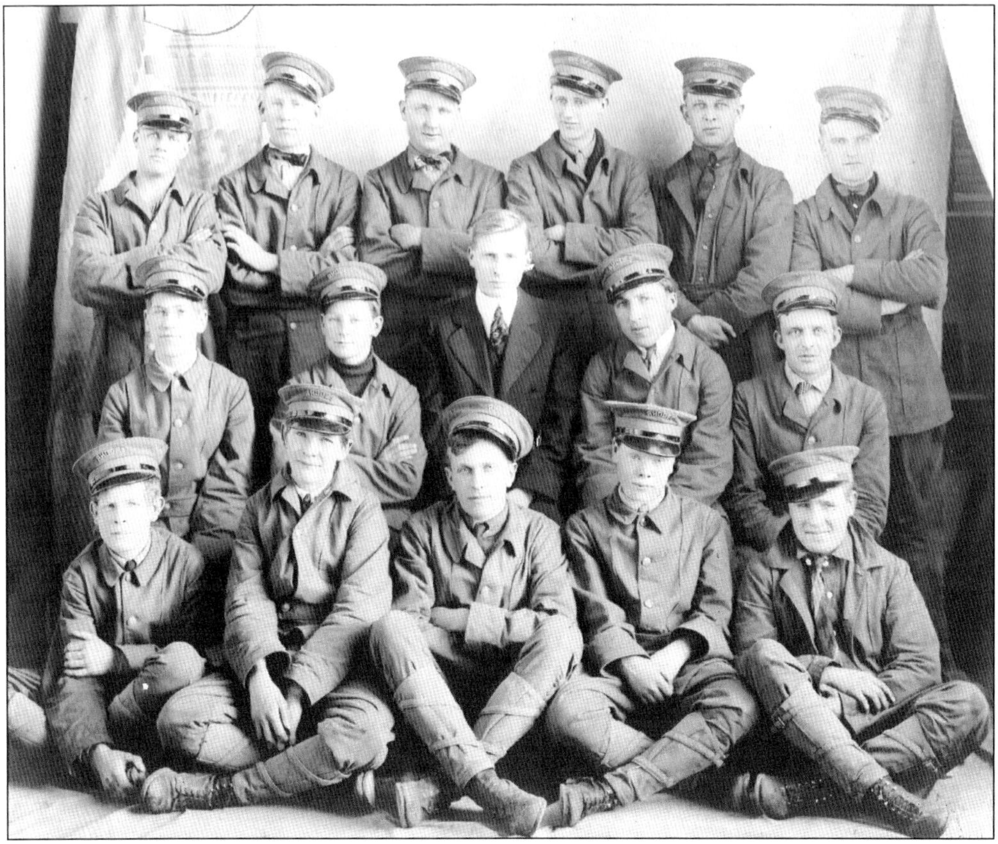

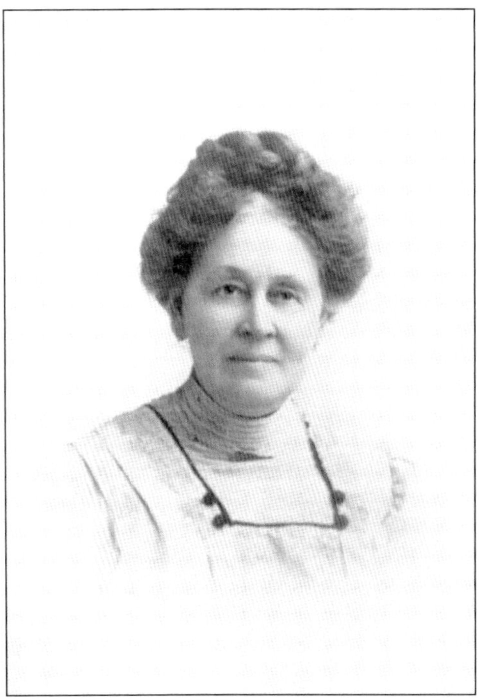

These were some of the employees of the Rhodes Brothers Department Store delivery department around 1908. Their uniforms had the 1907 style "puttee" leggings. Originally, these employees delivered their goods in horse-drawn wagons, and a special delivery boy rode in the wagon to deliver packages to the homes. Sometimes streetcars were used for deliveries, but by 1912, most deliveries were made by gas-powered trucks.

In 1905, Emma Smith De Voe, an activist with women's suffrage movements, moved with her husband to Tacoma. She was able to help the women of Washington get the right to vote in 1910, the fifth state to do so. After founding the National Council of Women Voters in 1911, she went on to help get women the right to vote nationally in 1920. She passed away in Tacoma at the age of 79 on September 3, 1927.

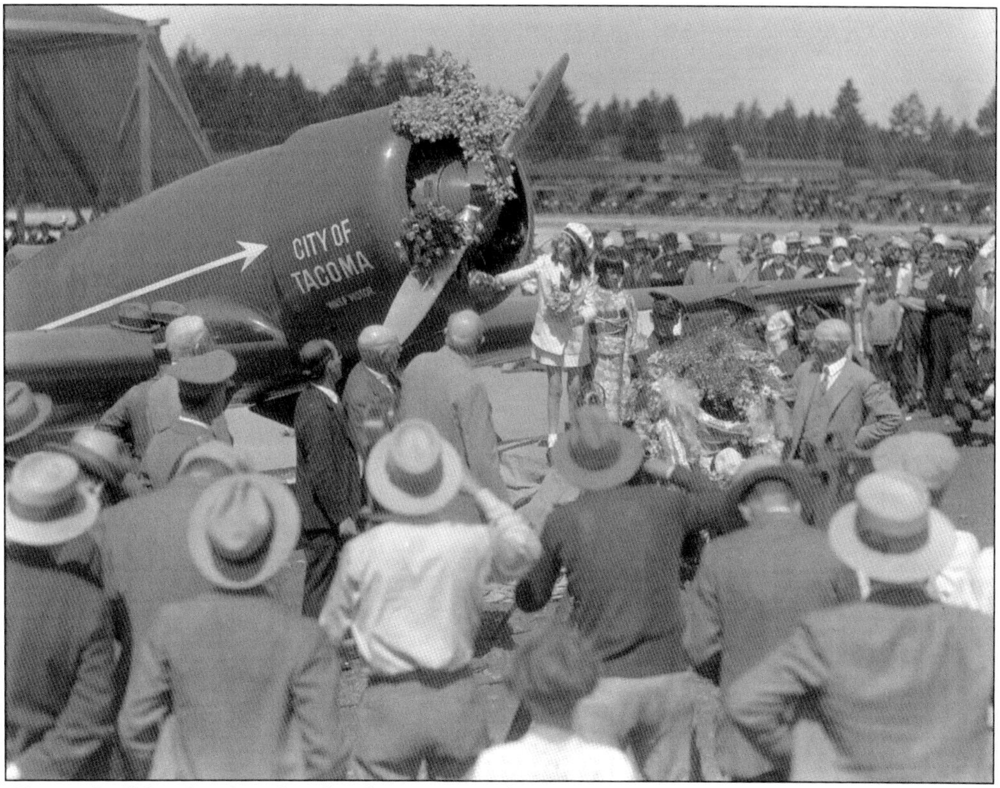

Clasina Buffelen breaks a bottle of Puget Sound water to christen Harold Bromley's Lockheed Vega, the *City of Tacoma*. Standing beside her is Evelyn R. Miyazaki, dressed in a kimono to represent the trans-Pacific flight Bromley was planning to make to Japan. Regretfully, on July 28, the flight ended in failure when gasoline from an overfilled tank caused the plane to crash on takeoff. Bromley was unhurt.

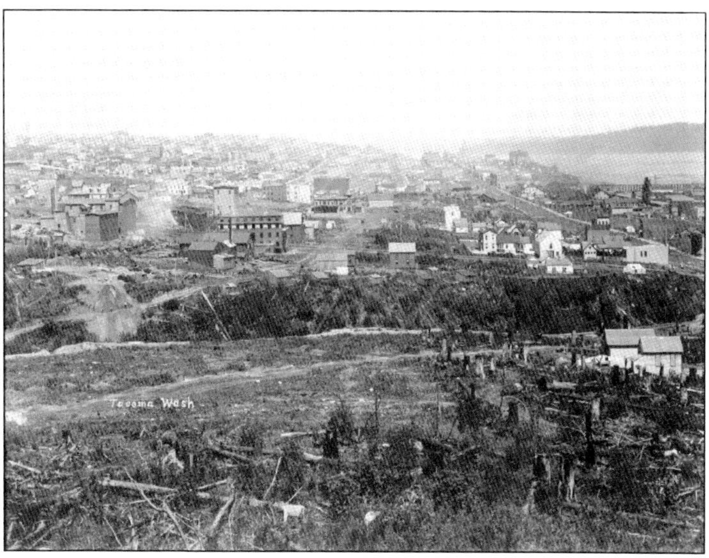

This is what Tacoma looked like in 1888, with Pacific Avenue at upper right. There are many buildings already constructed, and a few are also perched on the edge of what was known as Galliher's Gulch. To the left of center is the Pacific Brewing & Malting Co. malt house.

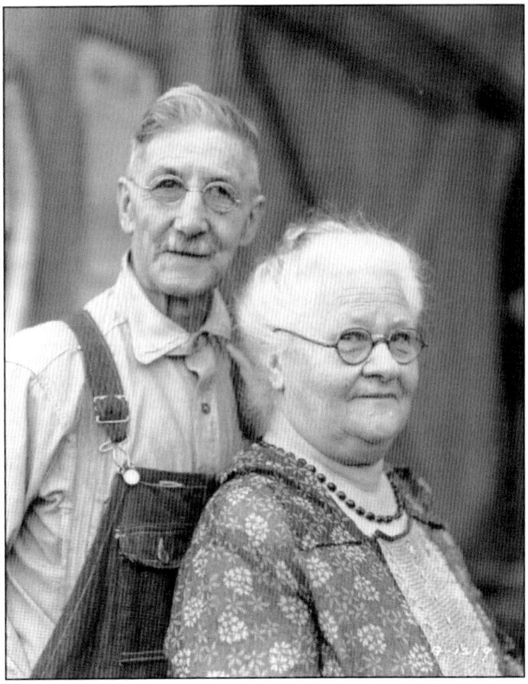

James Sales, shown here, was the first white child born within what would eventually become the city limits of Tacoma. He is shown here on his 75th birthday with his wife, Josephine, on October 28, 1928. He was born on October 20, 1853, near what was called the Delin Mill in a log cabin. The present-day address would be on South Twenty-Third and Dock Streets.

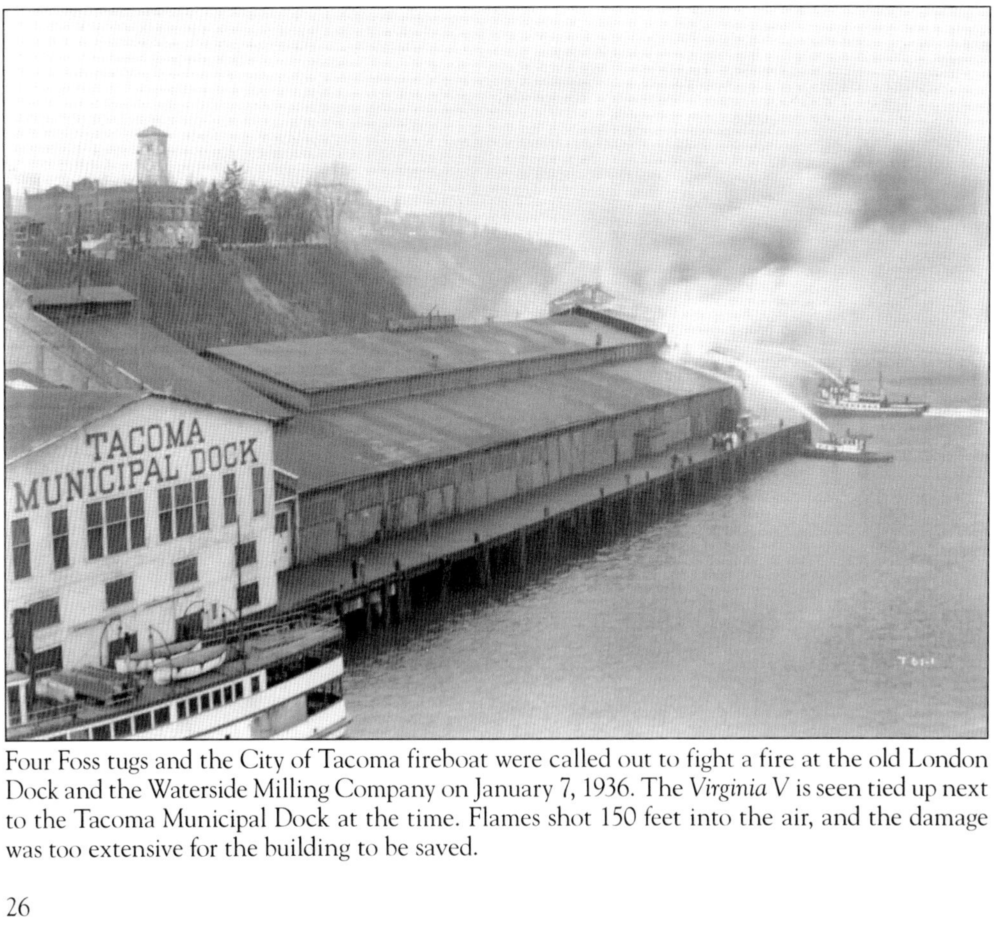

Four Foss tugs and the City of Tacoma fireboat were called out to fight a fire at the old London Dock and the Waterside Milling Company on January 7, 1936. The *Virginia V* is seen tied up next to the Tacoma Municipal Dock at the time. Flames shot 150 feet into the air, and the damage was too extensive for the building to be saved.

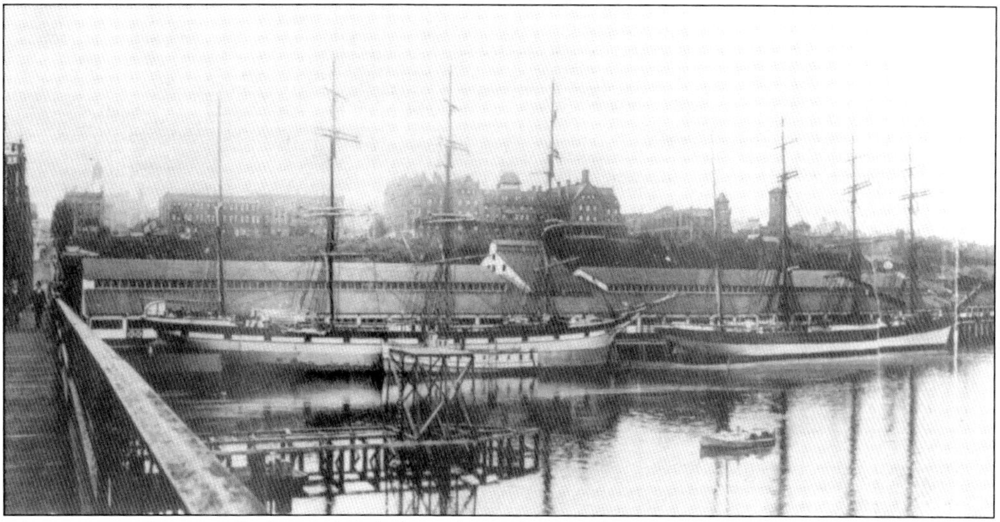

This c. 1900 photograph shows the skyline above the Northwestern Warehouse Company, which was later converted to the Tacoma Municipal dock on Thea Foss Waterway. The "Mosquito Fleet" used this dock as the water transportation hub for Tacoma on the Puget Sound.

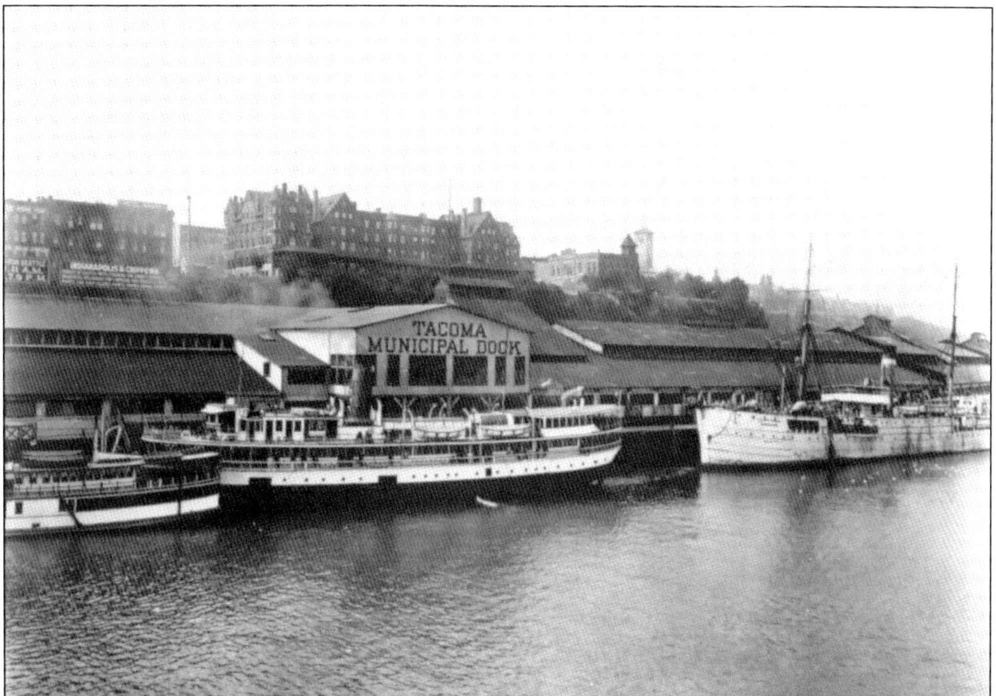

Two ferry boats of the Mosquito Fleet are shown in front of the Tacoma Municipal Dock around 1915. The Tacoma Hotel dominates the skyline on the bluff overlooking the waterfront. Tacoma City Hall is also visible along with the tip of the Northern Pacific headquarters building.

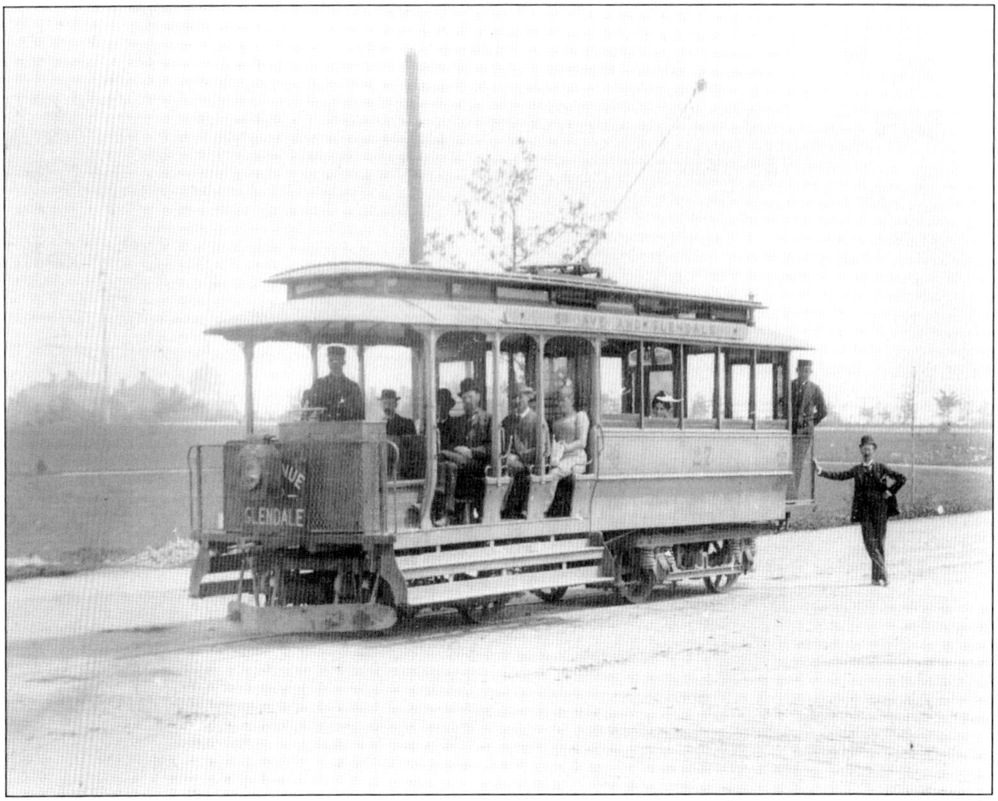

This streetcar operated by Tacoma Railway and Motor Company is shown in 1893 near Sixth Avenue. In the background is a treeless Wright Park, which was started when 20 acres were donated by Charles Wright to the City of Tacoma in 1886. Following the donation, 350 trees were planted in the park.

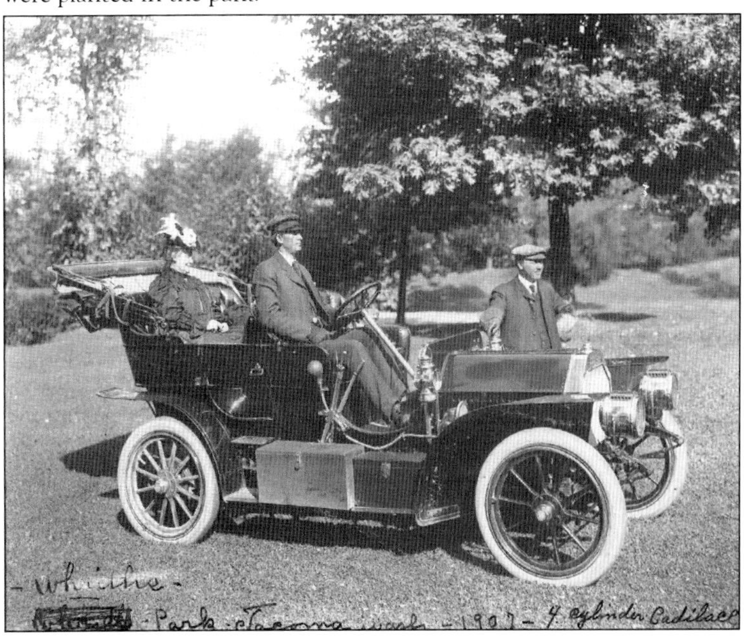

Dorcas Spalt is shown riding through Wright Park in her new 1906 Cadillac, which was reportedly the first Cadillac in Tacoma. She is being driven by her son Worthy Morris. Spalt passed away on September 3, 1931.

When William H. Taft came to Tacoma on September 7, 1907, while he was secretary of war, this dinner was held in his honor at the Tacoma Hotel. This photograph shows 300 prominent members of the chamber of commerce and other local businessmen. Taft had spoken earlier to a crowd of 12,000 at Wright Park. He came to Tacoma to review the potential site for Camp Lewis. On March 4, 1909, he became the 27th president of the United States.

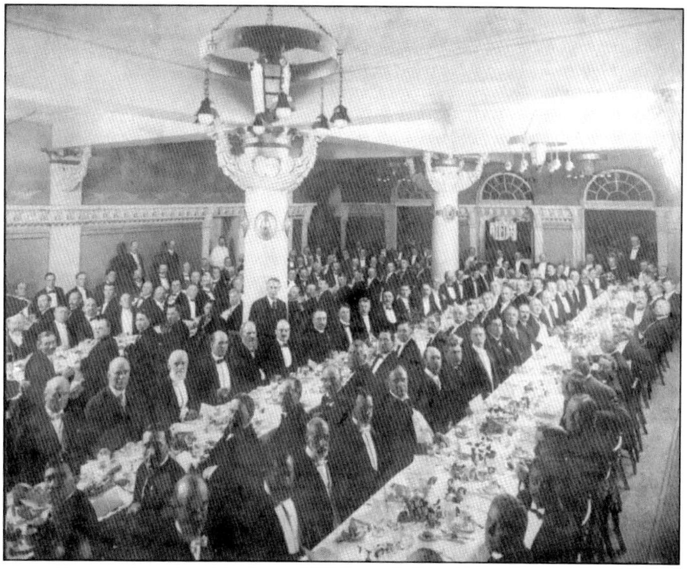

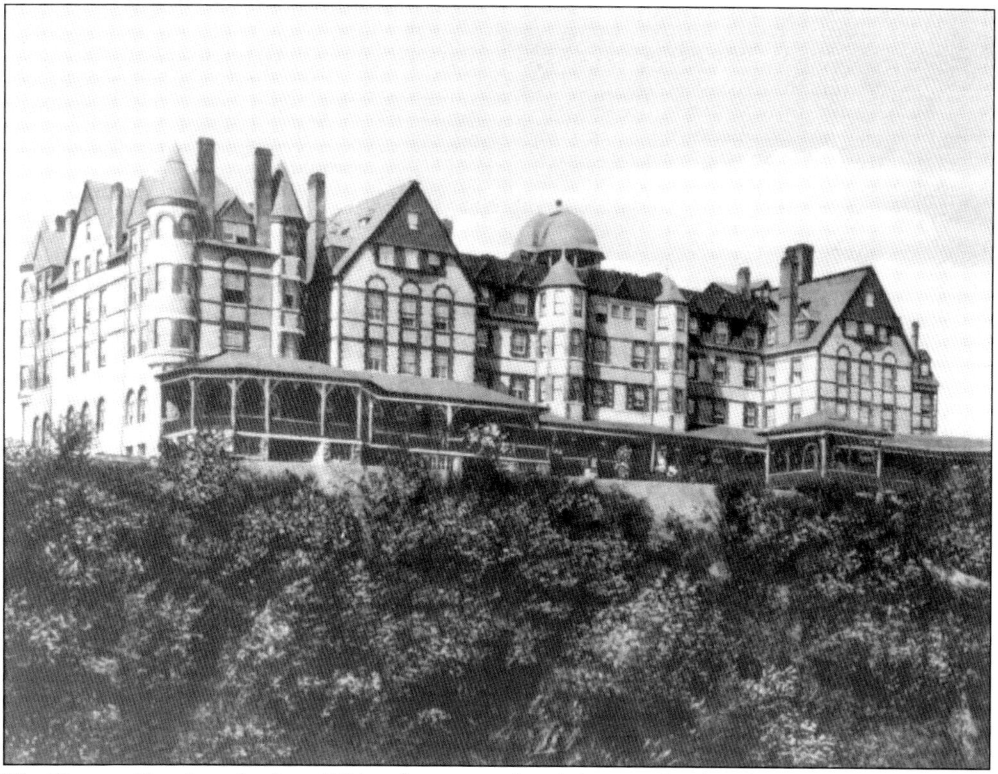

The Tacoma Hotel was built in 1884 and was considered the grandest hotel north of San Francisco. It occupied an entire block of A Street between South Ninth and Tenth Streets. The five-story, 185-room structure, a creation of noted architect Stanford White, burned down in 1935.

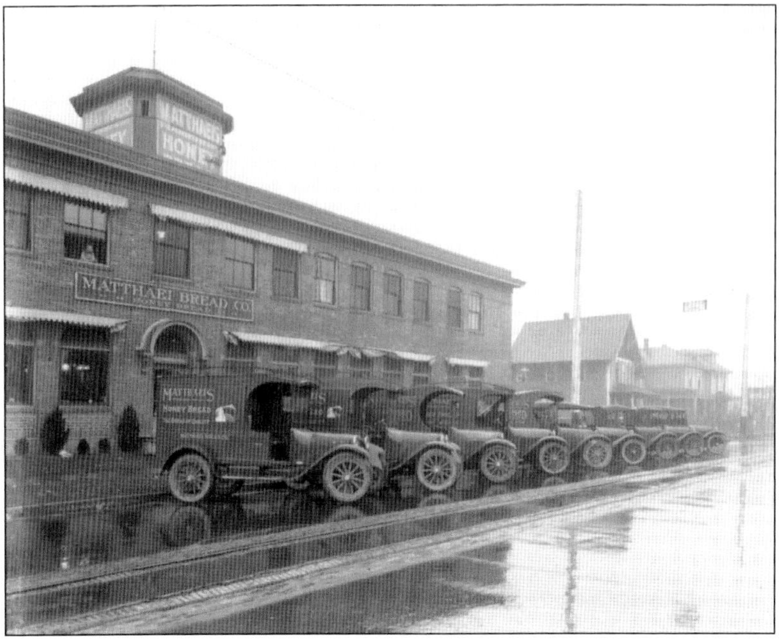

This is a photograph of the Matthaei Bread Company truck fleet in the 1920s. The company's building at 703 South Sprague Street was opened in April 1913 and eventually became home to Continental Baking Company; for over 70 years, it was the home of Wonder Bread in Tacoma.

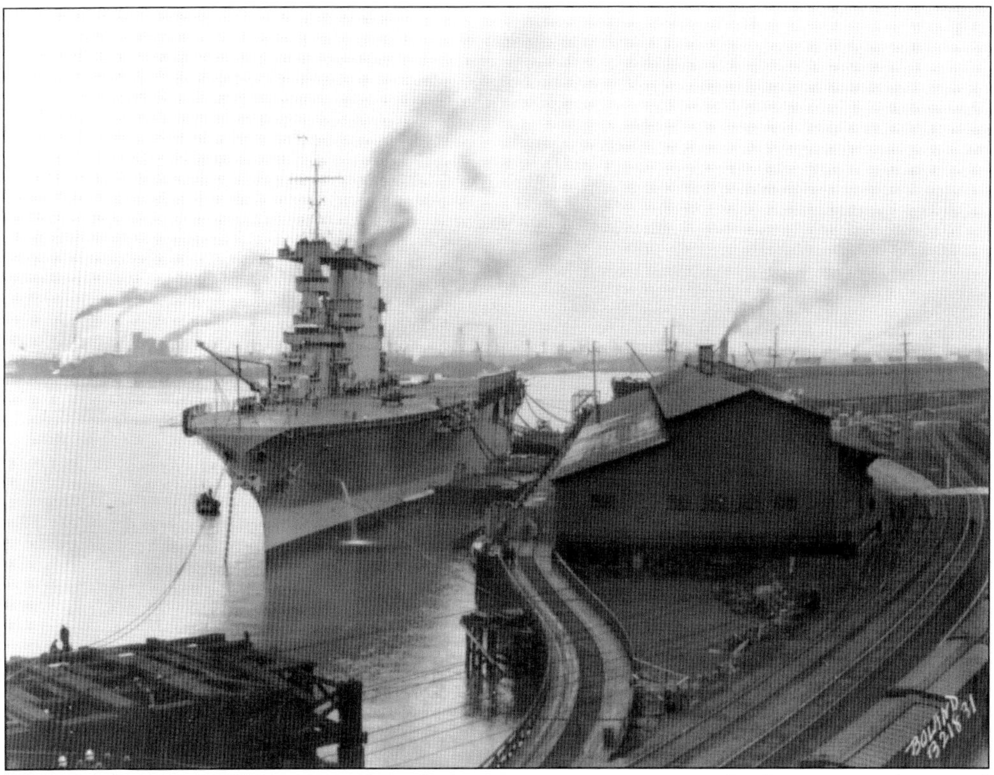

The aircraft carrier USS *Lexington* shared its generating power to provide electricity to the city of Tacoma from mid-December 1929 until mid-January 1930. It was docked at Baker Dock to provide electricity because a summer drought reduced the amount of electricity available from the city's hydroelectric system. The *Lexington* was able to furnish 25 percent of the city's power needs.

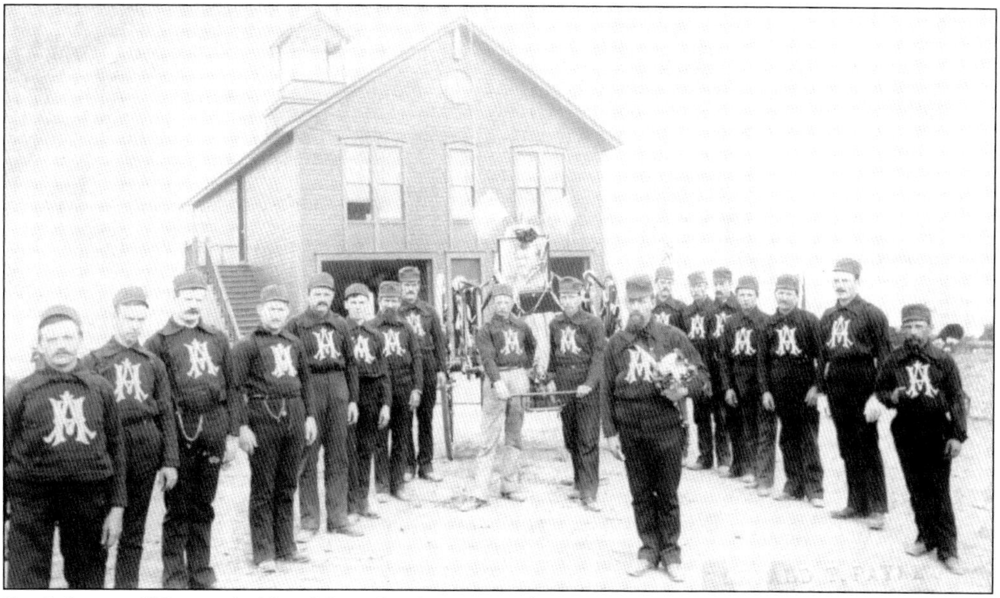

Firefighters of Tacoma's Alert Hose Co. No. 2 are shown in uniform as they prepare for a parade on August 8, 1885. Ulysses S. Grant had died on July 23, 1885, and the Washington territorial governor Watson Carvosso Squire had declared that the day of his funeral be an official day of mourning. The firehouse was located at 13th and A Streets. The captain of the station, Adelbert Uriah Mills, is shown holding a bouquet of flowers.

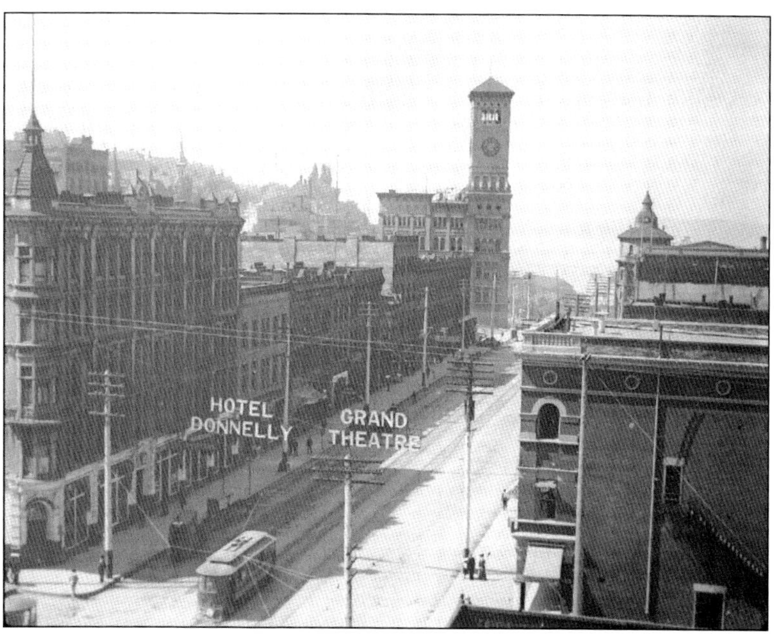

This photograph shows Pacific Avenue as it looked in 1900, with city hall towering to the left and the Northern Pacific headquarters building tower to the right, above the buildings. The Hotel Donnelly and Grand Theatre were on opposite sides of Pacific Avenue.

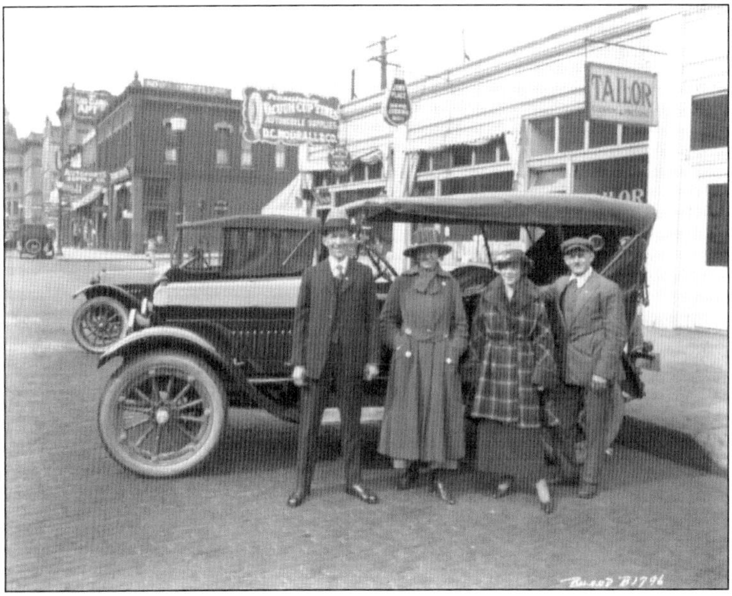

This party of four were parked on the east side of Pacific Avenue near South Eighth Street in May 1919. Being so well dressed, they were probably out for a Sunday drive. In the background are the Eau-Claire Apartments, Auto Parts Supply Co., D.C. Modrall & Co., Jim's Place, and a tailoring establishment.

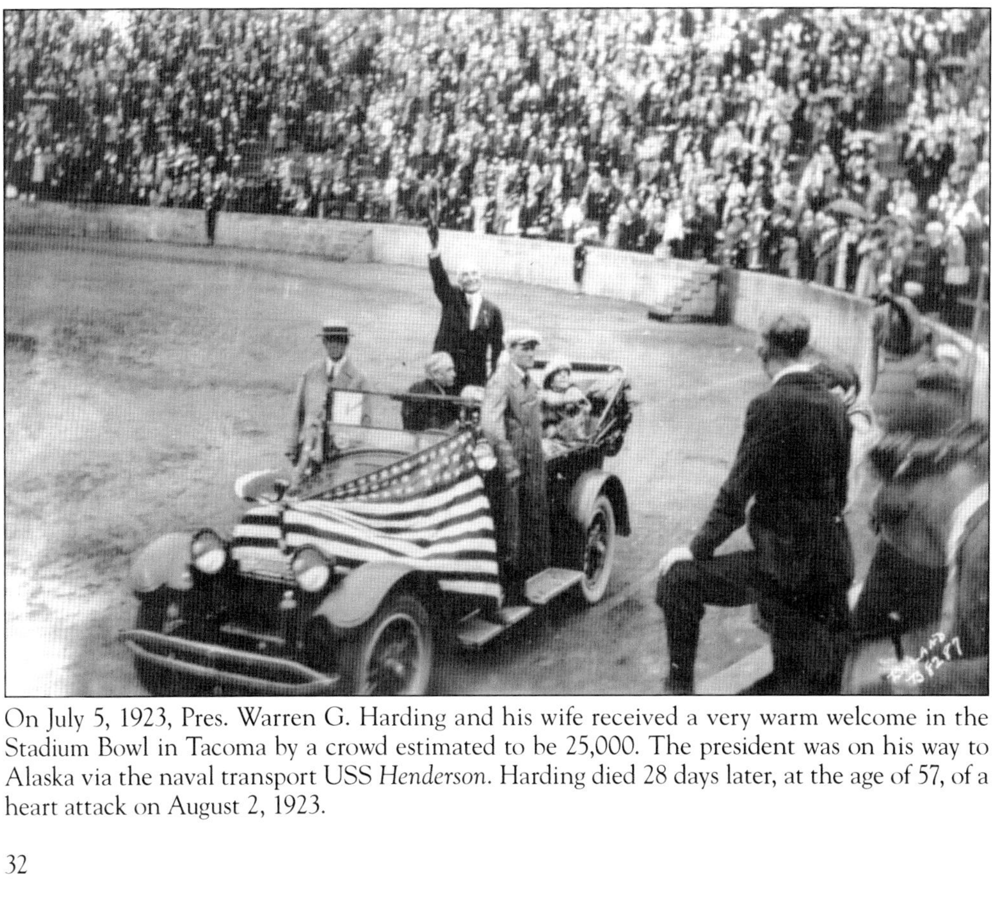

On July 5, 1923, Pres. Warren G. Harding and his wife received a very warm welcome in the Stadium Bowl in Tacoma by a crowd estimated to be 25,000. The president was on his way to Alaska via the naval transport USS *Henderson*. Harding died 28 days later, at the age of 57, of a heart attack on August 2, 1923.

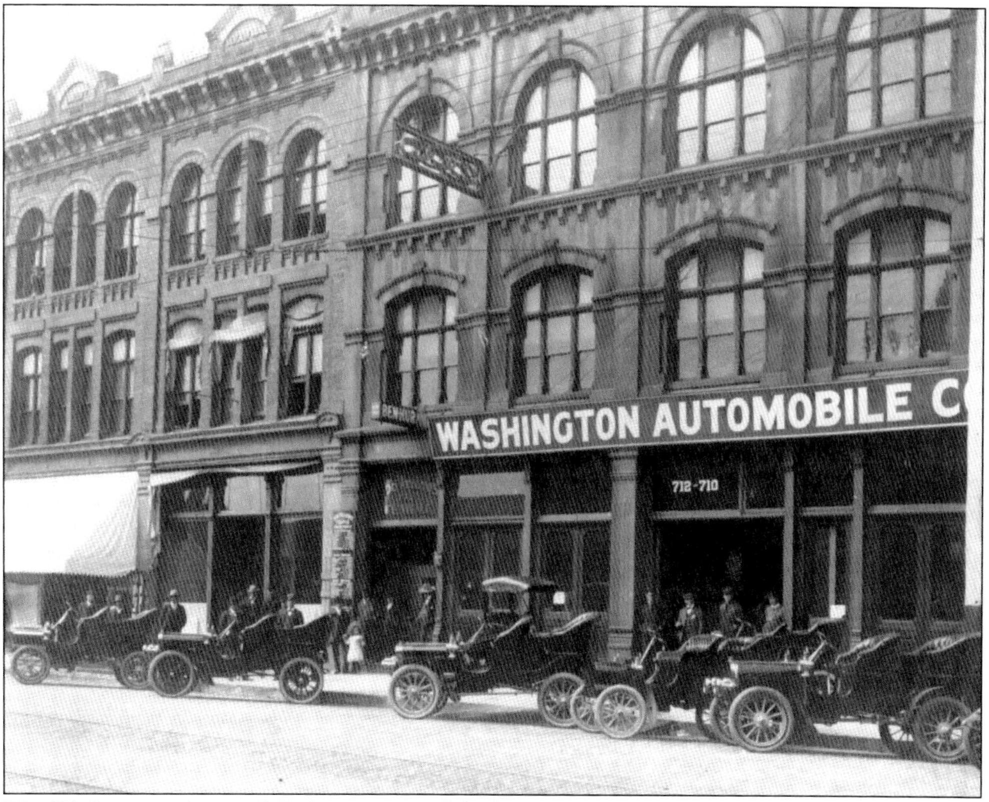

The Washington Automobile Co. was one of the first auto dealerships in Tacoma. These spectators are admiring the new fleet of Fords lined up outside the dealership on Pacific Avenue. W.W. Pickerill operated this dealership from 1905 until 1909. Before that time, this building was the home of the Chas. W. Langert Liquor Co. and the Tacoma Athletic Club. It later became the Odd Fellows Lodge.

This street scene of Pacific Avenue was taken around 1887 looking north from Tenth Street. The home of the *Tacoma News* is most obvious and was at 930 Pacific Avenue. At that time, the *Tacoma News* was an evening paper, and the *Daily Ledger* was a morning paper. They were later combined and taken over by the *News Tribune*.

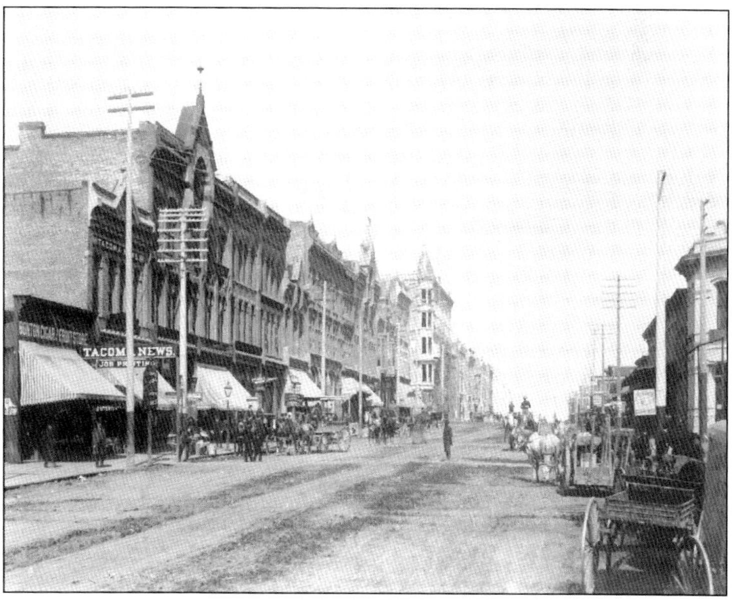

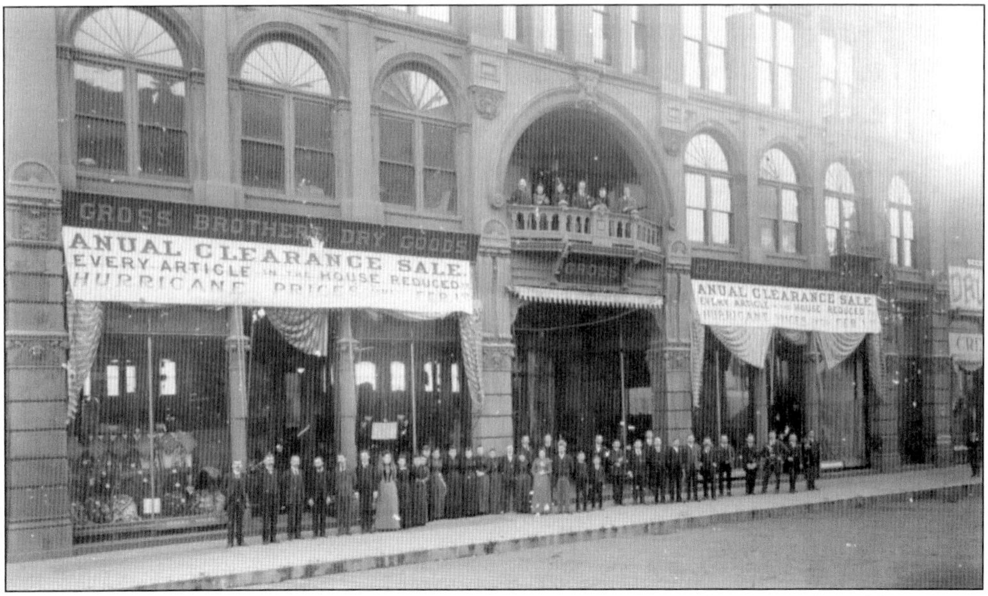

The large staff of Gross Brothers store at 901 Broadway is shown on the sidewalk and balcony to promote their annual clearance sale in the winter of 1890. This building was erected in 1889 and was eventually demolished in 1916 so that the Pantages Theater could be built on the site.

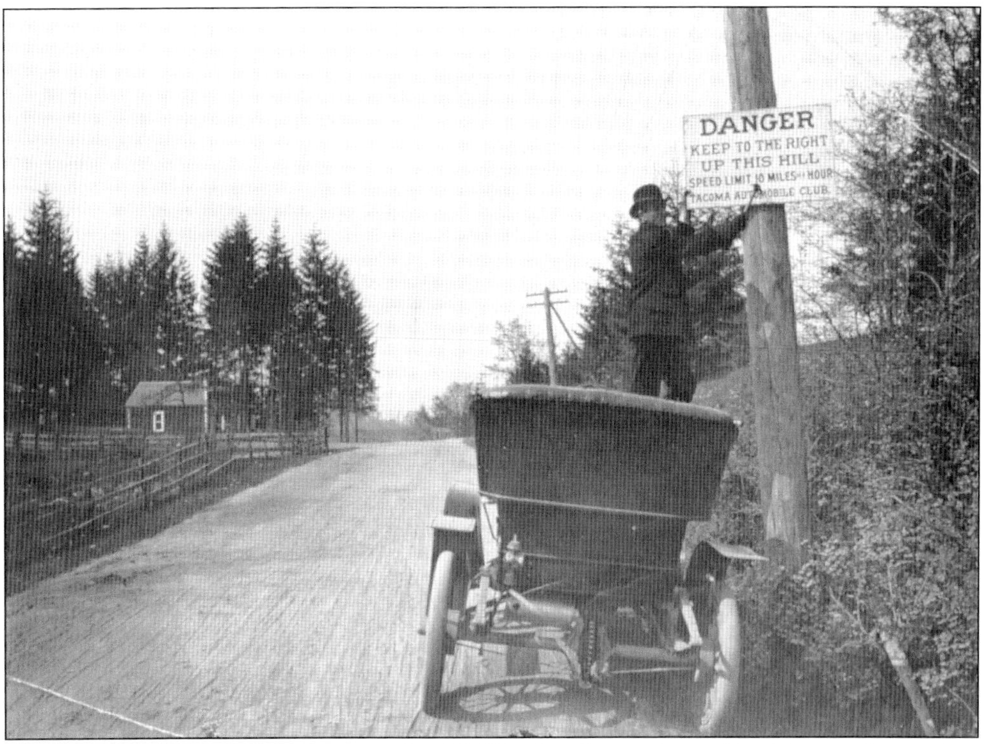

This "Danger" sign has just been posted by W.W. Pickerill, president of the Tacoma Automobile Club at that time. At the time, the legal speed limit within the Tacoma city limits was 12 mph. This sign warned drivers to stay to the right and keep their speed under 10 mph.

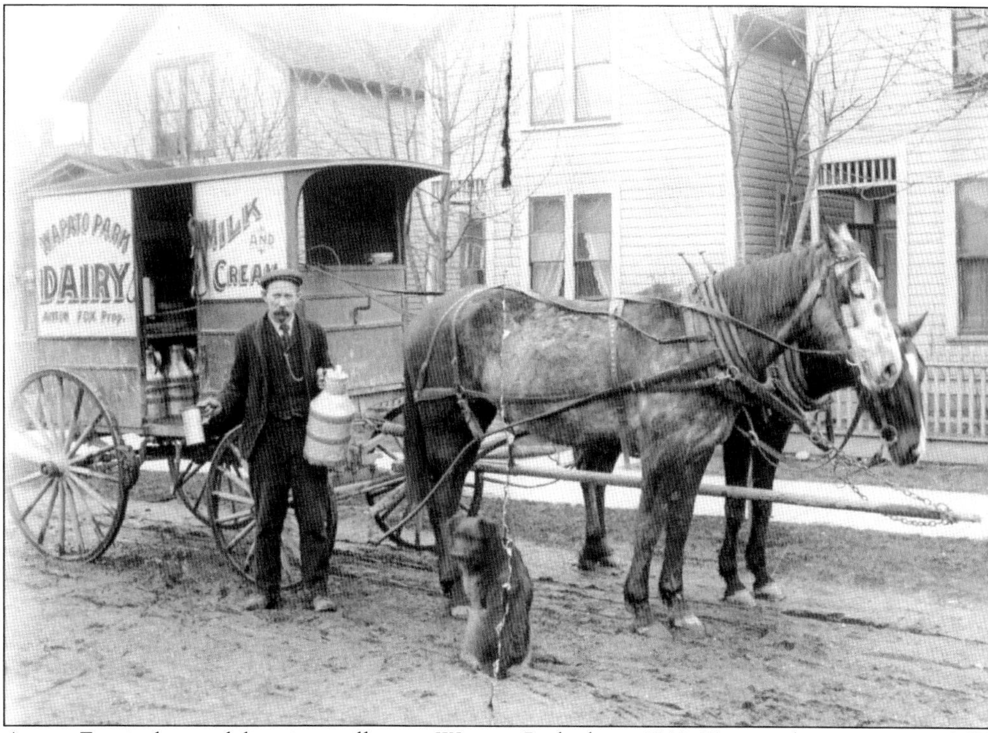

Anton Fox is shown delivering milk near Wapato Park about 1910. He was the proprietor of the Wapato Park Dairy and, along with his horses Daisy and Billy and the family dog Teddy Bear, delivered milk and cream in metal milk cans to his customers.

This photograph shows one of Tacoma's first ladder trucks, drawn by three horses. Harry White is driving, and L.S. Finney is at the tiller. Charles W. Nichols is next to the driver's seat. On the ground, from left to right, are S.F. Buck, William F. Bing, A.I. Hooten, and Edward Evans.

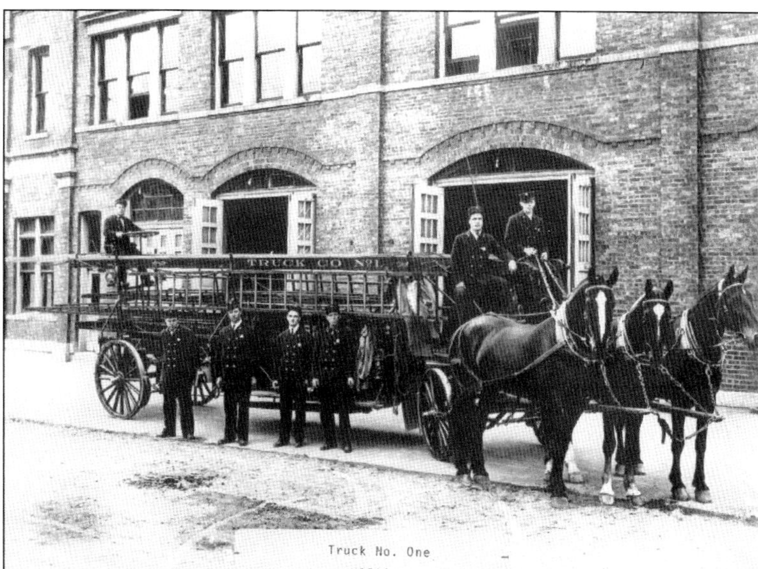

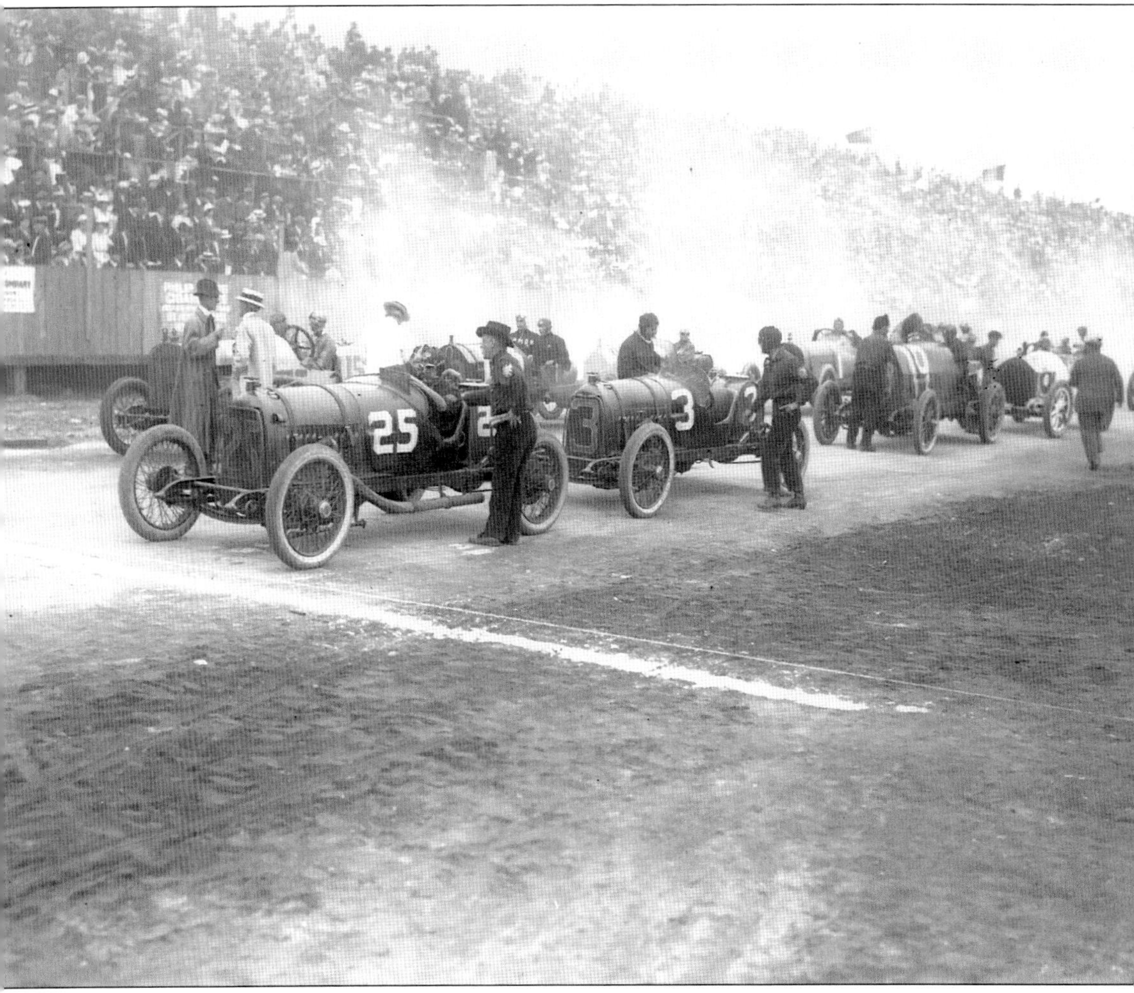

Racers would come from out of town, including Californian Billy Carlson, seated in car No. 25, and "Terrible Teddy" Tetzlaff, in No. 3, both with Maxwell racing cars. Billy Carlson and his mechanic Paul Franzen were both killed in an accident at the speedway the next year, on July 4, 1914.

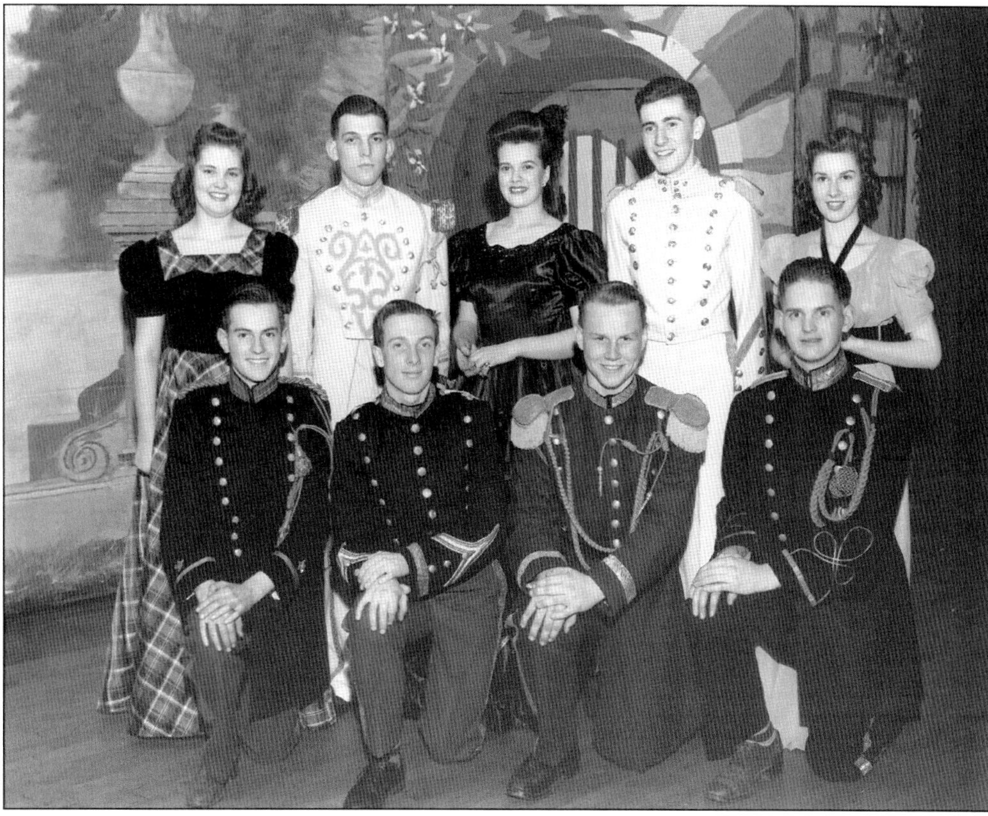

Stadium High School produced *The Merry Widow* on March 13, 14, and 15th in 1941. Donna Mae Jaden, who had the lead role, is shown at center in the second row. She was born in Tacoma on September 16, 1922, and graduated from Stadium High School before going to Hollywood and starting her very successful acting career, using the name of Janis Paige.

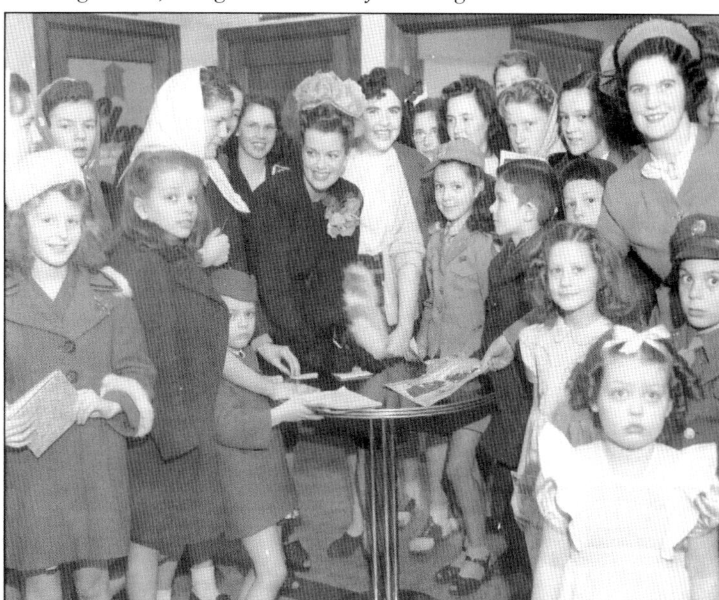

Janis Paige is shown left of center on January 16, 1946, signing autographs at Tacoma's KMO Studios for children while visiting her hometown. She acted in movies, documentaries, television shows, and stage productions. Her star was placed on the Hollywood Walk of Fame on February 9, 1960.

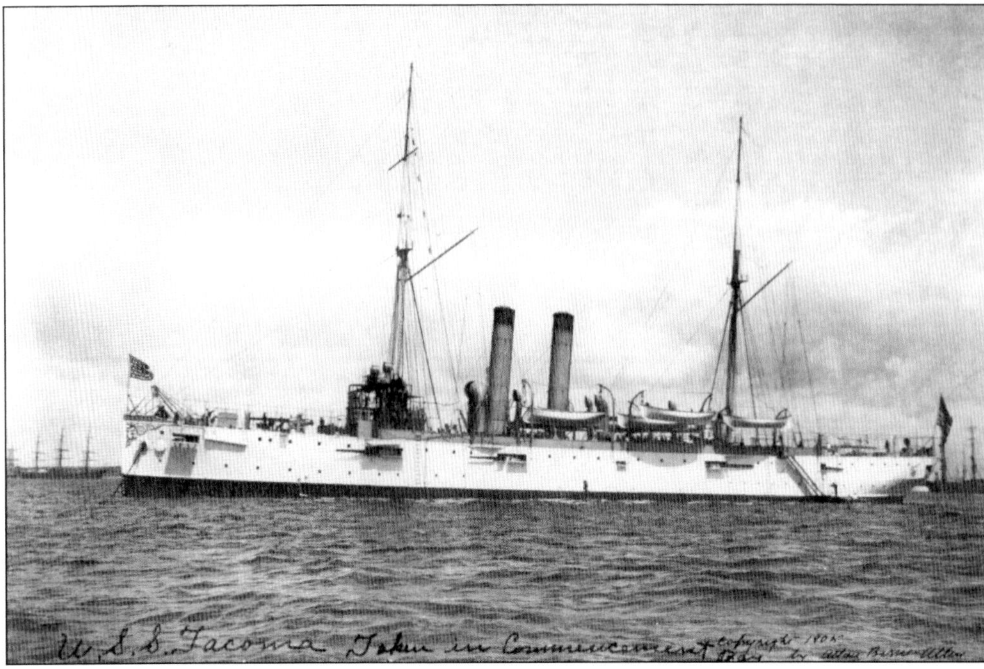

The USS *Tacoma* is shown on its maiden voyage to Tacoma shortly after being commissioned on January 30, 1904. She was built at Mare Island, California, by Union Iron Works and launched on June 2, 1903. After many successful deployments in World War I, she unfortunately ran aground on January 16, 1924, near Veracruz, Mexico, and was struck from the Navy list on February 7, 1924. The original ship's bell is currently on display in Tacoma at War Memorial Park.

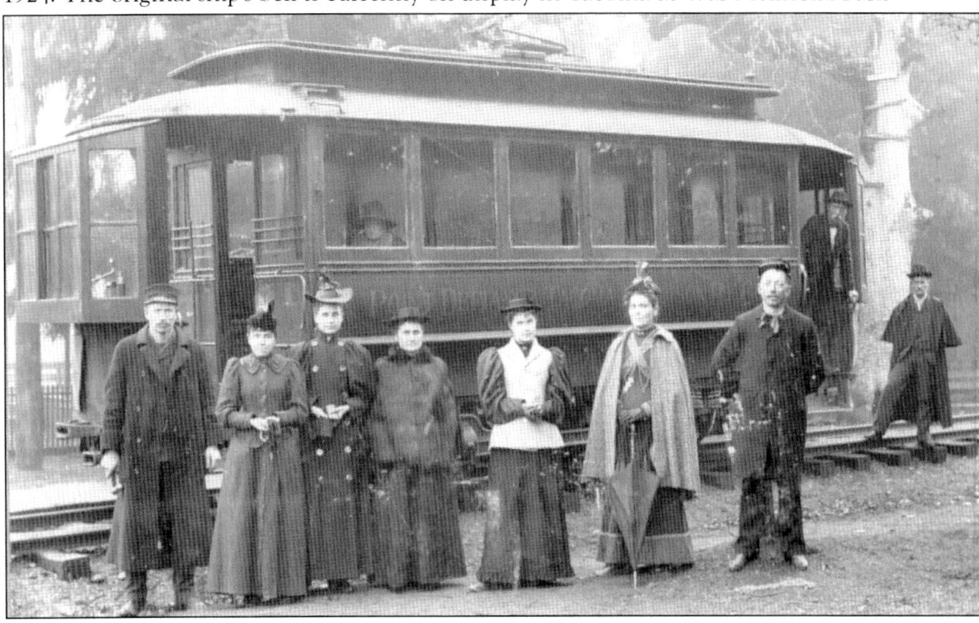

The Point Defiance Line trolley system was completed in 1890 and later sold to Tacoma Railway & Power Company by North End real estate developer Allen C. Mason. He was a major influence in the growth of Tacoma's Proctor District and is credited with coining the name "City of Destiny" for Tacoma.

On July 4, 1924, the Tacoma Yacht Club held a Bathing Girl Revue. Contestants posed in one-piece bathing suits with stockings rolled down, or no stockings at all, and showed bare arms and legs. This year, out of 32 contestants, Grace Copeland was judged the most beautiful bathing girl.

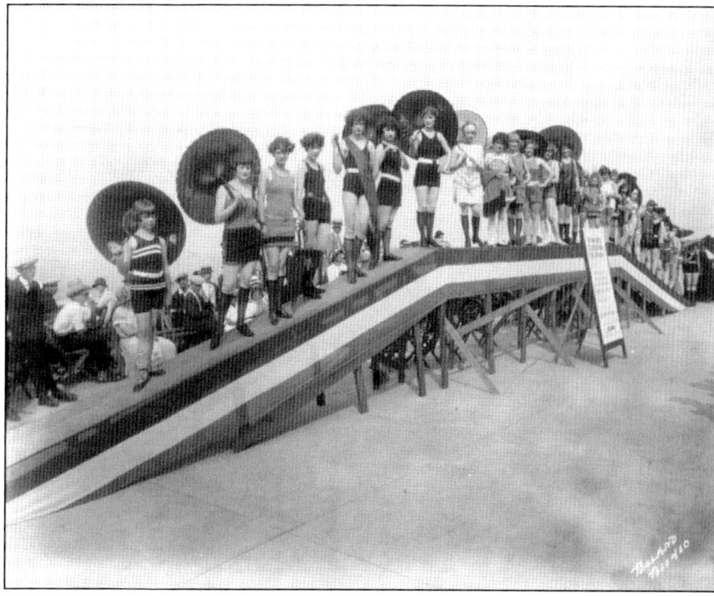

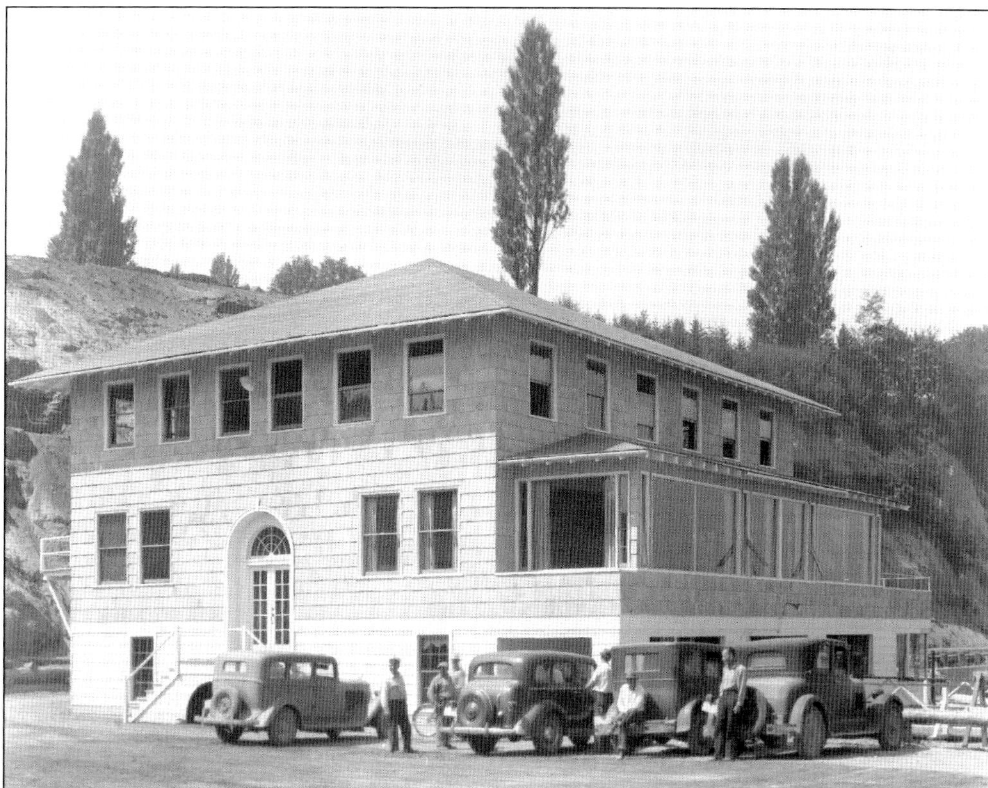

This is what the Tacoma Yacht Club looked like in August 1936. In 1916, this clubhouse was headquarters for the Seabourne Shipyards, before being moved to this site by a scow in 1923. The first floor was the quarters for Captain and Mrs. Swanson, the club caretaker, while the second floor was the lobby, lounge, and billiard room, including a 50-by-35-foot sun porch. The top floor was the meeting room and dance hall.

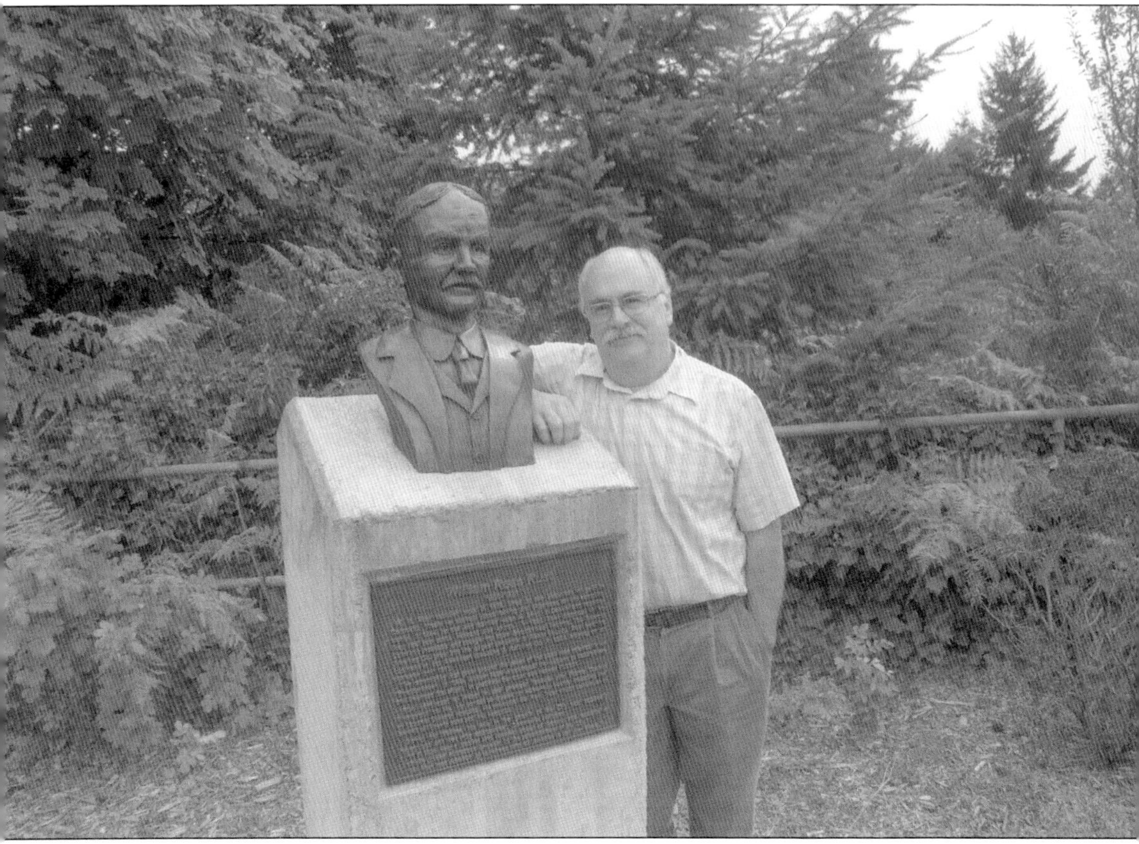

Paul R. Michaels is shown alongside a sculpture he created of William R. Rust, for whom the City of Ruston was named. Rust came to Tacoma in 1887 and became manager of the Tacoma Smelting & Refining Company in the spring of 1890. With only $30,000 cash, he gained control of the smelter and worked there until he retired on January 1, 1916, a very rich man. Before retiring, he was able to sell the smelter for $5 million, and it became a unit of the American Smelters Securities Company. (Photograph by author.)

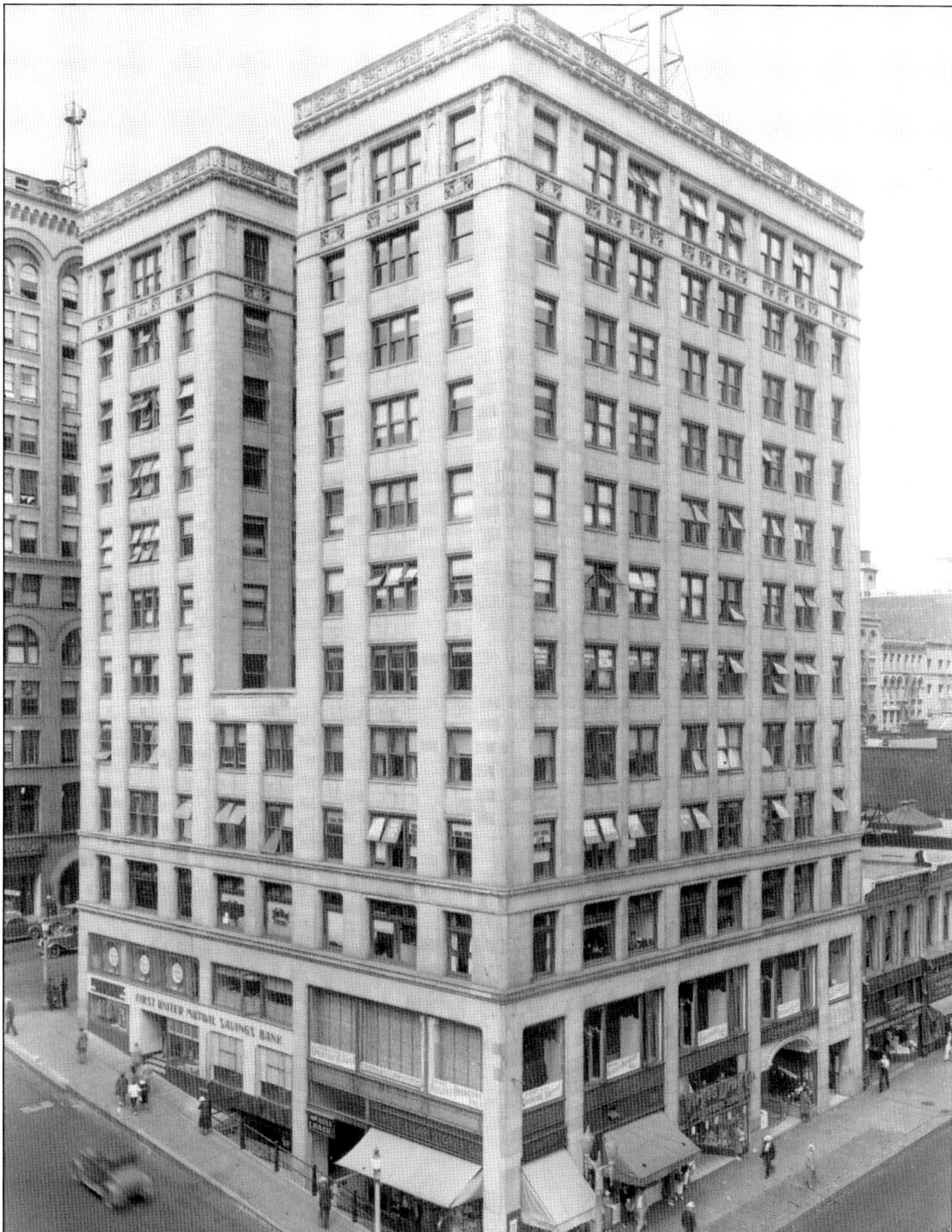

This photograph, taken in 1937 at South Eleventh Street and Pacific Avenue, shows the Rust Building, named for its builder, William R. Rust. The 12-story building opened in 1920 and has had various names through the years, including Commerce Building, Townsend Building, and the Seafirst Financial Center.

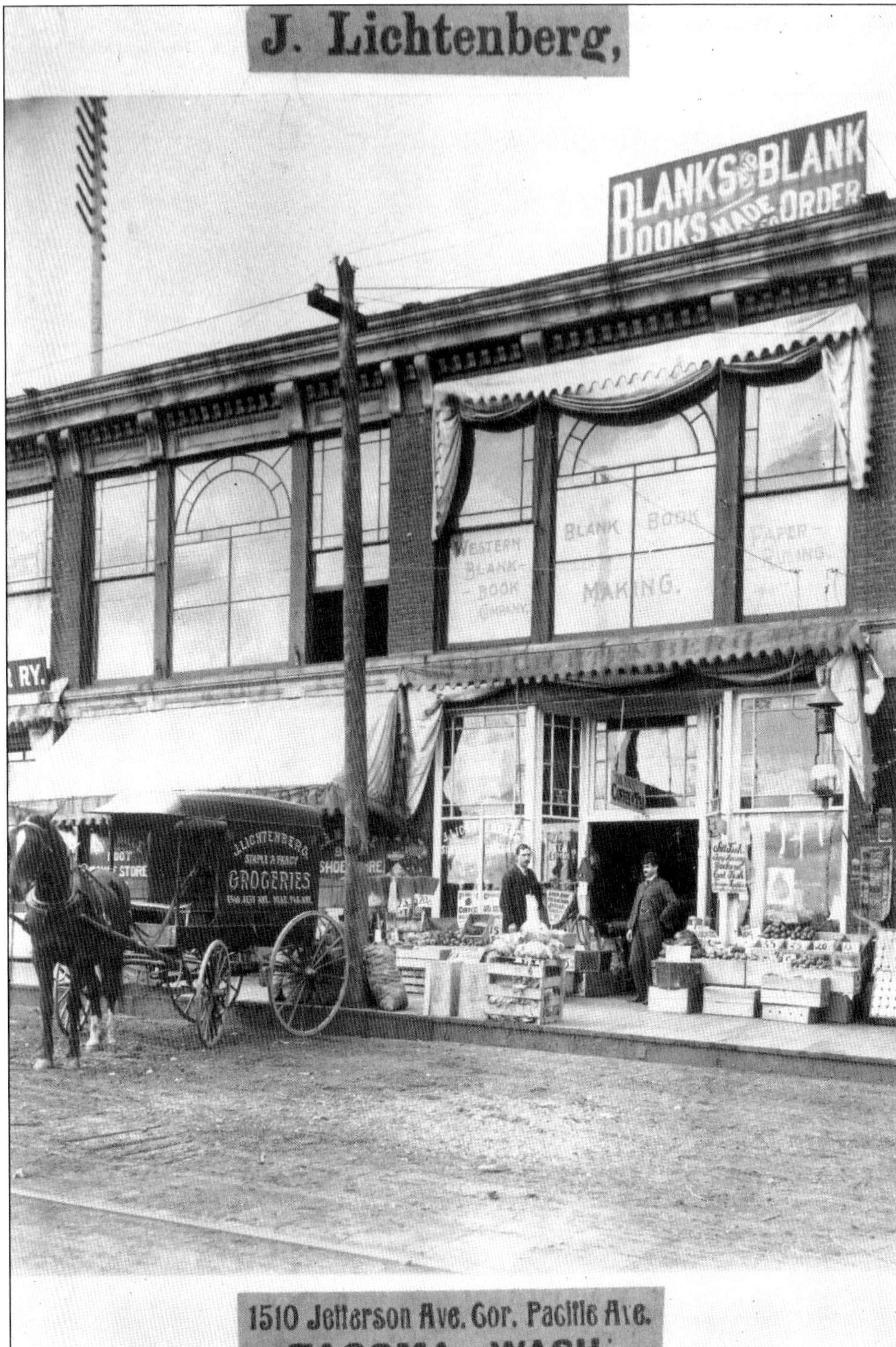

In 1903, the Lichtenberg store, which was located at 1510 Jefferson Avenue, would have been a good choice for grocery shopping. This store was founded by Julius Lichtenberg and operated from 1897 until 1909. The Western Blank Book Company on the second floor was in business from 1893 until 1912.

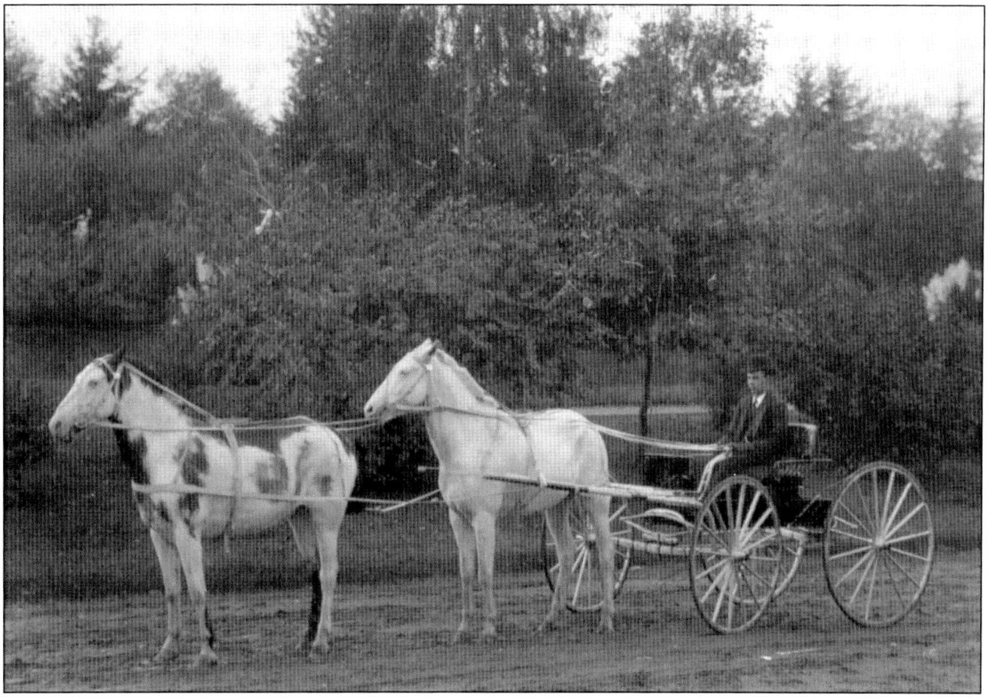

Before car rental agencies there was Roy J. Clark, proprietor of Clark's Livery and Club Stables. These horses and buggies were available to rent on short notice or for weddings and funerals. Clark is shown in 1904 near his place of business at 1210 A Street.

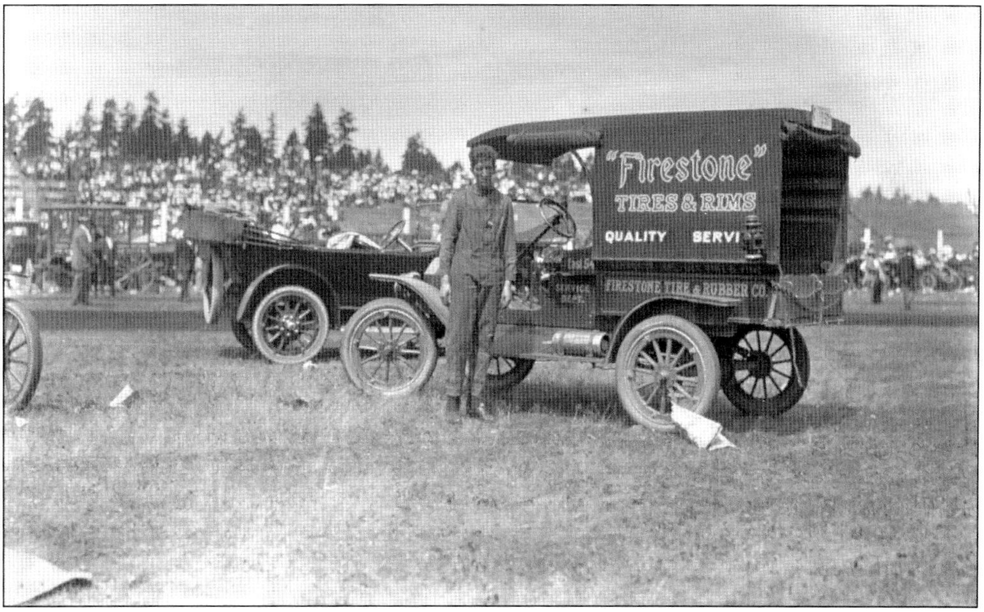

During the races at the Tacoma Speedway, the Firestone tire service truck was always ready to replace a tire for the racers on a moment's notice. The racetrack was a two-mile wooden board track for automobile racing that operated from 1914 to 1922 and was considered by some to be second only to the Indianapolis Speedway at the time. The races were usually 100, 200, or 250 miles in length.

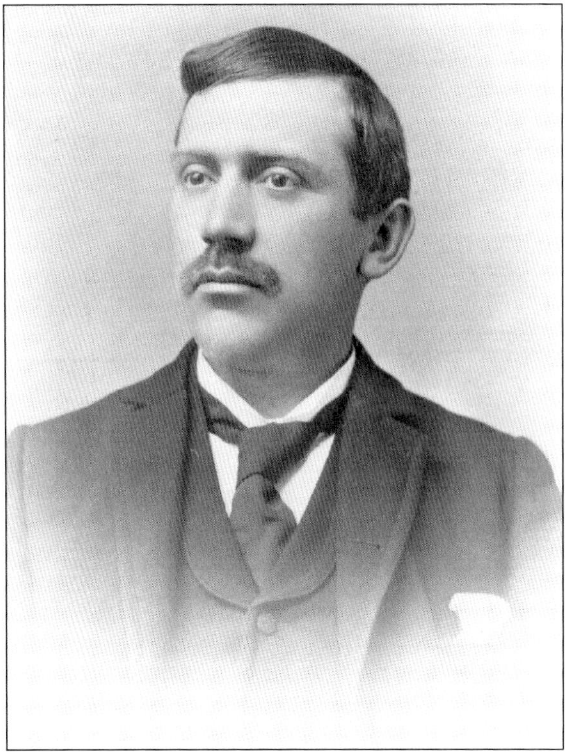

Aaron R. Titlow became the Pierce County prosecuting attorney after moving from Ohio. He was also the owner of the Hotel Hesperides located on the site of what is now the Titlow Lodge, owned by Metro Parks Tacoma. Originally the hotel had three floors, but Metro Parks removed the top two floors to make it the one-floor facility it is today.

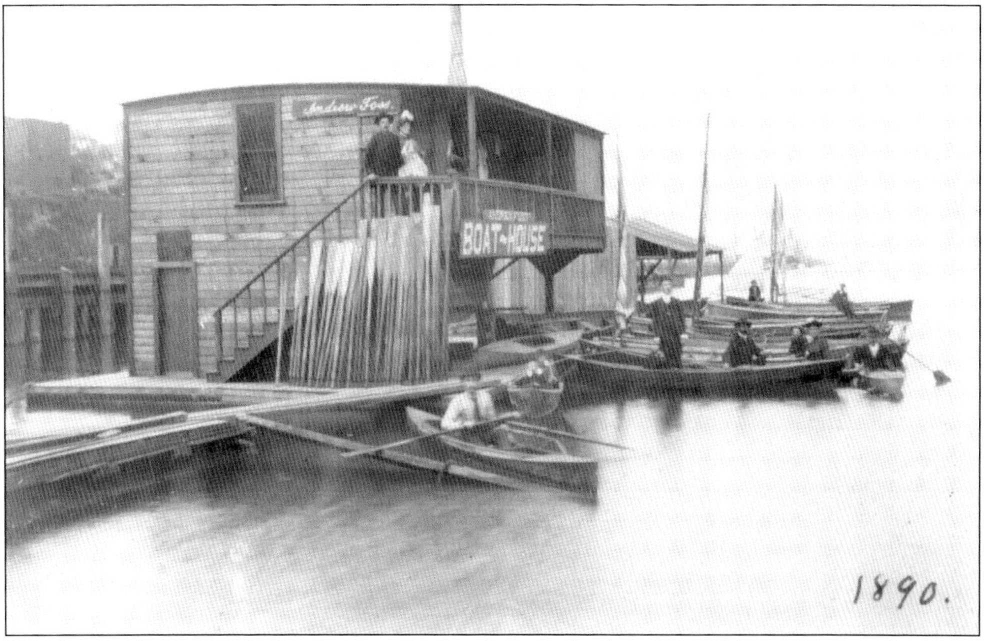

Standing at the top of the landing on this boathouse, the first one in Tacoma, are Andrew and Thea Foss shortly after arriving from Norway in 1889. Thea is holding their daughter Lillian. Henry Foss would be born about three months later and carried on the business his mother Thea started, by buying a used rowboat. Her business became Foss Launch Company, which later became the Foss Maritime Company.

Three

Development Years

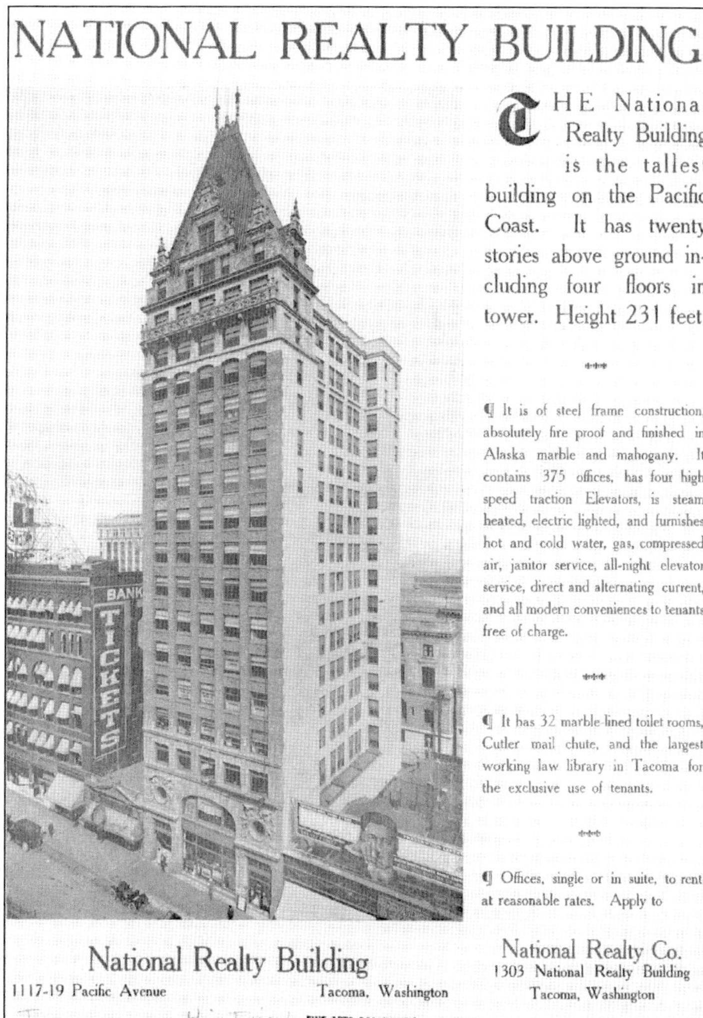

Construction started on the National Realty Building in 1909, and it was completed in 1911, when it was put up for sale by the National Realty Company. It was the tallest building in Washington State until surpassed in 1914 by the Smith Tower in Seattle. When Puget Sound National Bank purchased this building in 1917, it was the largest single real estate transaction in Tacoma's history.

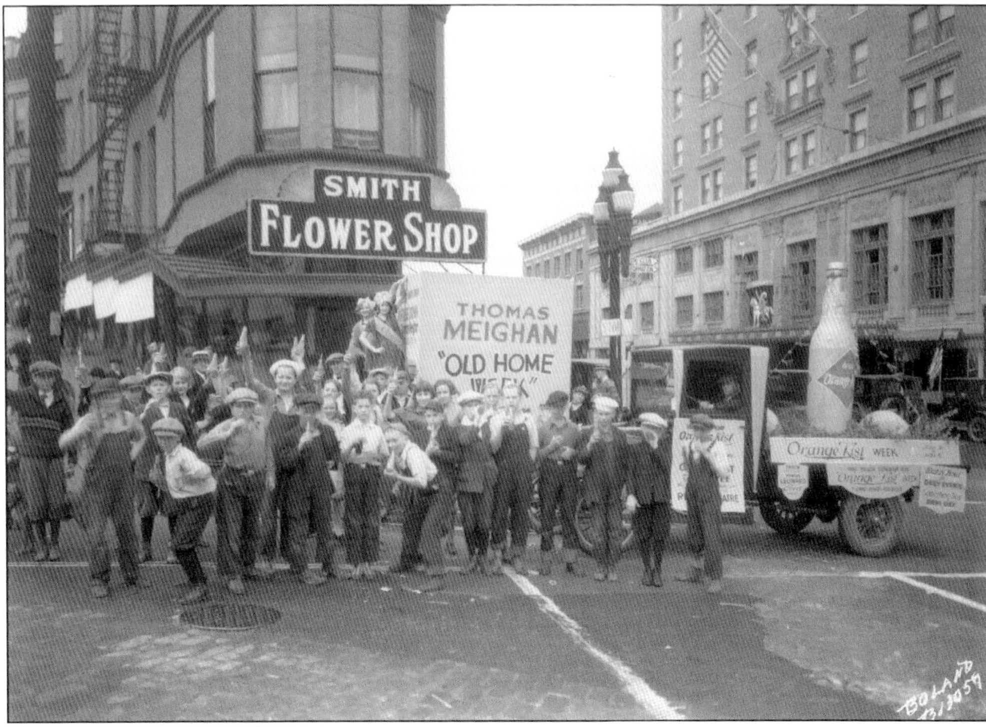

The image above shows schoolchildren celebrating Orange Kist Week on August 1, 1925, in front of Smith's Flower Shop. The Bostwick Building on Saint Helens Avenue is a Tacoma historical landmark and was erected in 1899. In June 1937, John "Lee" Kress opened his first malt shop in Tacoma in the Bostwick Building. It could seat 40 customers and had a configuration similar to today. Lee Kress passed away in 1959 at the age of 45. This site is now home to rental apartments and the Bostwick Café.

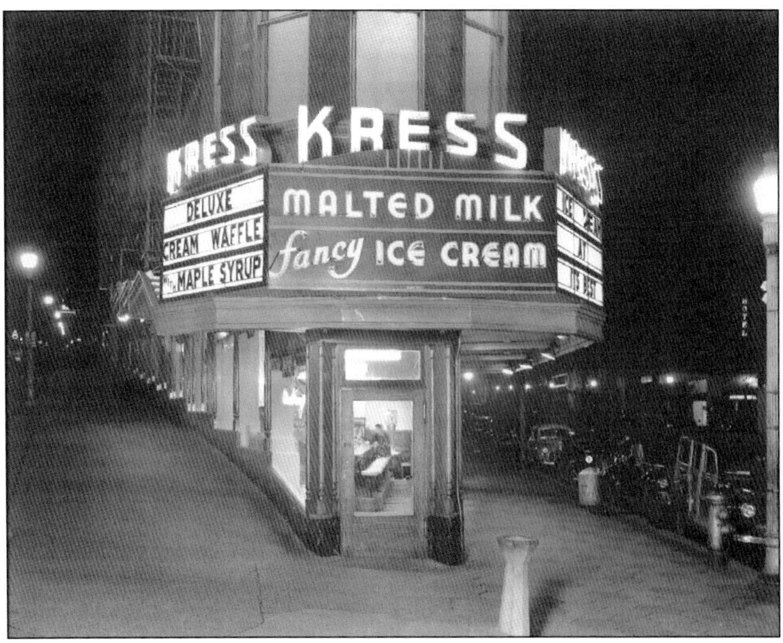

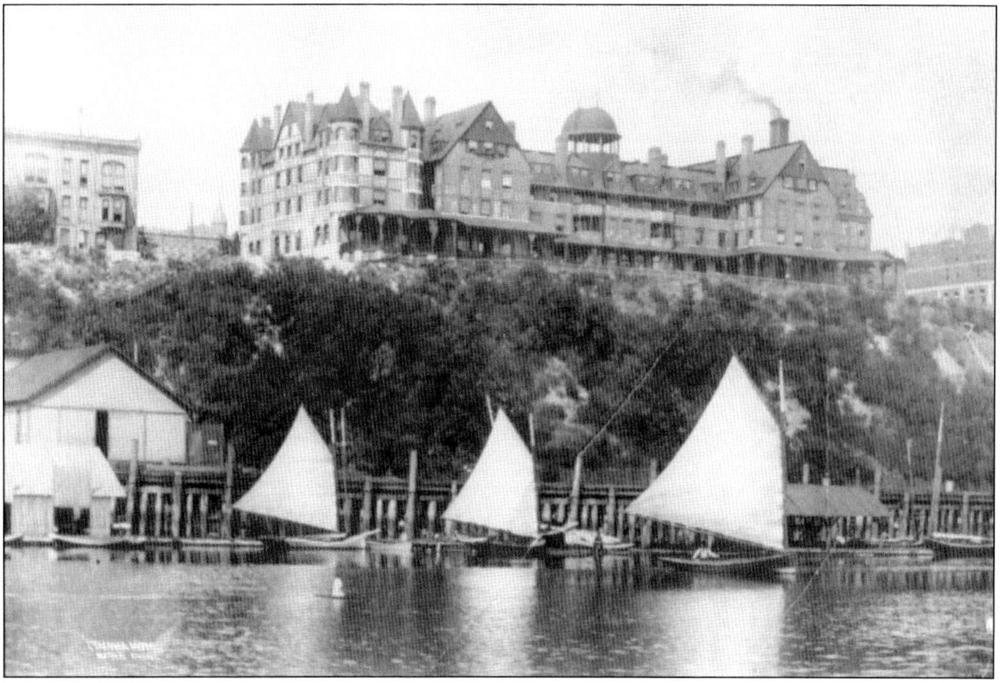

These photographs are of the majestic Tacoma Hotel that started construction in July 1883 and had its grand opening on August 8, 1884. The hotel was built of brick and faced with stone and occupied an entire city block on A Street, between Ninth and Tenth Streets. It had 125 guest rooms along with a 12-foot-square oven with a daily capacity of 500 pies or 250 loaves of bread. October 17, 1935, was the end of the Tacoma Hotel, when a fire broke out early in the morning. No lives were lost, but the hotel was not rebuilt. In 1986, construction began on this site for the Frank Russell Building, owned by George and Jane Russell. It was finished in 1988. That building was later sold by the Russells and is currently owned by State Farm Mutual Auto Insurance Company.

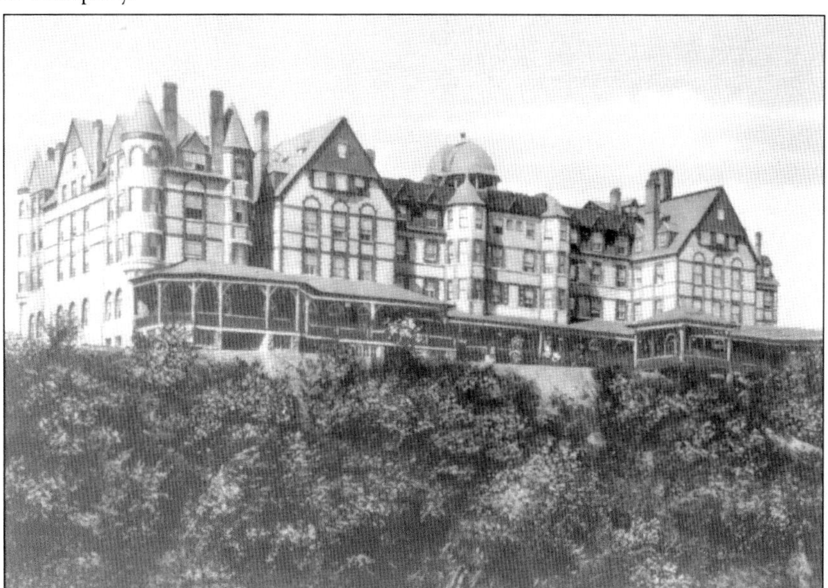

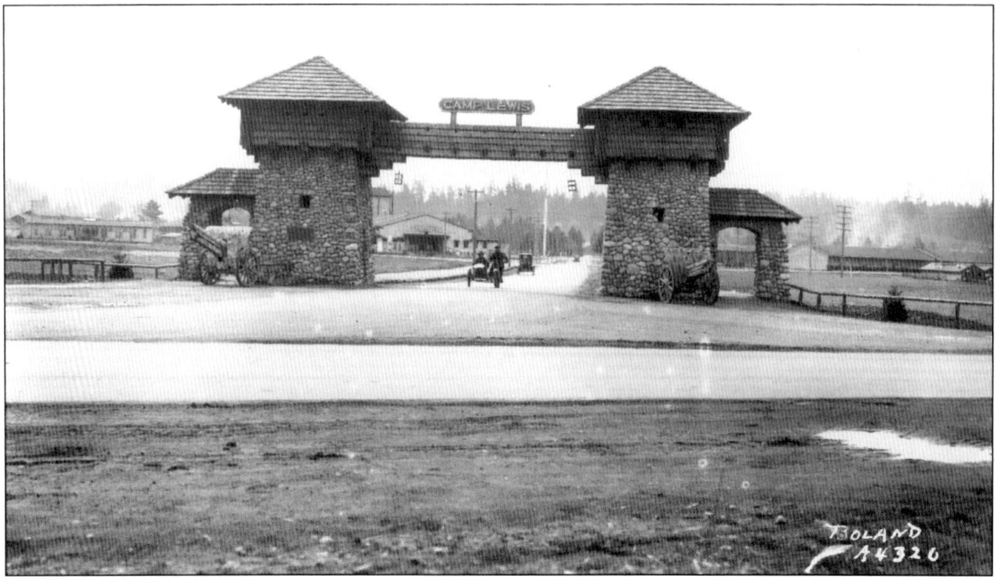

This gate to Camp Lewis was built in 1917 and paid for by employees who built the initial main buildings for the camp. In 1917, Pierce County donated 70,000 acres to the government for the establishment of this military base. This gate cost $4,000 to build and is still standing, although it was moved to make room for the Interstate 5 freeway around 1960.

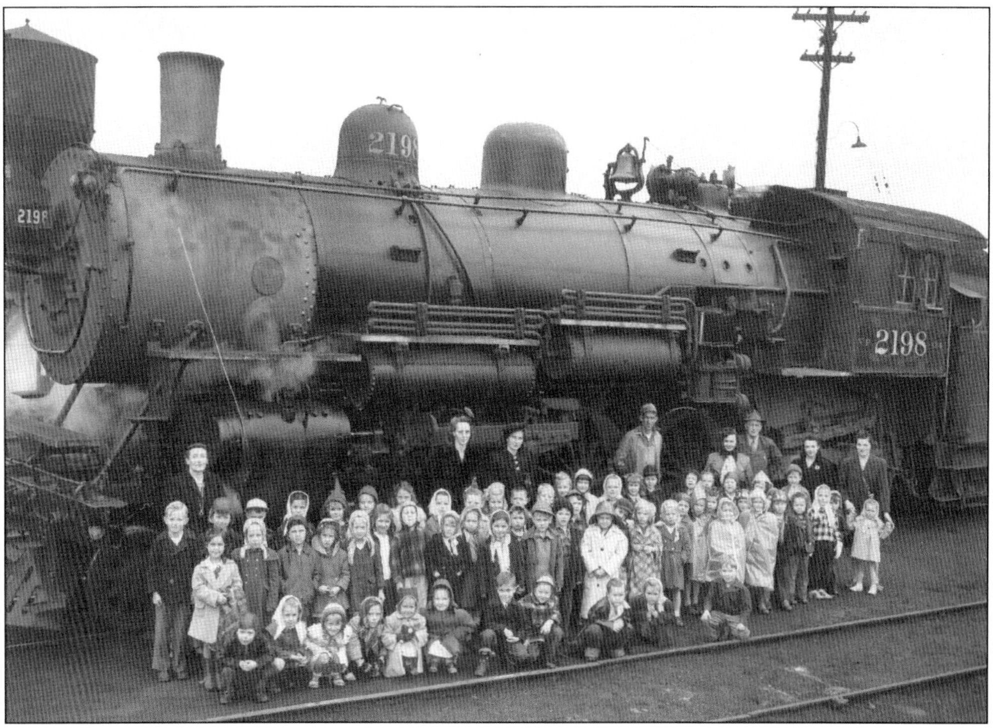

These students from Fern Hill School were guests of the Union Pacific Depot and the Northern Pacific roundhouse for a field trip in November 1947. The children were able to go on a short railroad trip and inspect the equipment on these much-anticipated and fun field trips that were part of the Tacoma schools' reading readiness program.

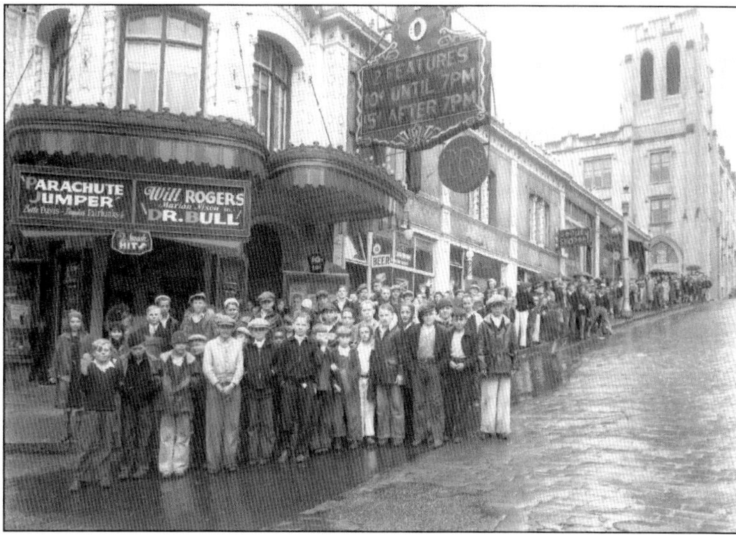

Children are lined outside the Rialto Theater to see Bette Davis and Douglas Fairbanks in *Parachute Jumper.* In 1934, the film industry was starting to enforce the Hays Production Code to eliminate sex and violence from movies.

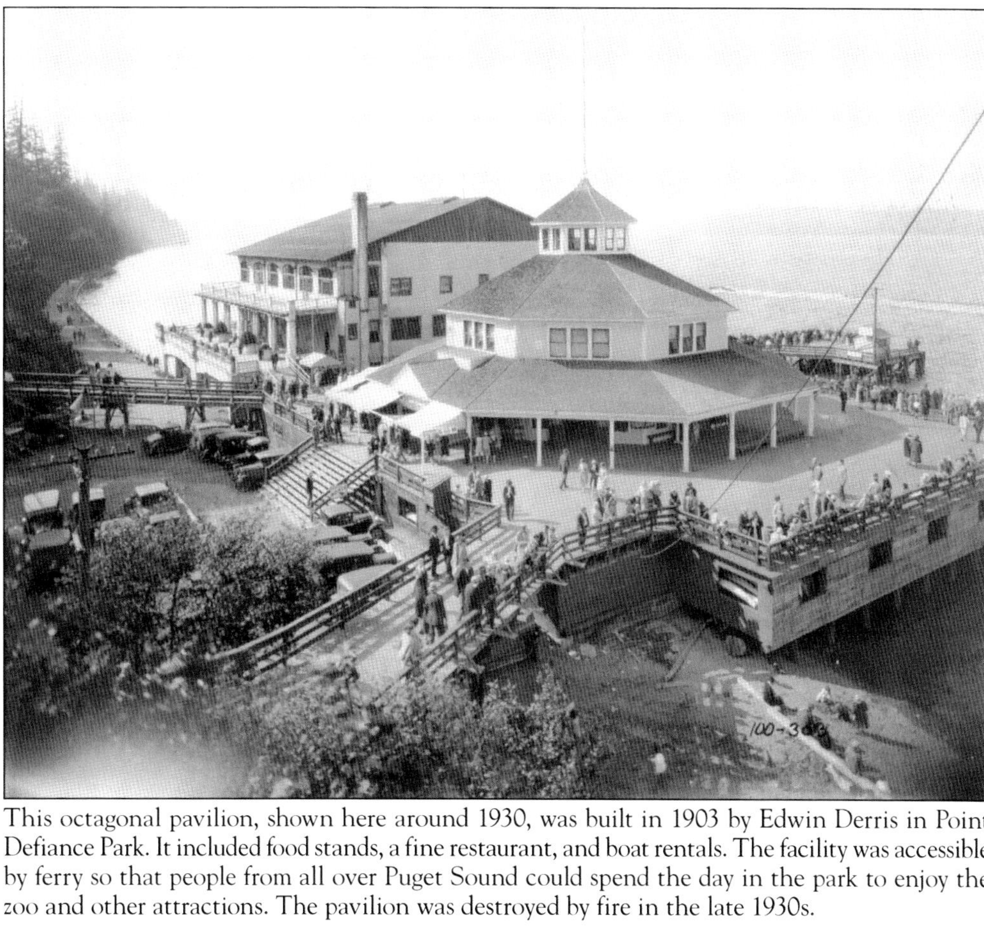

This octagonal pavilion, shown here around 1930, was built in 1903 by Edwin Derris in Point Defiance Park. It included food stands, a fine restaurant, and boat rentals. The facility was accessible by ferry so that people from all over Puget Sound could spend the day in the park to enjoy the zoo and other attractions. The pavilion was destroyed by fire in the late 1930s.

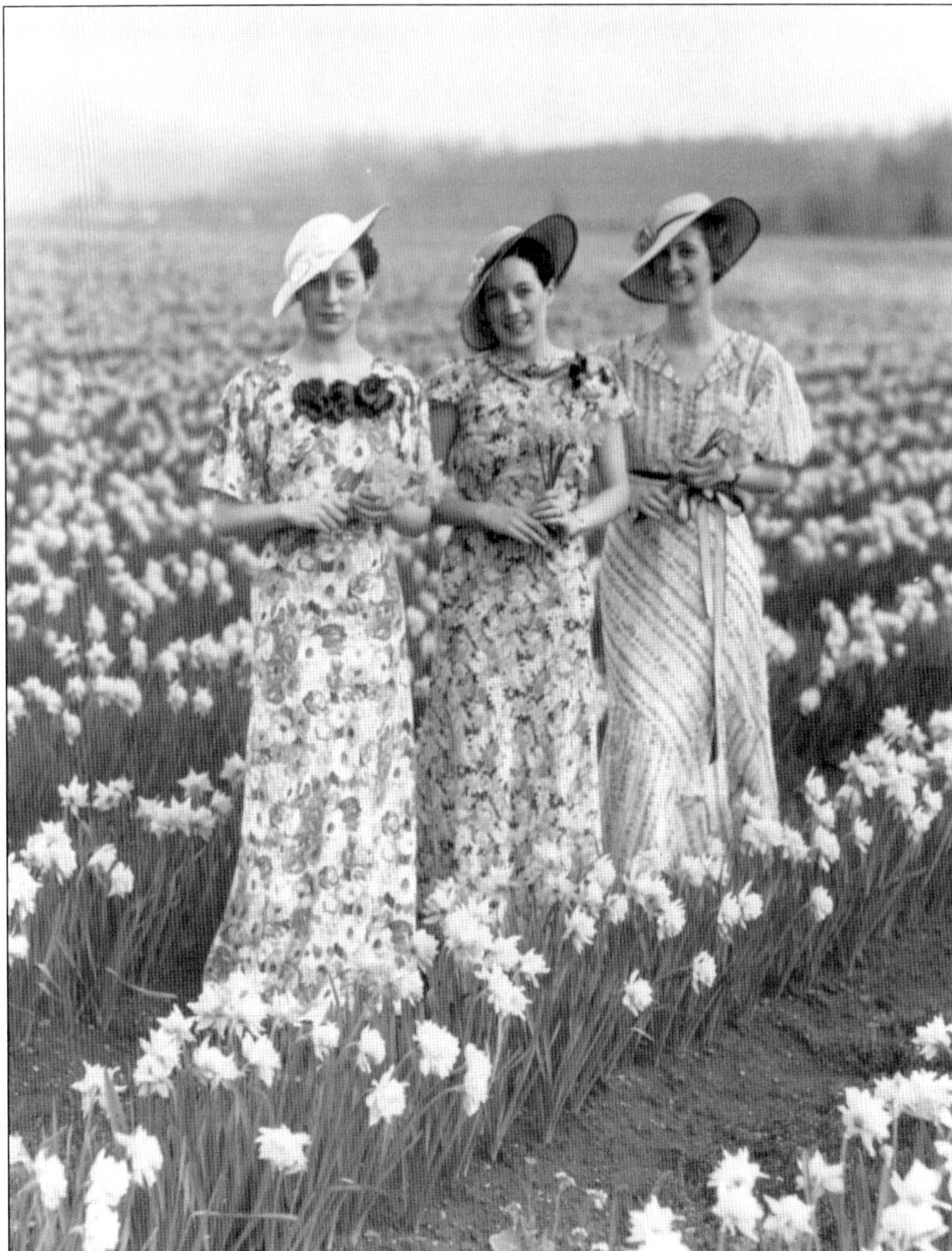

The first-ever Puyallup Valley Daffodil Festival was held in 1934, and these three ladies are posing in a field of bright yellow daffodils to help advertise this new event. The parade gradually grew to involve the communities of Puyallup, Sumner, Orting, and Tacoma. From left to right are Frankie Cowan, Billye Fairchild, and Betty Brumbaugh wearing long spring dresses and stylish hats.

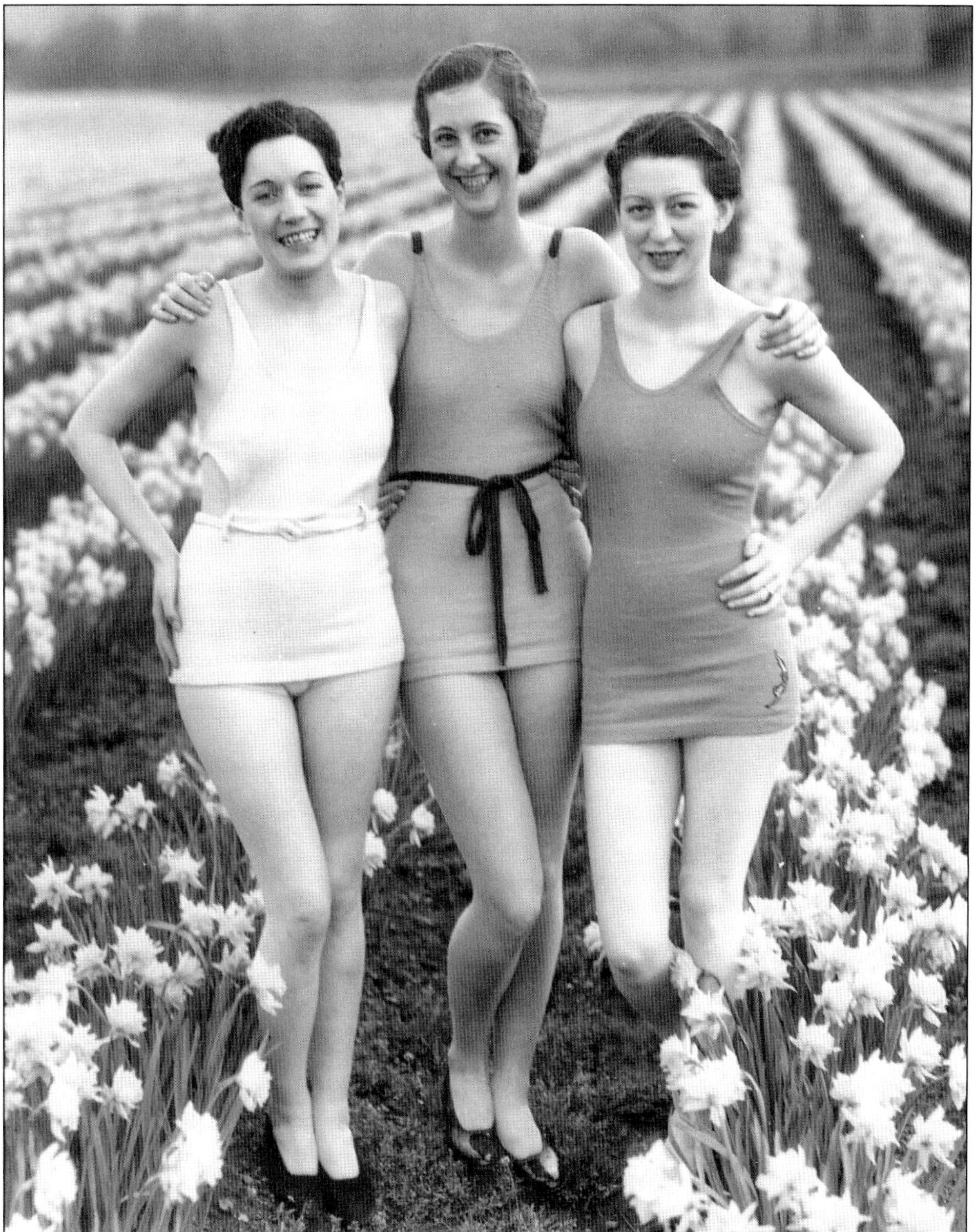

A little "cheesecake" was used to advertise the new flower festival that was to become the annual Puyallup Valley Daffodil Festival, which was held March 17–18, 1934. The very first festival was organized with a budget of $600 and has now grown to be one of America's oldest flower extravaganzas. From left to right are Frankie Cowan, Betty Brumbaugh, and Billye Fairchild.

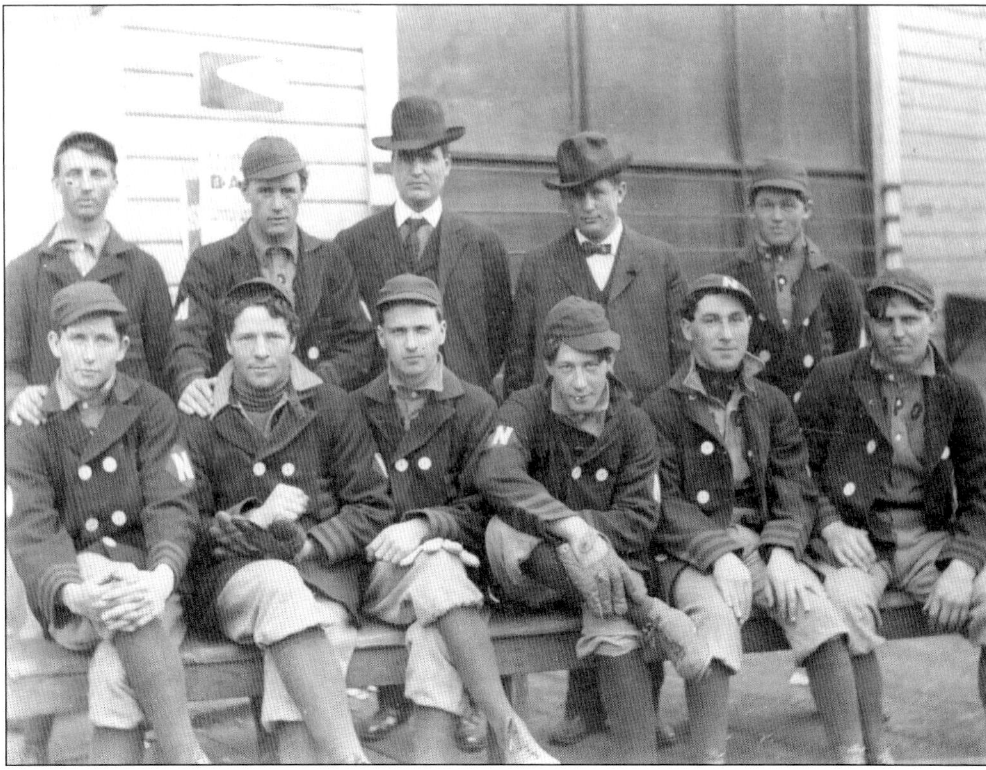

The Newports, an amateur baseball team in Tacoma, pose in 1908. From left to right are (first row) Ed Ballard, Jack Clark, Vic Olson, F. Burgeson, Frank Cozza, and Rudy Johnson; (second row) Arnold Levenhagen, Jack Clancy, Grant Clark (manager), Mike Knelp, and L. Furlatt. The team was named after the Newport Saloon at 1544 Commerce in the Newport Hotel.

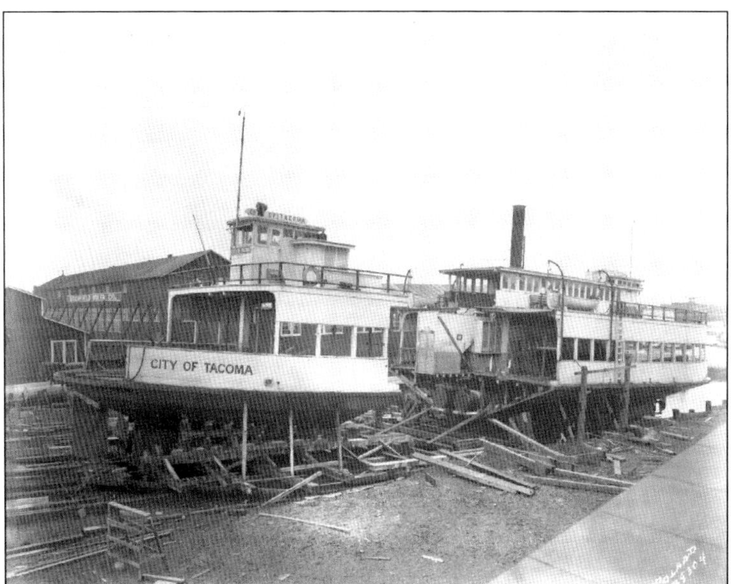

In 1924, the ferry *City of Tacoma* underwent a major remodel. This ferry operated between Point Defiance and Gig Harbor. This work was being done at Western Boat Building to have 34 feet added just aft of her engine to increase her length so that the carrying capacity could be increased to 50 automobiles. The ferry was only out of service for 30 days to accomplish this feat.

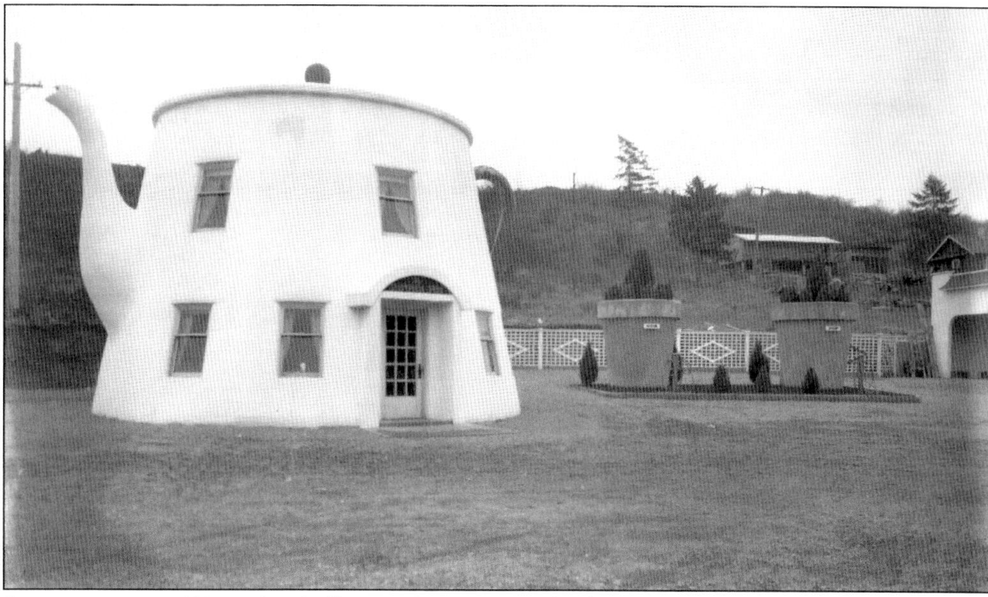

Starting out in 1929 as the Coffee Pot Restaurant, this became known later as Bob's Java Jive. After a few other short-time names, it was sold to Bob Radonich in 1955. The 1960s band the Ventures used to play here regularly when surf music was at its height. The structure was listed in the Tacoma Register of Historic Places on September 30, 2003, as Bob's Java Jive. The Coffee Pot Restaurant, at 2101 South Tacoma Way, was listed in the National Register of Historic Places on April 21, 2014.

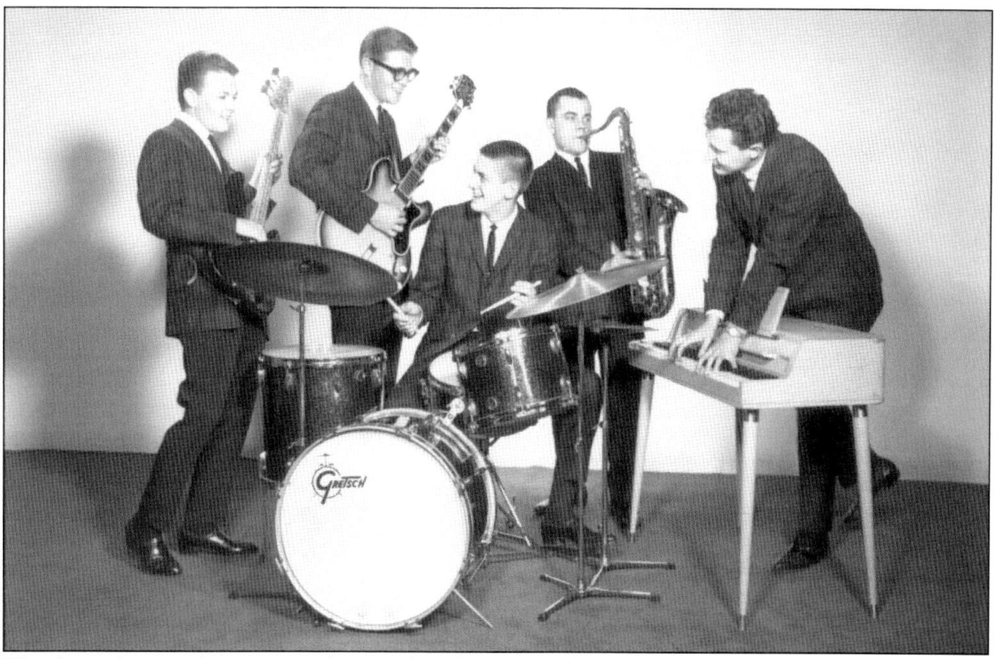

The legendary rock pioneers the Wailers (1958–1969) are, from left to right, Buck Ormsby, Richard (Rick) Dangel, Mike Burk, Mark Marush, and Kent Morrill. Besides being nationally recognized in the 1960s, the Wailers played regularly at Bob's Java Jive and the Spanish Castle, a major ballroom halfway between Seattle and Tacoma, which is now destroyed.

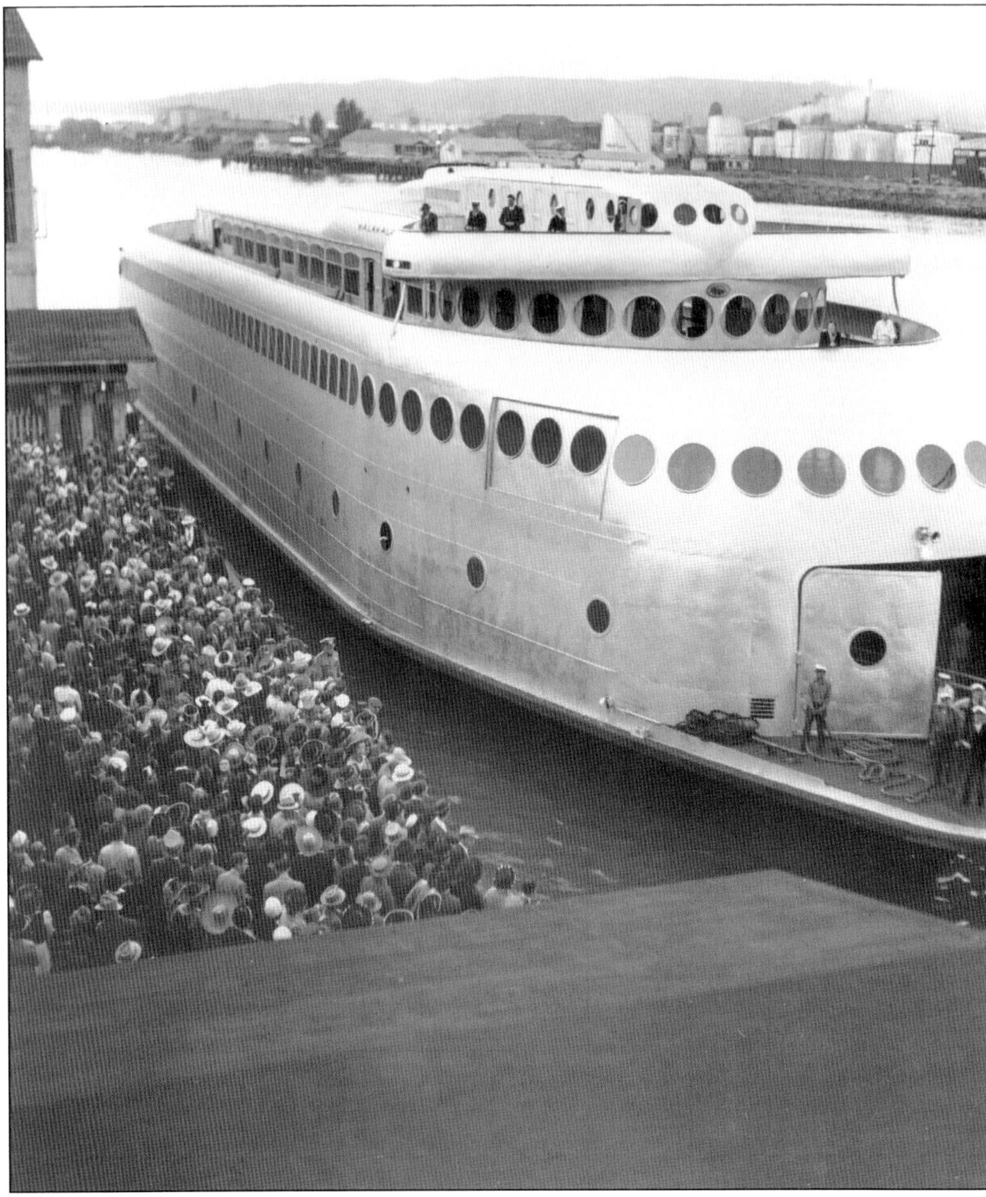

The Washington state ferry *Kalakala* transported passengers for the last ferry ride prior to the Narrows Bridge opening on July 2, 1940. These passengers are waiting at the Tacoma Municipal Dock for the last ride to Gig Harbor. A party was held aboard with over 1,400 revelers who celebrated with music and dancing sponsored by the Young Men's Business Club.

An Official Event of Tacoma Narrows Bridge-McChord Field Celebration

DANCE! FROLIC! JUBILATE! CELEBRATE!

A FOUR-HOUR LAST FERRY-BOAT RIDE

Another Golden Jubilee on the "KALAKALA"

TUESDAY, JULY 2, 1940

LEAVE TACOMA MUNICIPAL DOCK, 8 P. M.

Sponsored by Tacoma Young Men's Business Club.

No 757

ONE DOLLAR

From Tacoma to Bremerton via the Four Ferry Landings

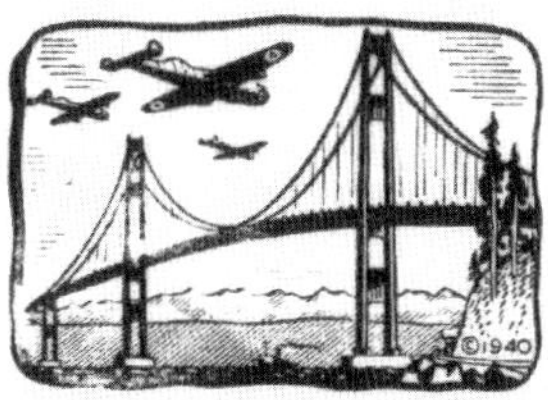

Twice under the Bridge on the "KALAKALA"

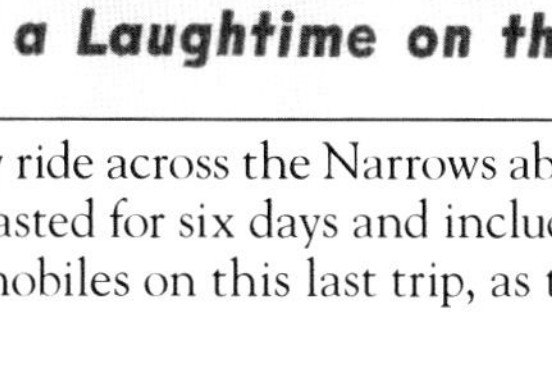

LEAVING
Tacoma Municipal Dock,
8:00 P. M.
Pt. Defiance Ferry Landing,
8:30 P. M.
Gig Harbor Ferry Landing,
9:00 P. M.
—
Passengers Only—No Autos

UNLOADING AT
Gig Harbor Ferry Landing.
Pt. Defiance Ferry Landing.
Tacoma Municipal Dock.
—
Come in Costume If Possible

The Thrill of a Laughtime on the Last Ferry!

This is a $1 ticket for the last ferry ride across the Narrows aboard the *Kalakala*. The celebrations for opening the Narrows Bridge lasted for six days and included dancing, parades, speeches, and ceremonies. There were no automobiles on this last trip, as the ferry became a party boat.

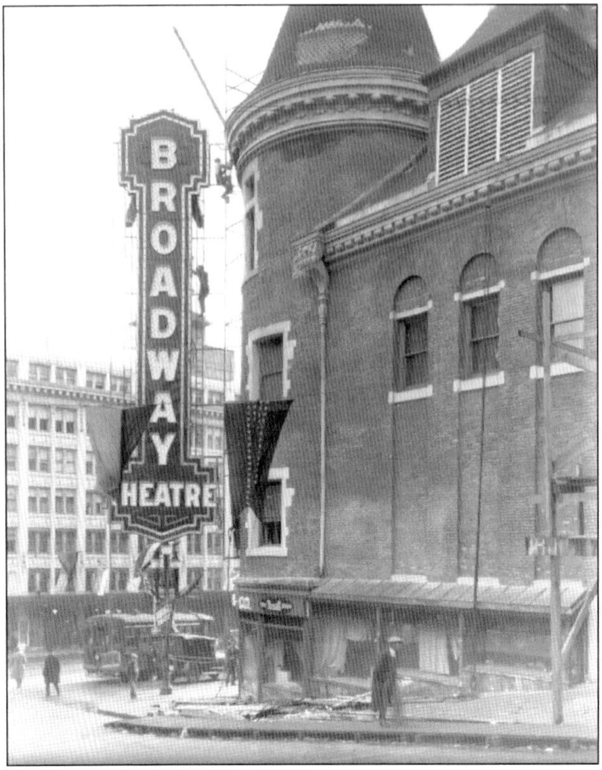

The Tacoma Theatre was built in 1889 and located at 902 Broadway. Originally, it was a grand opera house and then converted to a motion picture theater in 1927 and renamed the Broadway Theatre, as shown. It was later renamed the Music Box Theater in 1933 and was eventually destroyed by a fire on April 30, 1963.

The Beverly Theater opened in 1934 and was named after the daughter of Michael "Mike" Barovic, the owner. Previously, this building housed the Colonial Theatre but was completely remodeled in 1931. It was eventually replaced by the Telenews Theater in 1945, and the building was demolished in 1988. Mike Barovic passed away on May 31, 1994, at the age of 97.

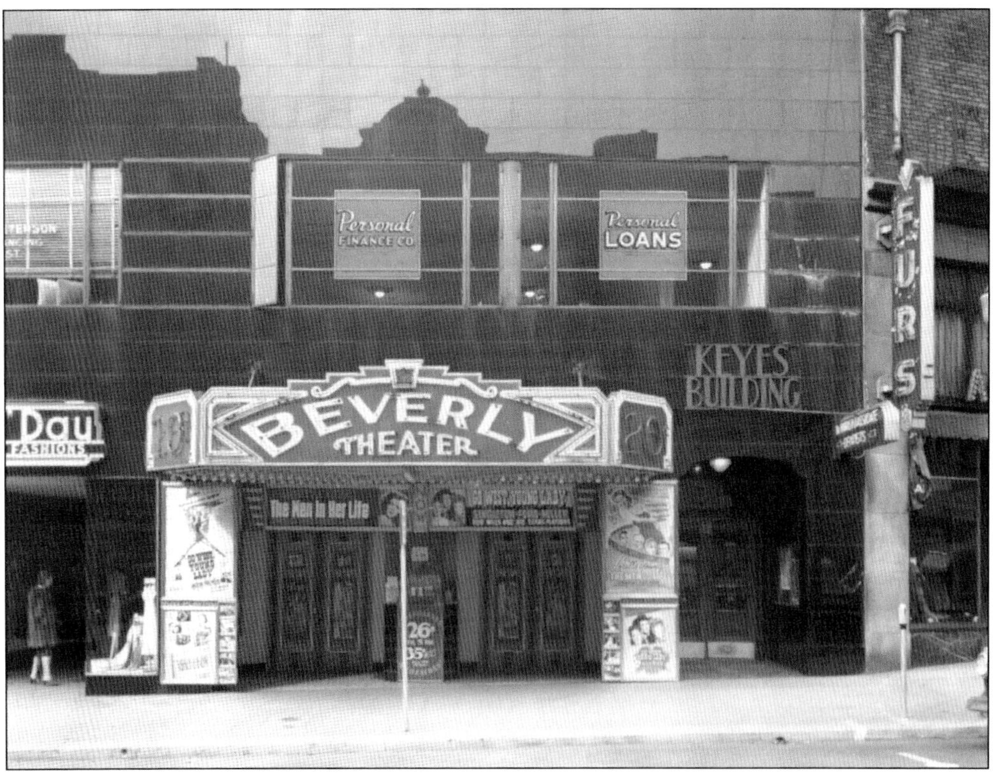

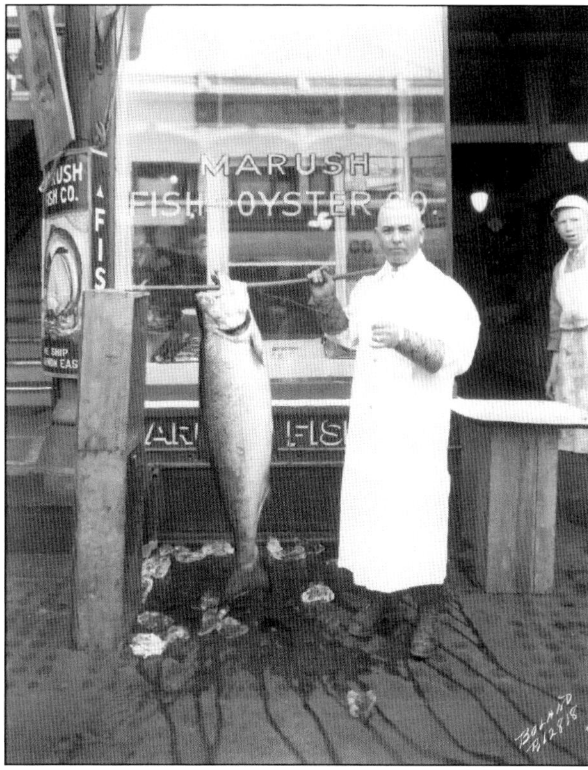

Mike Marush is shown in this photograph, taken in June 1925, with a king salmon, believed to be the largest ever caught locally on hook and line. The fish weighed 47 pounds and was caught and dressed by G.C. Crawford of Gig Harbor, not far from where the Narrows Bridge would eventually be built.

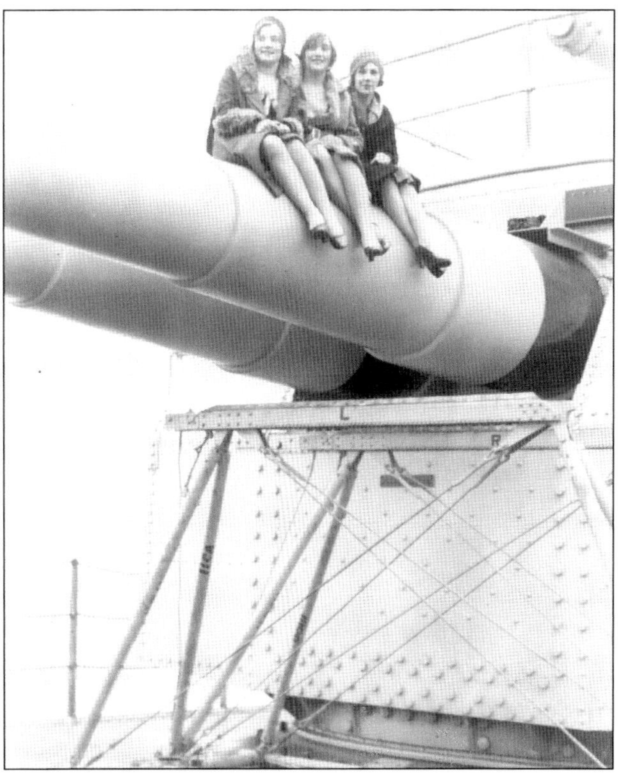

Perched on the eight-inch guns of the USS *Lexington* on December 23, 1929, are Freda Gardner, of the Tacoma Chamber of Commerce; Ethel Haasarud, RKO cashier; and Naomi Dykernan, head usher, Fox Rialto. They were promoting the chamber of commerce's dance for the *Lexington's* enlisted men to be held at the Greenwich Coliseum. Visitors were allowed to tour the *Lexington* while it was docked at Tacoma in the winter of 1929 to supplement the city's electrical power.

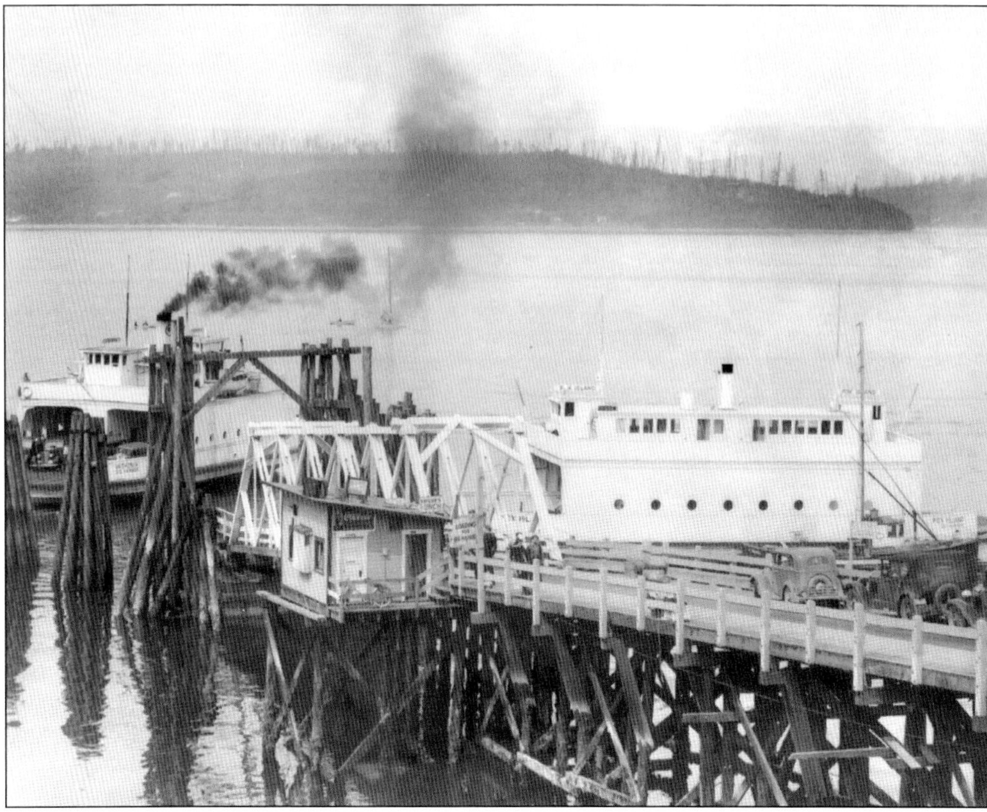

This photograph at the Point Defiance ferry landing shows the *Vashonia* coming in to dock with the smaller ferry boat *Fox Island* to the right. The Washington Navigation Company ran the ferries between Tacoma and the peninsula under the direction of Mitchell Skansie of Gig Harbor. The people and cars on the right are waiting to load for their trip to Gig Harbor.

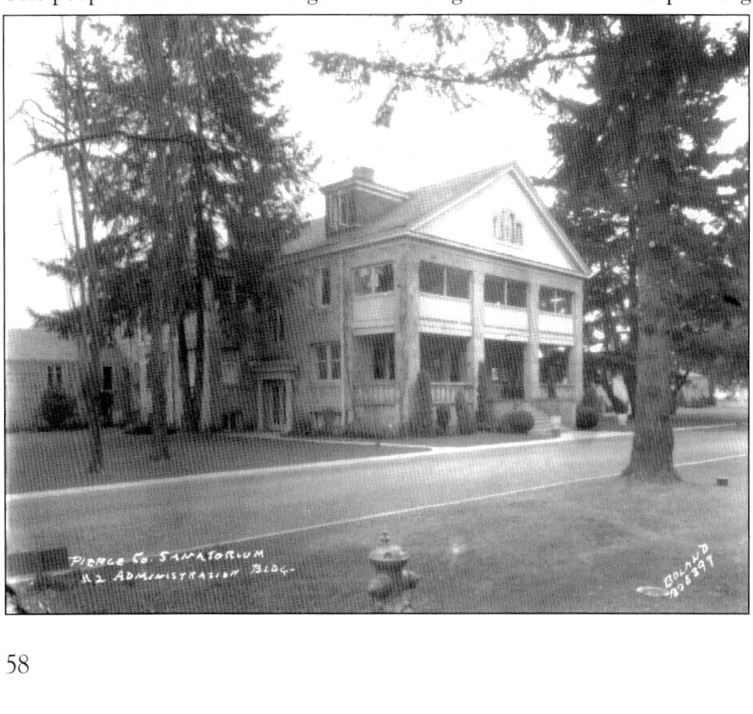

This is Lakeview Sanatorium, more formally known as Pierce County Sanatorium, as seen on March 24, 1934. Adults and children were treated for tuberculosis in separate wards in this facility. In 1955, this hospital campus was purchased by McChord Air Force Base, and patients were treated at the Mountain View Sanatorium in Tacoma.

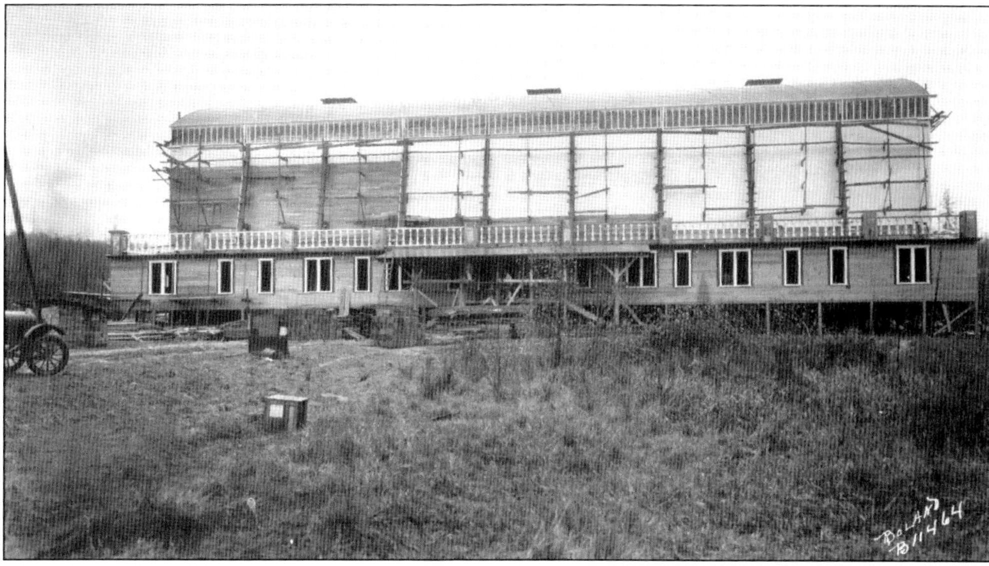

Near the end of 1924, serious motion picture production came to Tacoma–Pierce County. This photograph shows the H.C. Weaver Productions studios located on five and a half acres near Titlow Beach at the end of Sixth Avenue. The administration building in front of the soundstage had the executive offices, a projection room, 15-star dressing rooms, and dressing rooms for extras. The elaborate dedication, which was open to the public, was held on December 14, 1924.

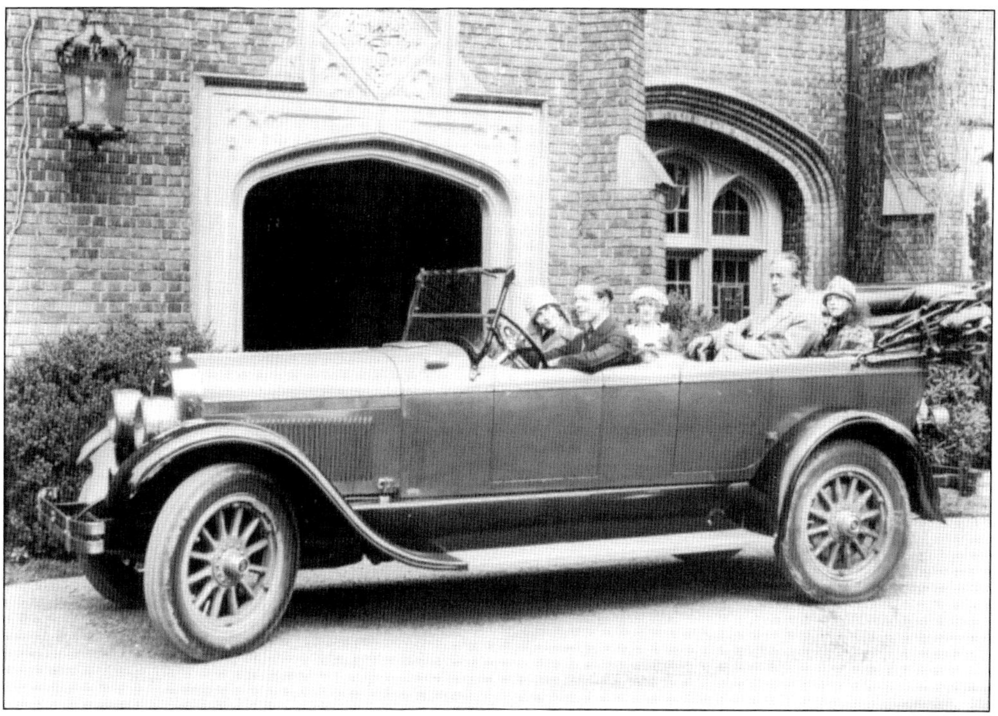

During March 1926, H.C. Weaver Productions used Thornewood, seen here, as a set for the filming of *Eyes of the Totem*. This silent film was released on May 15, 1927, and then lost for decades until recently. Other local sites used for filming were the Tacoma Totem Pole, the Winthrop Hotel, and Annie Wright Seminary.

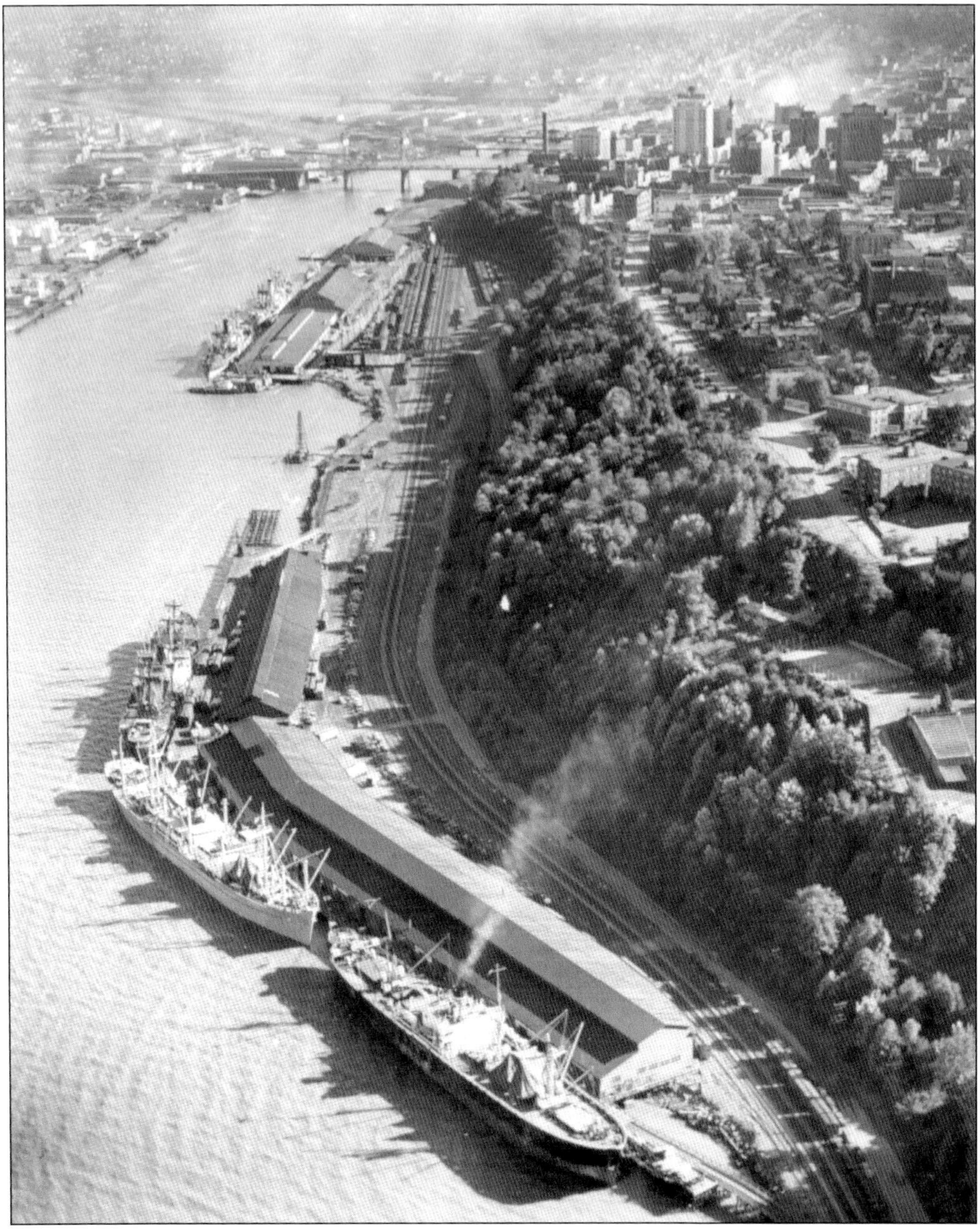

This photograph of Tacoma shows Baker Dock, Schaffer No. 1, Commercial Dock, McCormick Dock, Municipal Dock, and the Associated Grocers Co-operative warehouse on the Thea Foss Waterway on September 9, 1948. The Eleventh Street bridge is at top center.

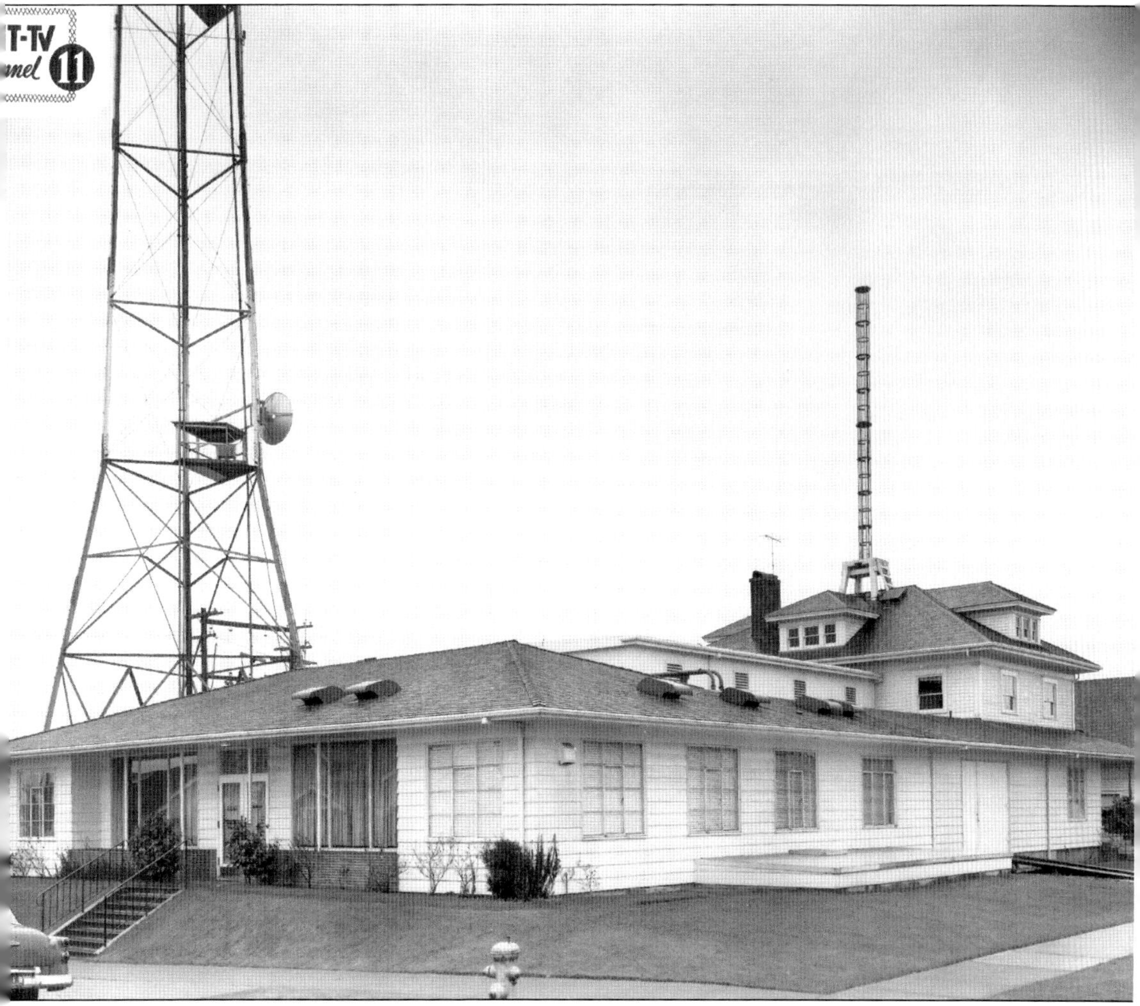

Locally produced television shows in the 1950s emanated from this simple, wood-frame building on the corner of South Eleventh Street and Grant Avenue. KTNT began broadcasting with a 289-foot tower in March 1953 as a Channel 11, a CBS affiliate. Early shows such as *Brakeman Bill* and *Pantry Playhouse* were produced from this facility.

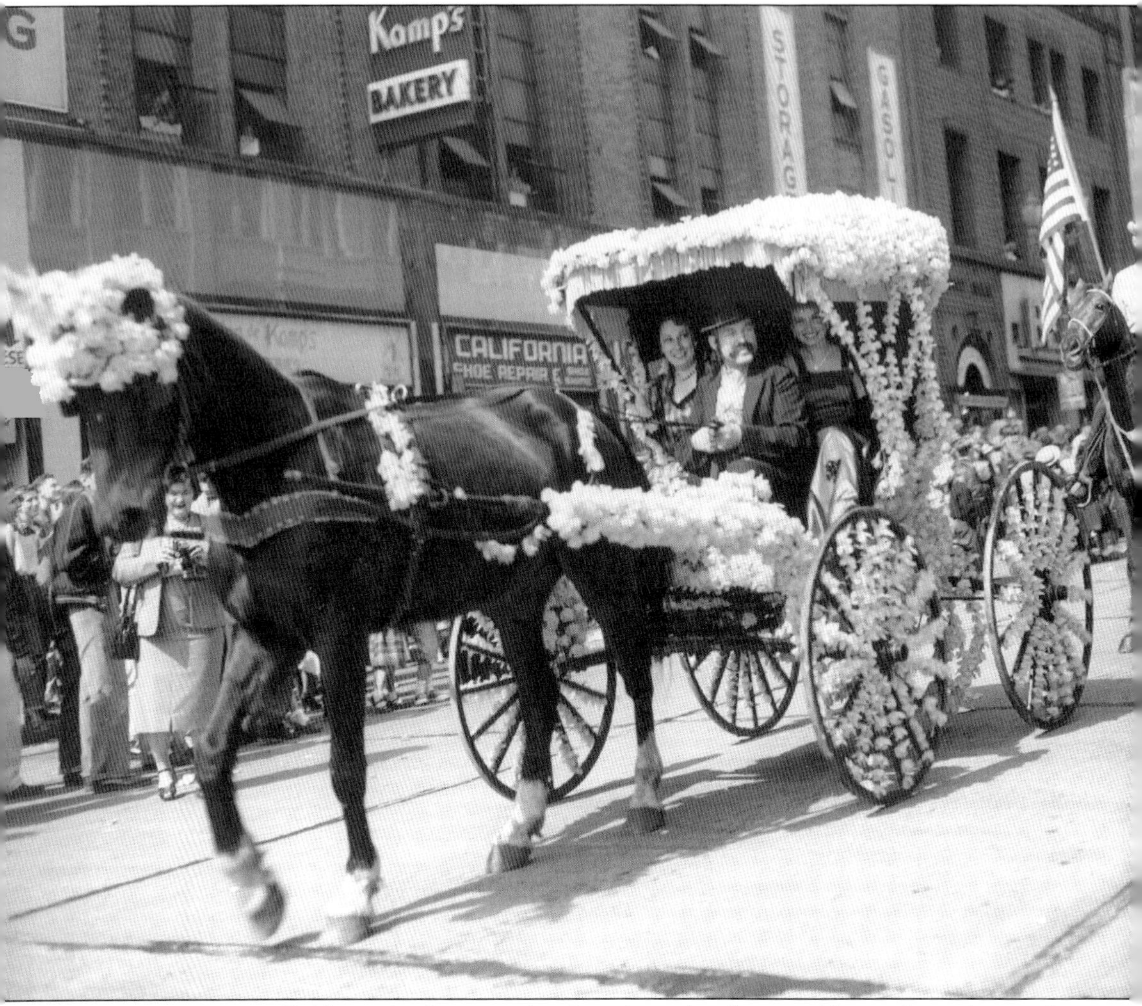

For the 1952 Daffodil Parade, the Pease family rode in this decorated horse-drawn buggy. Steve Pease is shown with his wife, Mary, and daughter Dorothy Jean. Steve was the owner of Steve's Gay 90's and was often referred to as the mayor of South Tacoma. Steve's Gay 90's was a very popular restaurant from 1951 until it closed in 1977.

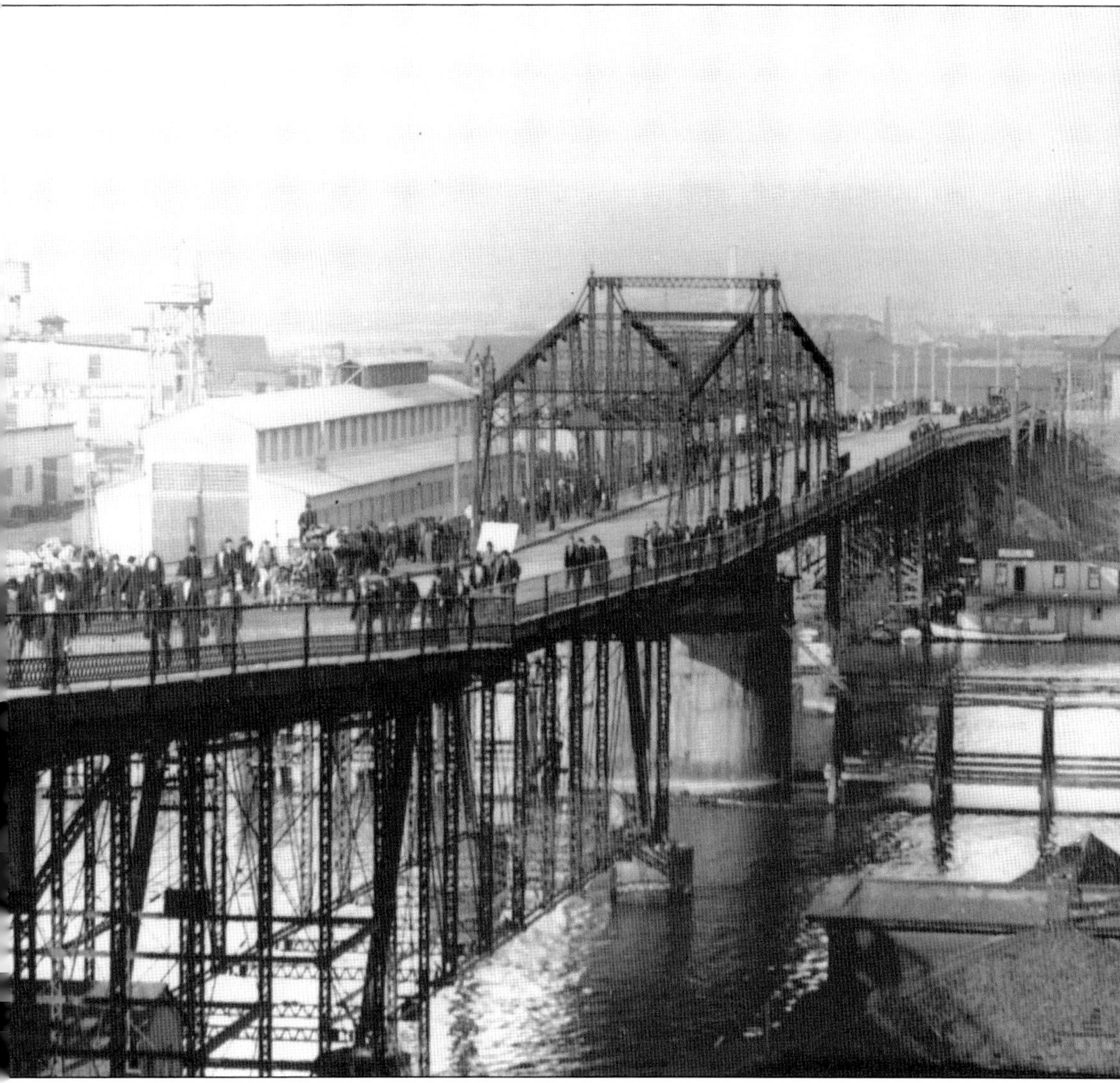

The first contract to build a bridge to span the Foss waterway on Eleventh Street was let in 1894, and construction was completed in 1895. This initial bridge was closed in 1911 and replaced with the current Murray Morgan Bridge, which was closed between 2007 and 2014 for rehabilitation.

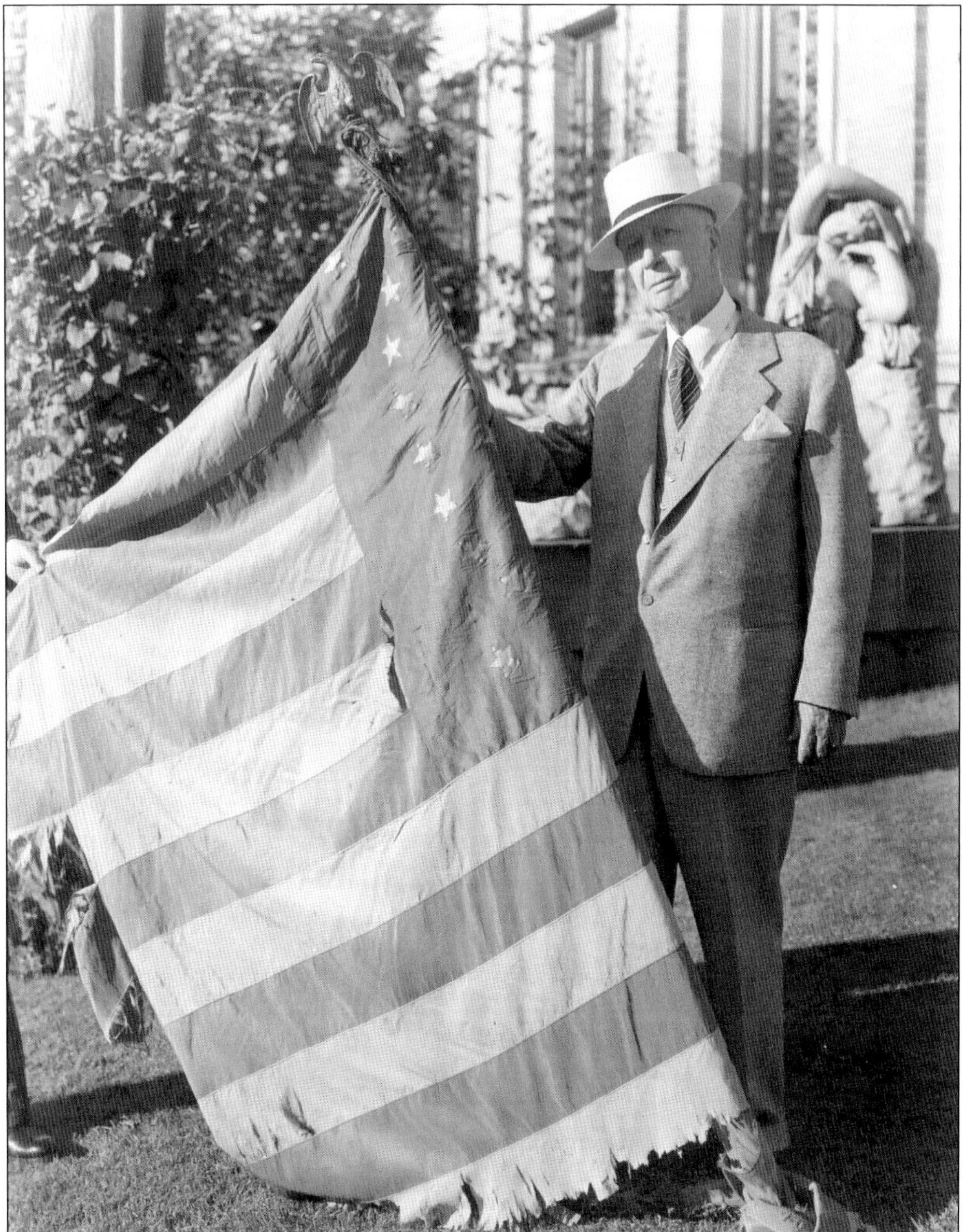

Gen. James M. Ashton is shown in 1935 in front of what was then known as the Ferry Museum with an old cavalry guidon. This flag was presented to Elisha P. Ferry, the first governor of Washington State, by his nephew Clinton P. Ferry during his inaugural ceremonies.

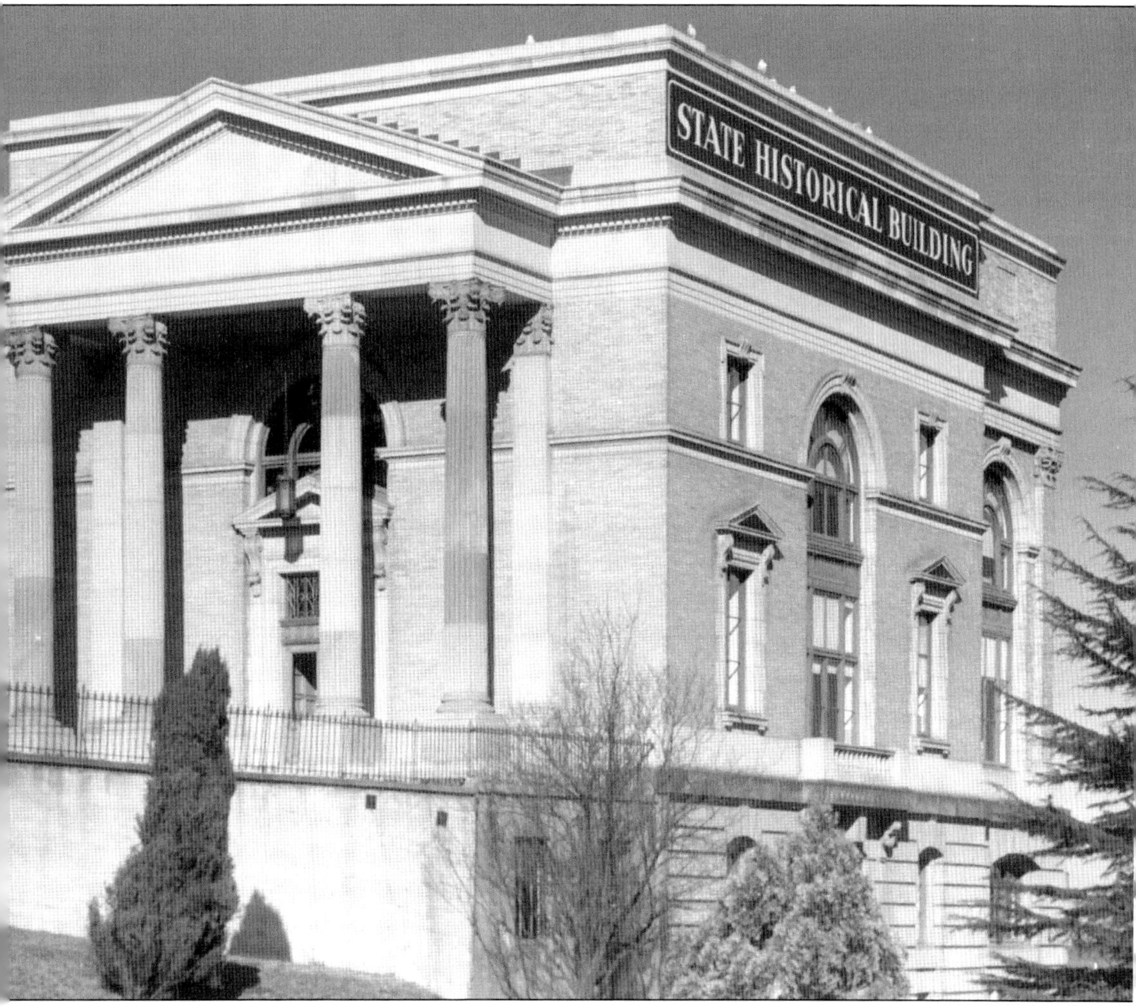

Originally, what was called the Ferry Museum was built at 315 North Stadium Way in 1911. This building is now the Washington State History Research Center and is open to researchers by appointment only. The library's reading room has over 16,000 books, 600,000 photographs and negatives, 3,300 maps, and 1.5 million archives. It was converted to a research facility when the newer Washington State Historical Society Museum opened on Pacific Avenue in 1996.

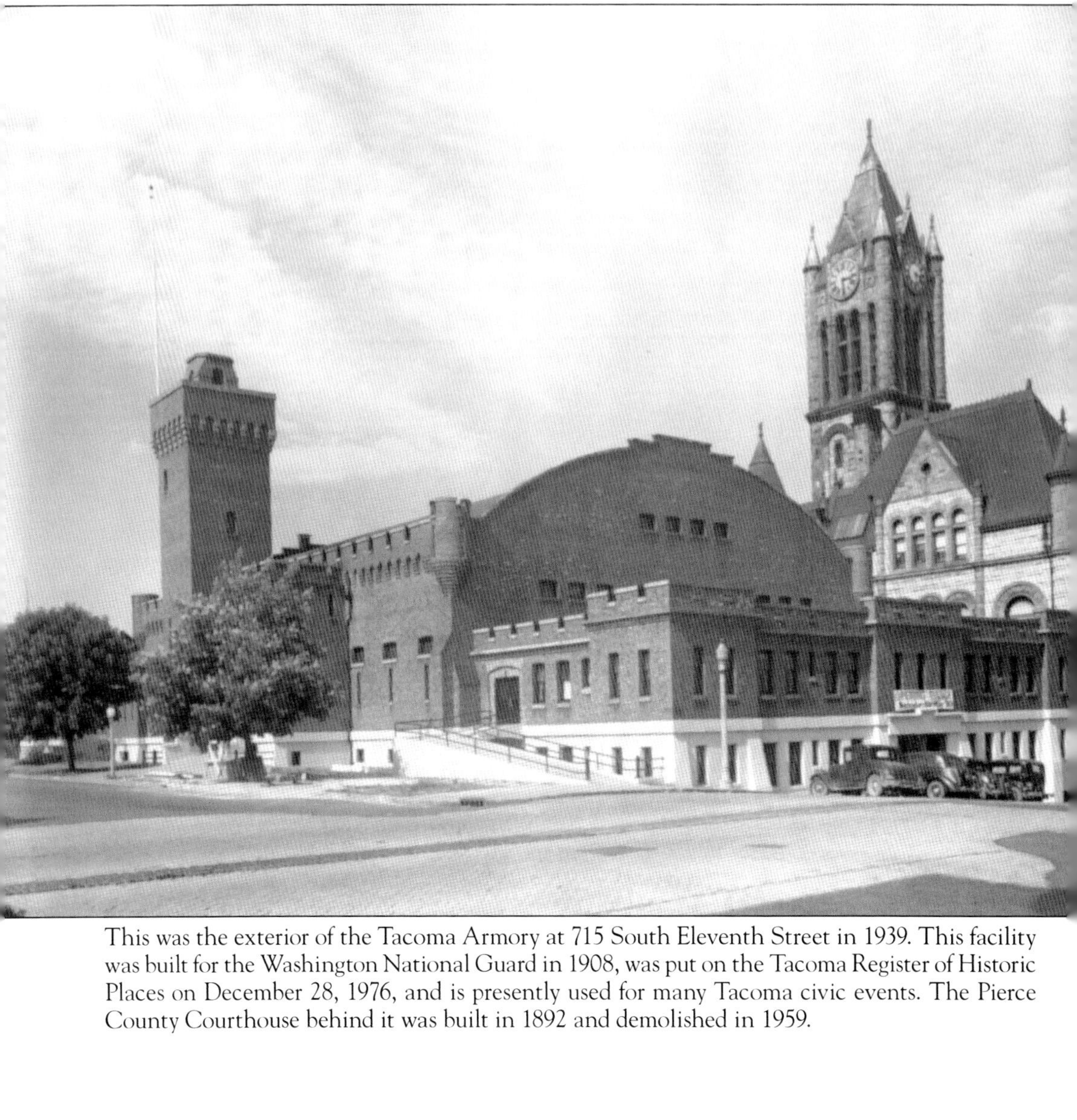

This was the exterior of the Tacoma Armory at 715 South Eleventh Street in 1939. This facility was built for the Washington National Guard in 1908, was put on the Tacoma Register of Historic Places on December 28, 1976, and is presently used for many Tacoma civic events. The Pierce County Courthouse behind it was built in 1892 and demolished in 1959.

Four

MATURING YEARS

Construction on the first Narrows Bridge began on September 27, 1938. Even while the bridge was under construction, workers gave it the nickname of "Galloping Gertie." These brave workmen, atop a tower of the bridge, have no safety harnesses on as they pose for a photograph. The first Narrows Bridge opened on July 1, 1940, and collapsed on November 7.

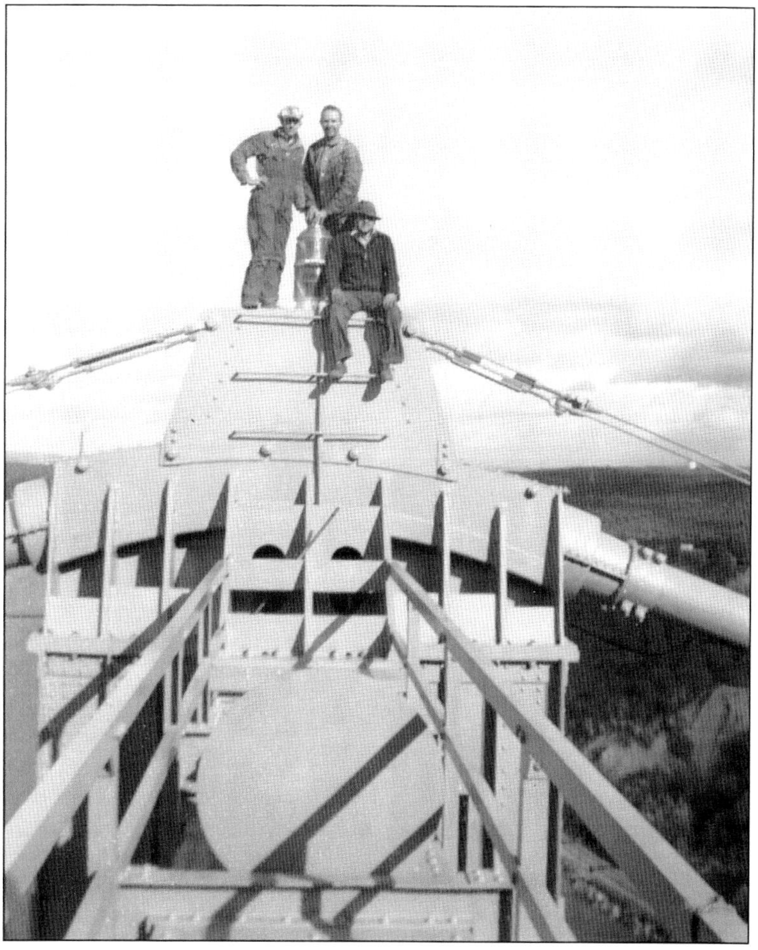

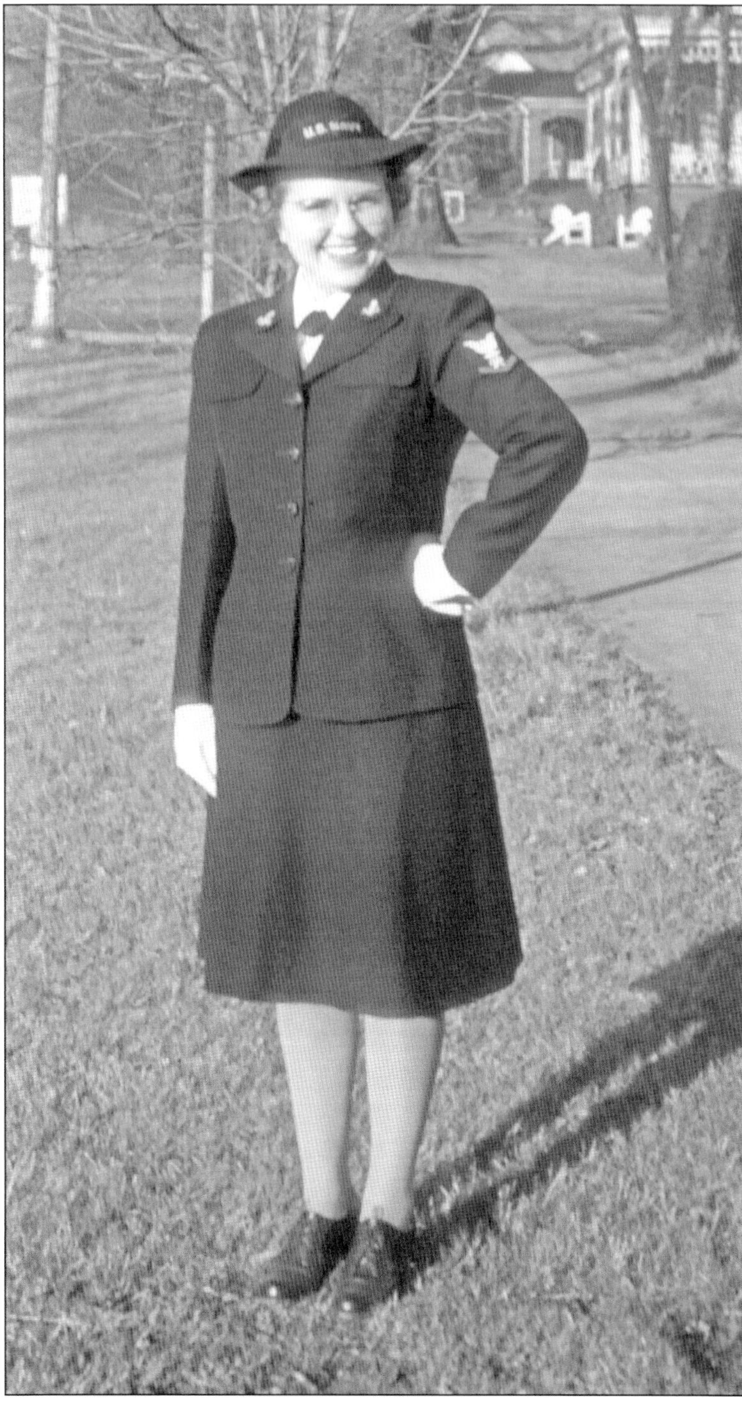

Betty Jo Alexander, a longtime Tacoma resident, is showing off her new uniform shortly after completing her training for the US Navy's women's reserves, better known as Women Accepted for Volunteer Emergency Service (WAVES). Alexander served as a payroll clerk during World War II to the ships in Seattle and delivered payroll to many seamen, who were glad to see her on paydays. (Courtesy Alexander family.)

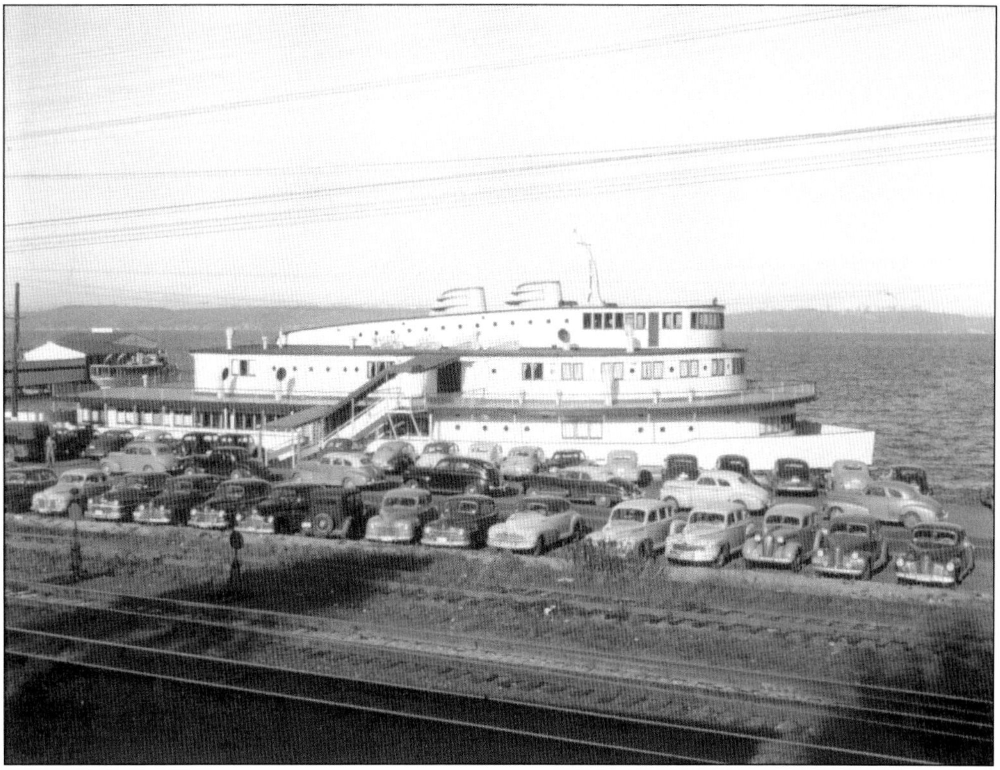

The Top of the Ocean opened on December 7, 1946, and was called the most beautiful luxury dine and dance liner until she burned down on April 3, 1977. There were four dining rooms plus a private suite for the Tacoma Athletic Club upstairs. The owners, Allen Rau and Bert Sundgren, had the restaurant constructed on pilings as it was never meant to be floated on the sound, or anywhere else.

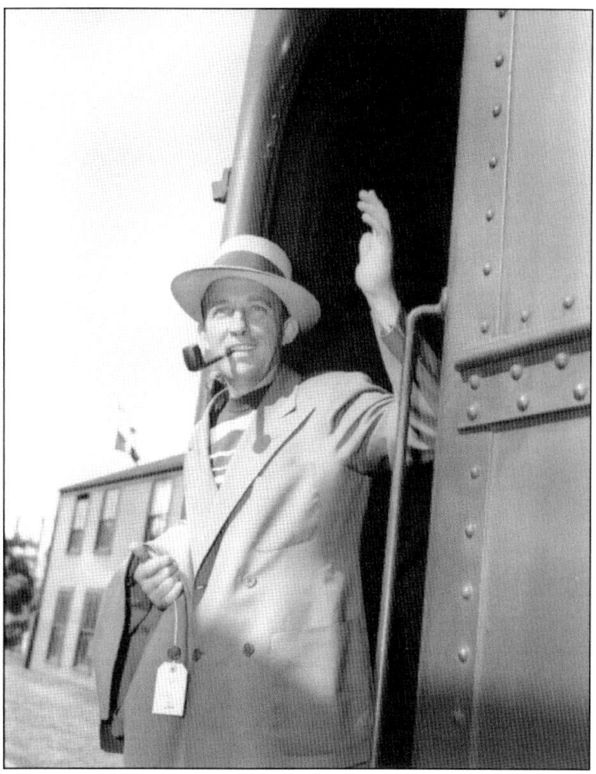

Bing Crosby is shown arriving at Tacoma's Union Station in 1942. He was headlining a war bond show at Tacoma's Liberty Center on August 6 with comedians Phil Silvers and Rags Ragland. Crosby also entertained the troops at Fort Lewis. His birth name was Harry Lillis Crosby, and he was born on May 3, 1903. His first childhood home was at 1112 North J Street in Tacoma.

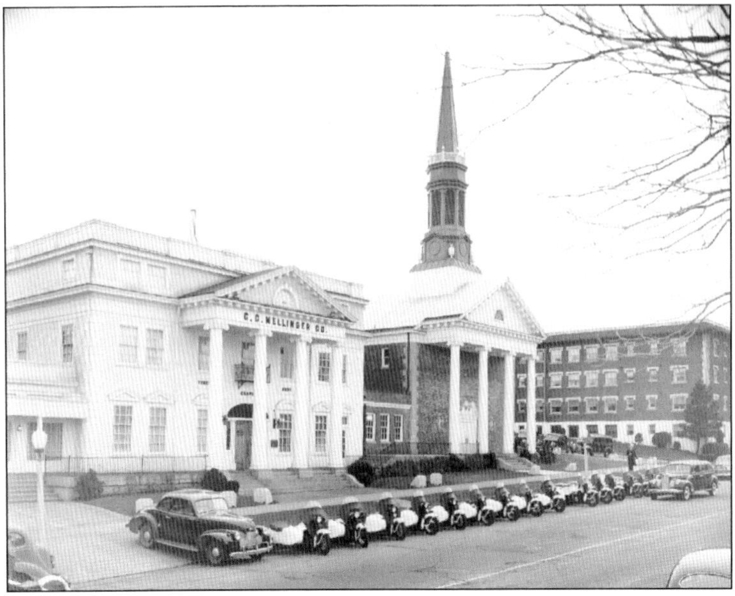

The funeral for Vincent J. Hansen, held on November 27, 1946, brought out almost the entire Tacoma Police Department to the C.C. Mellinger Company mortuary. The patrolman had died due to complications from yellow fever, which he contracted overseas during World War II. The mortuary, at 510 Tacoma Avenue South, is presently home to Pierce County Alliance.

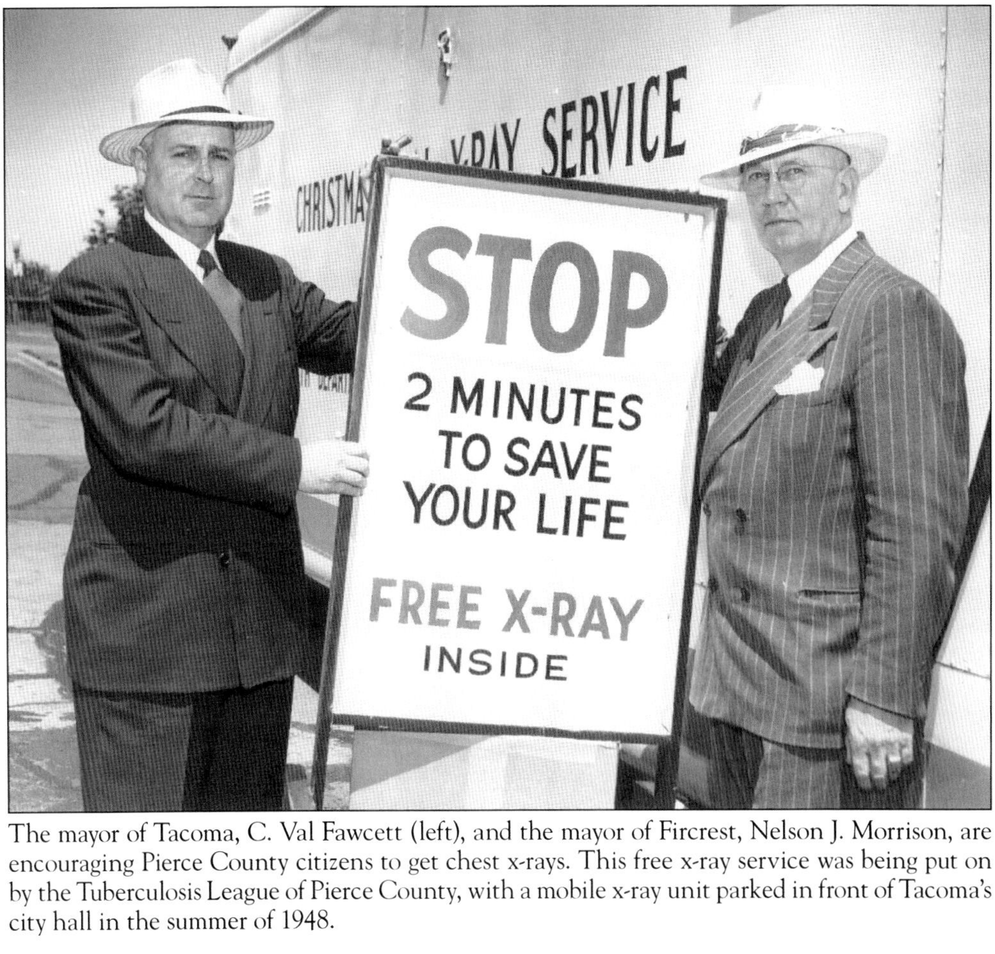

The mayor of Tacoma, C. Val Fawcett (left), and the mayor of Fircrest, Nelson J. Morrison, are encouraging Pierce County citizens to get chest x-rays. This free x-ray service was being put on by the Tuberculosis League of Pierce County, with a mobile x-ray unit parked in front of Tacoma's city hall in the summer of 1948.

On June 10, 1948, President Truman was in Tacoma and gave a speech to an estimated crowd of 9,000. This photograph shows him seated in a 1948 Cadillac convertible with Gov. Monrad Wallgren. Sen. Warren G. Magnuson is standing by to greet the president.

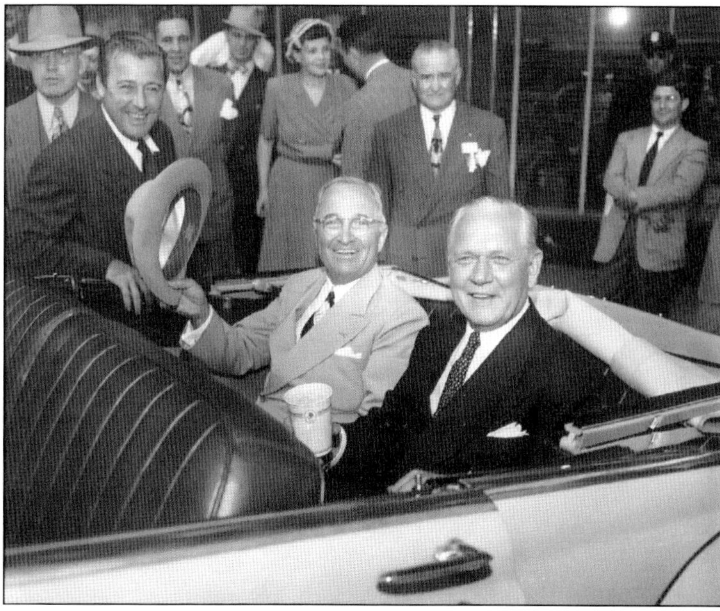

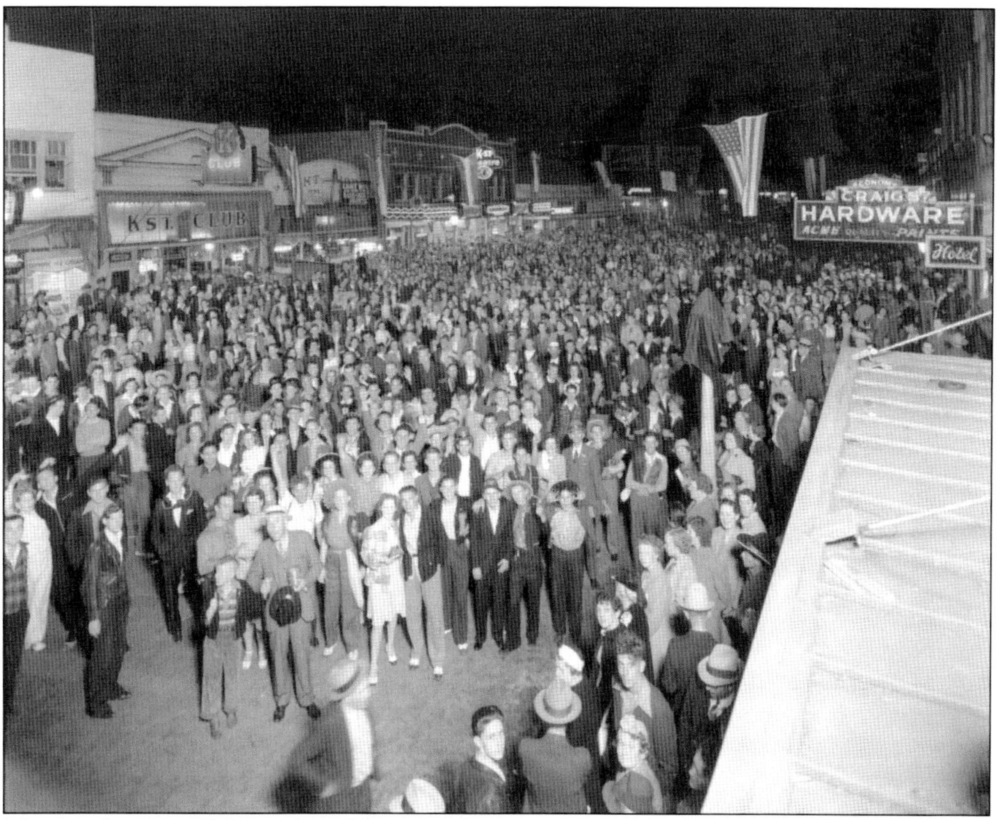

The merchants on K Street (now Martin Luther King Jr. Way) had a giant block party and street dance on July 3, 1940. This event celebrated both the opening of the Narrows Bridge two days earlier and the renaming of Tacoma Field to McChord Field. A Rite Aid drugstore replaced the entire block of buildings on the left in 1998.

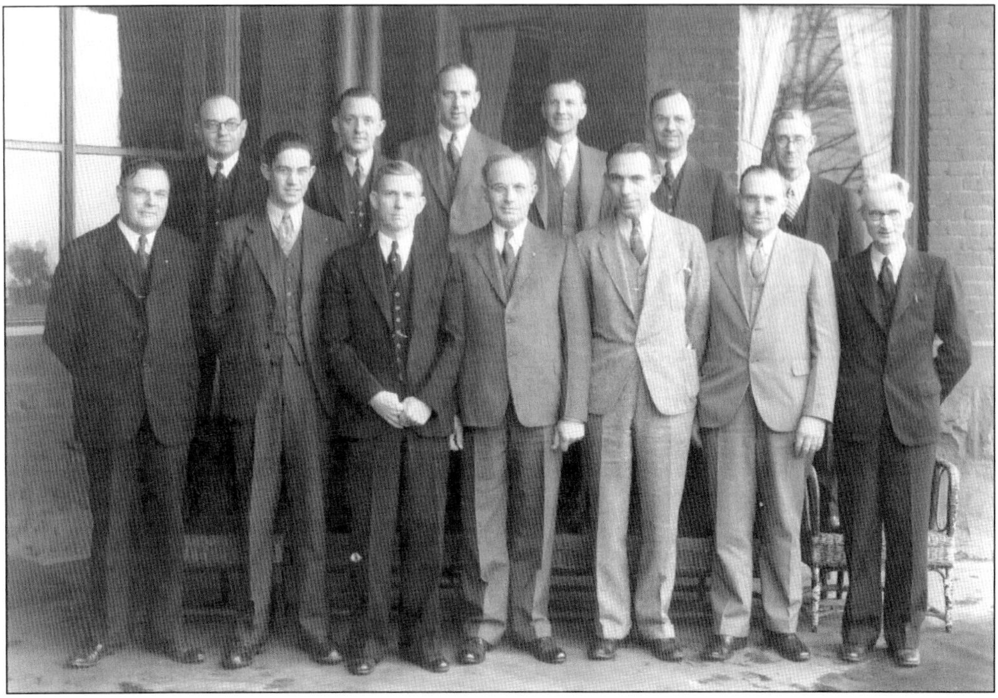

This image of Brown and Haley Candy Co. executives was taken in 1933, with Harry L. Brown in the center of the first row and Jonathan Clifford Haley third from left in the first row. Harry Brown initially learned how to make candy in 1902 at the Tacoma confectionery Josslyn's and started his own retail candy shop in 1907. In 1914, Brown partnered with Haley, and Oriole Chocolates became formalized—candy-making history in Tacoma began. The name was changed to Brown and Haley in 1919 and remains so to this day. Below, in 1953, employees on the manufacturing line make hand-dipped chocolates at the plant at 110 East Twenty-Sixth Street, which still stands.

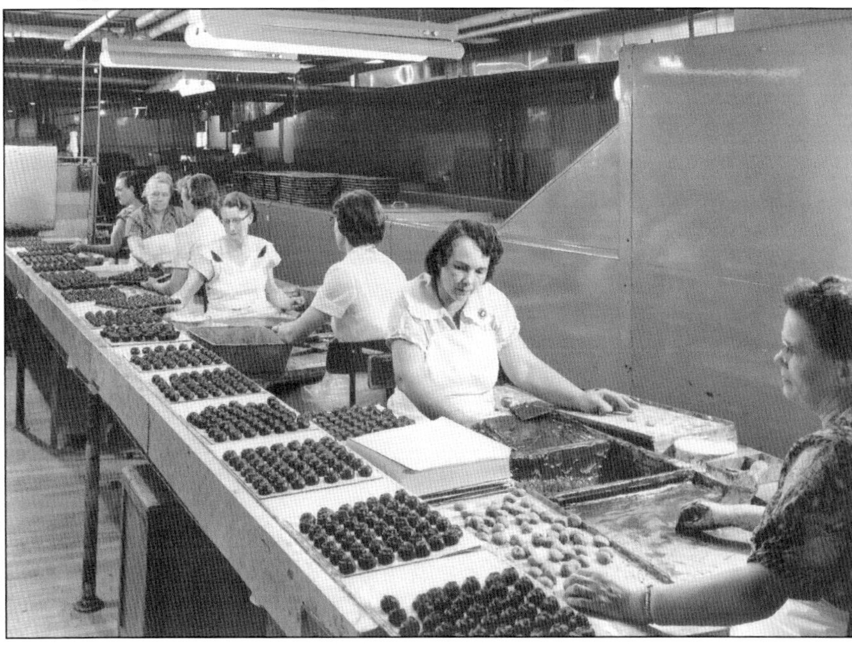

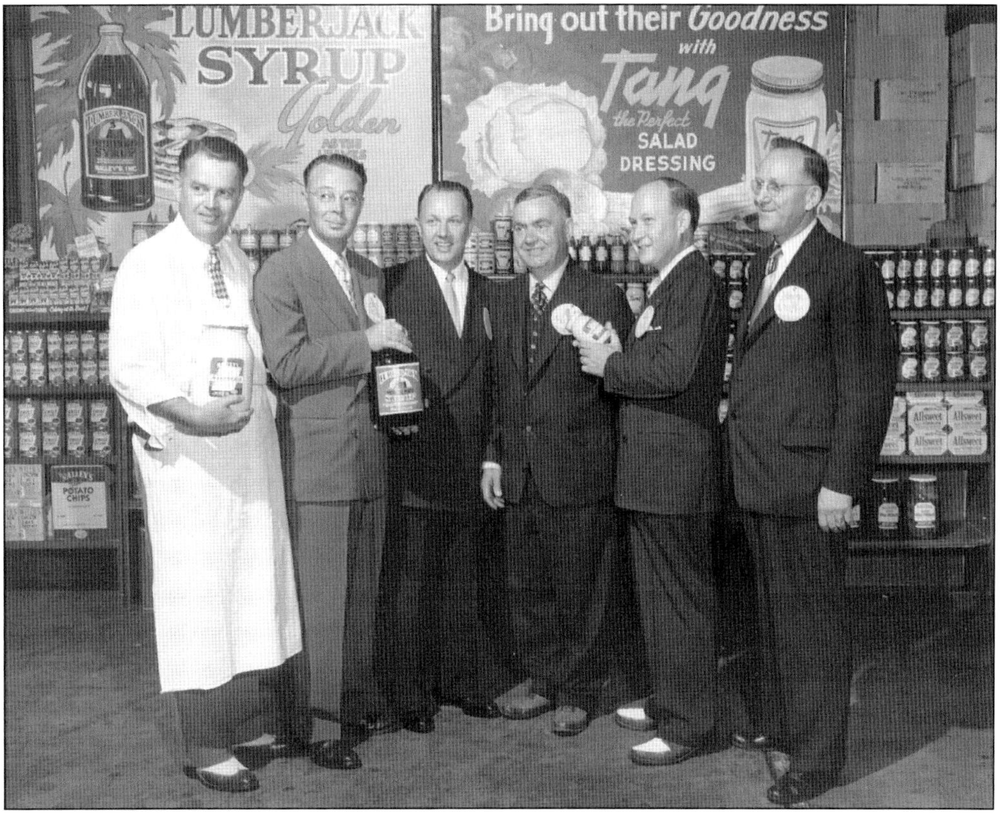

Above, from left to right, Cecil Walrath, Joe Lehman, Cliff Wold, Marcus Nalley, L. Evert Landon, and Henry Willis are pictured on August 24, 1949. The occasion was the 31st anniversary of the founding of Nalley's Inc. by Marcus Nalley. The company was founded in Tacoma in 1918 and had grown to a $10 million per year business. Various products are shown in the background. On the 10-acre site in the Center Street District, known as Nalley Valley, employees pictured below on the pickle assembly line pack cucumbers into glass jars for processing; they were sold as Nalley's Treasure Pickles. This factory was built in 1941, and the photograph was taken in 1946.

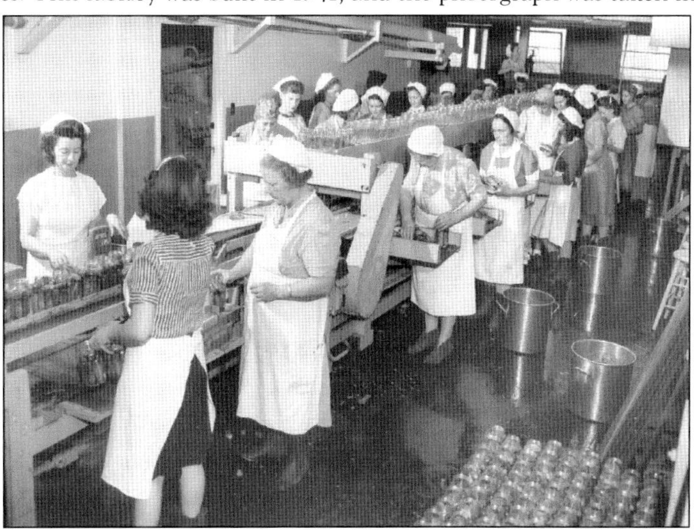

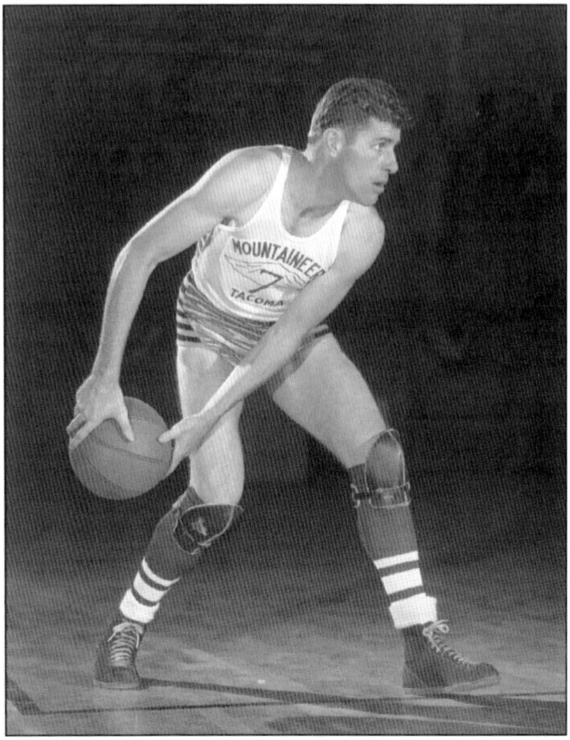

Bob Voelker was a forward on the Coast League Tacoma Mountaineers professional basketball team for the 1947–1948 season. He is shown here getting ready to play in his first game in the state armory against Bellingham. The Mountaineers' second game was against Astoria's Royal Chinooks in Oregon.

The entire Mountaineer team from Tacoma is shown here. From left to right are team leader and halftime show performer Helen Hays, John Katica, Hank Vallee, Sig Sigurdson, Bob Graf, Ernie Endress, Bob Voelker, Jack Voelker, coach Tom Werner, and co-owner and club president Milton Bay. The team played professionally for one year.

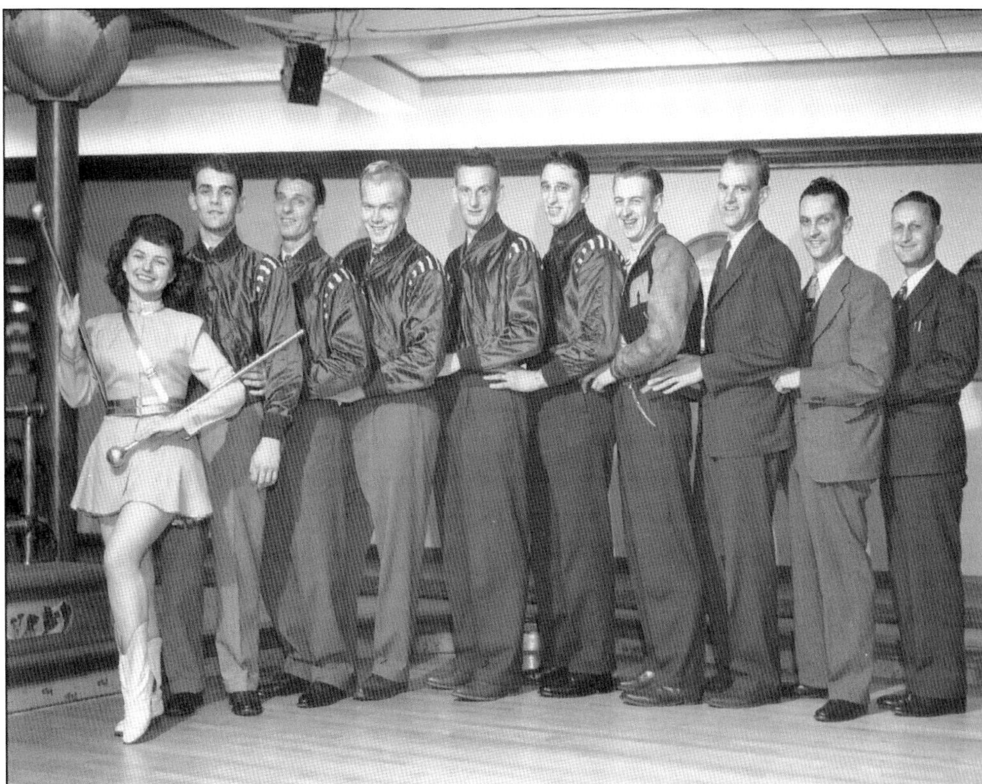

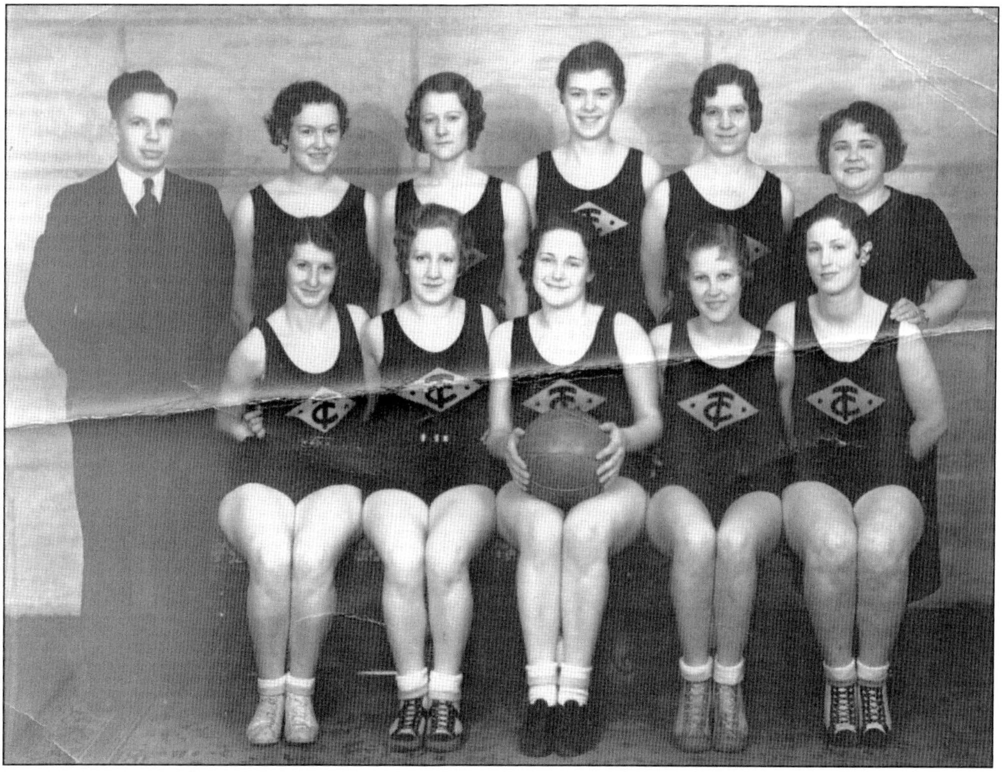

Competitive city league basketball was popular in Tacoma in the early 1930s. Shown here are the Carstens Packing Company Vagabonds. From left to right are (first row) Sally Reese, Freda Wingard, Eleanor Hiller, Grace Thorne, and Katherine Rivers; (second row) coach Paul Benton, Eleanor Foley, Vera Kemp, Mary Livesley, Dorothy Weingard, and manager Gladys Hult. In 1932, there were six women's teams in the city league sponsored by the Metropolitan Park District.

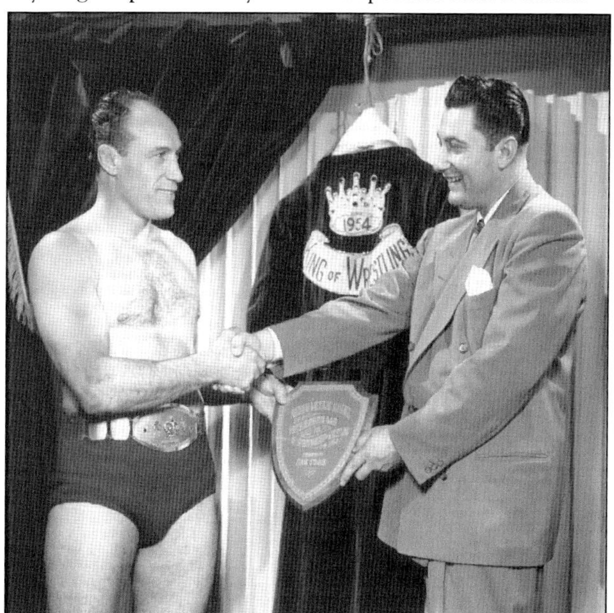

Frank Stojack, known as the "King of Wrestling," is shown shaking hands with his brother Pete Stojack upon receiving the National Wrestling Alliance Youth Inspiration Award for Sportsmanship and Wrestling for 1952. After graduating from Lincoln High School and Washington State College, Stojack played professional football for the Brooklyn Dodgers. He was later elected to Tacoma City Council in 1953 and then Pierce County sheriff until 1964.

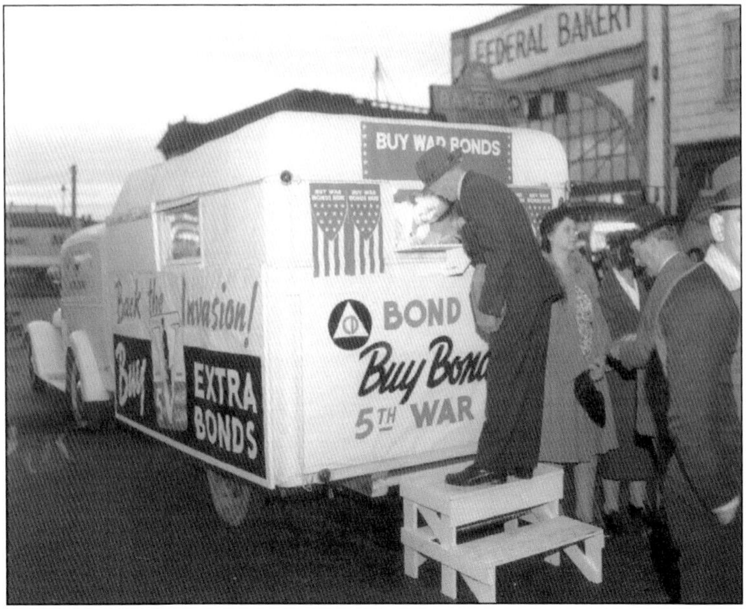

These citizens are purchasing war bonds at the civil defense wagon that traveled the neighborhoods of Tacoma to raise money for the World War II effort in 1944. The Federal Bakery is in the background of this photograph, taken at 1107 South K Street, now Martin Luther King Jr. Way.

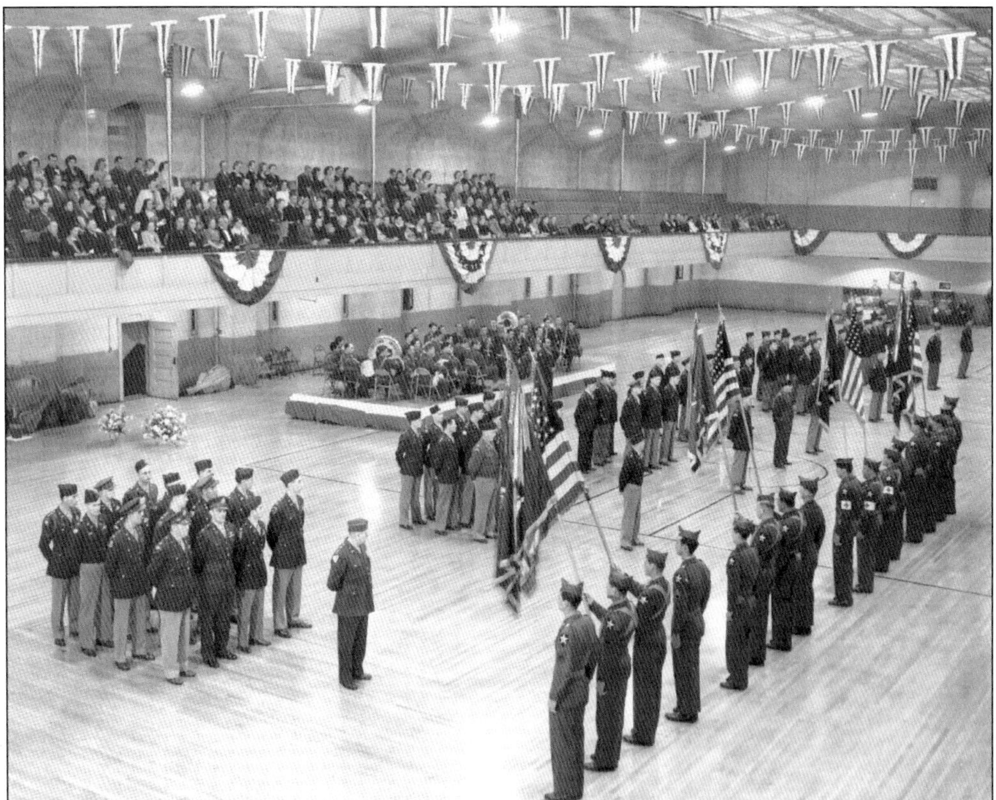

On November 11, 1947, a military ball was held at the armory to commemorate Armistice Day, later known as Veterans Day. This photograph shows the presentation of the colors to the local reserve units of the Army and Army Air Corps, which was one of the highlights of the evening. Approximately 1,500 people attended this military ball.

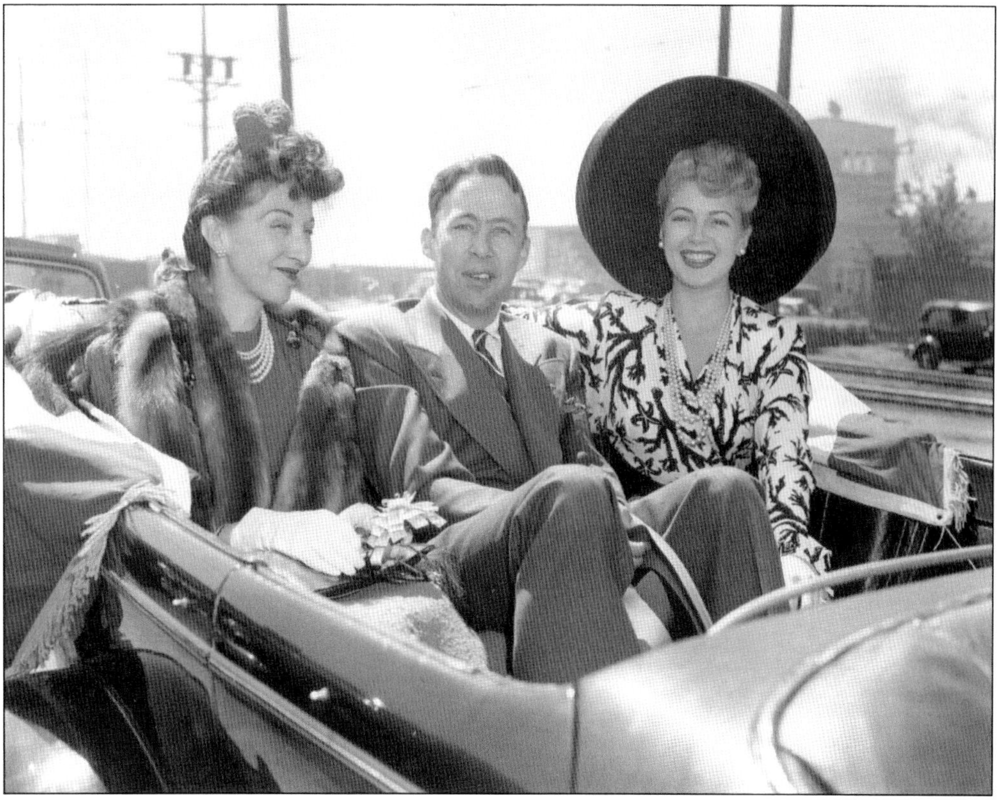

Tacoma mayor Harry Cain is shown on June 13, 1942, with actress Lana Turner on the right and her mother on the left. They are in the Titus Motor Company's 1924 Lincoln Touring car that is presently on display at the Lemay Car Museum. This was the first passenger vehicle across the first Narrows Bridge when it opened. In just one day of her visit for this rally, Turner sold more than $120,000 in war bonds.

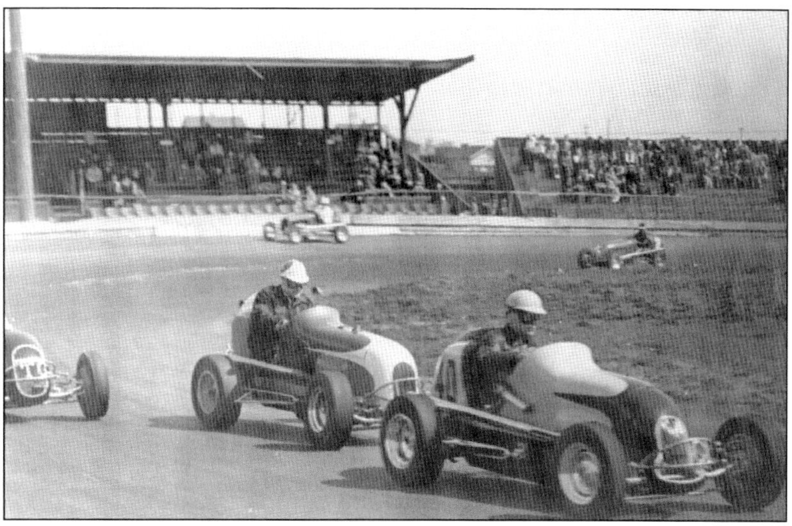

In 1946, midget racers are shown in a typical race at the Tacoma Speedway. Most races were held on Saturday nights starting in April. Drivers, along with their cars, would come from as far away as California.

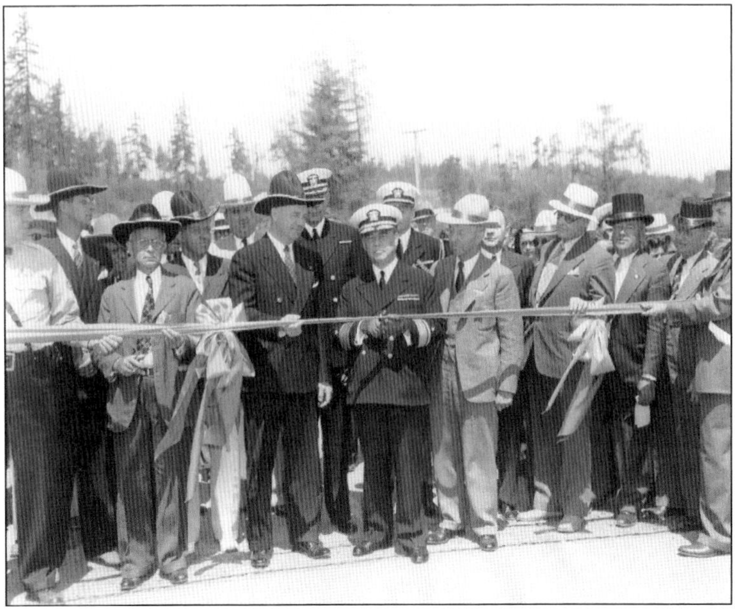

The first Narrows Bridge was formally opened with this ceremony on July 1, 1940. Adm. Edward B. Fenner, Bremerton Navy Yard commander, is shown cutting the ribbon. Shown flanking the admiral are Mayor Homer Jones of Bremerton (left) and John Schlarb, chairman of the Pierce County Board of Commissioners.

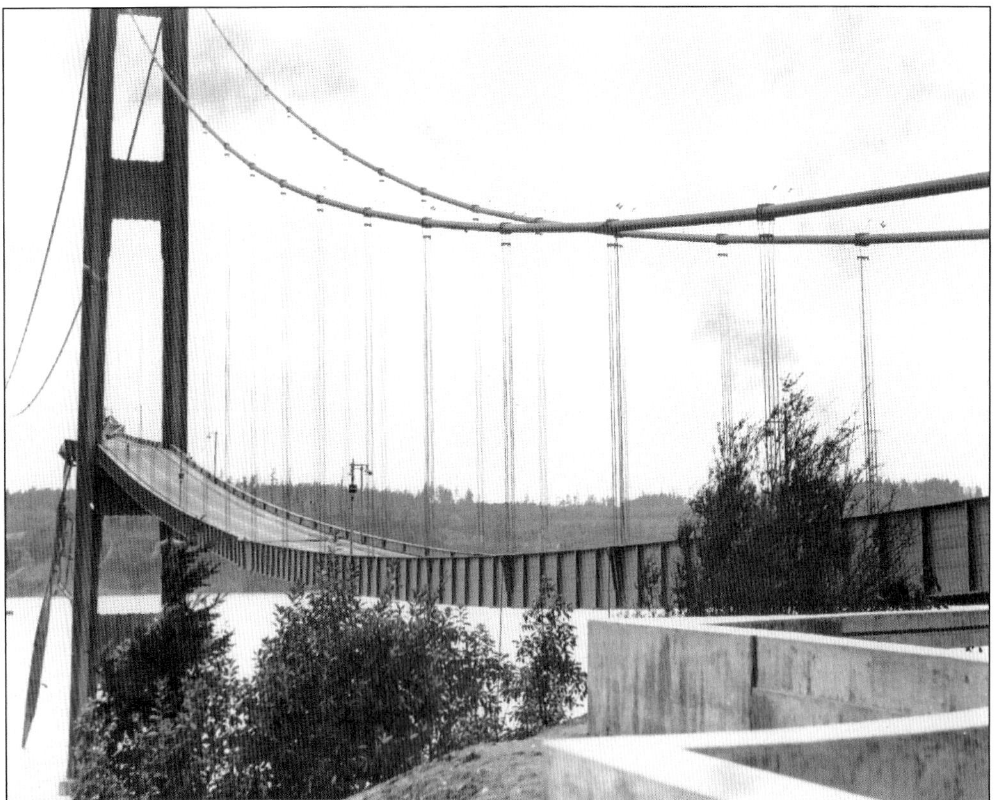

After opening on July 1, 1940, "Galloping Gertie" fell into the Narrows in Puget Sound on November 7 due to a design flaw and a 40-mile-per-hour wind. It took nearly 10 years until the replacement bridge could be opened on October 14, 1950.

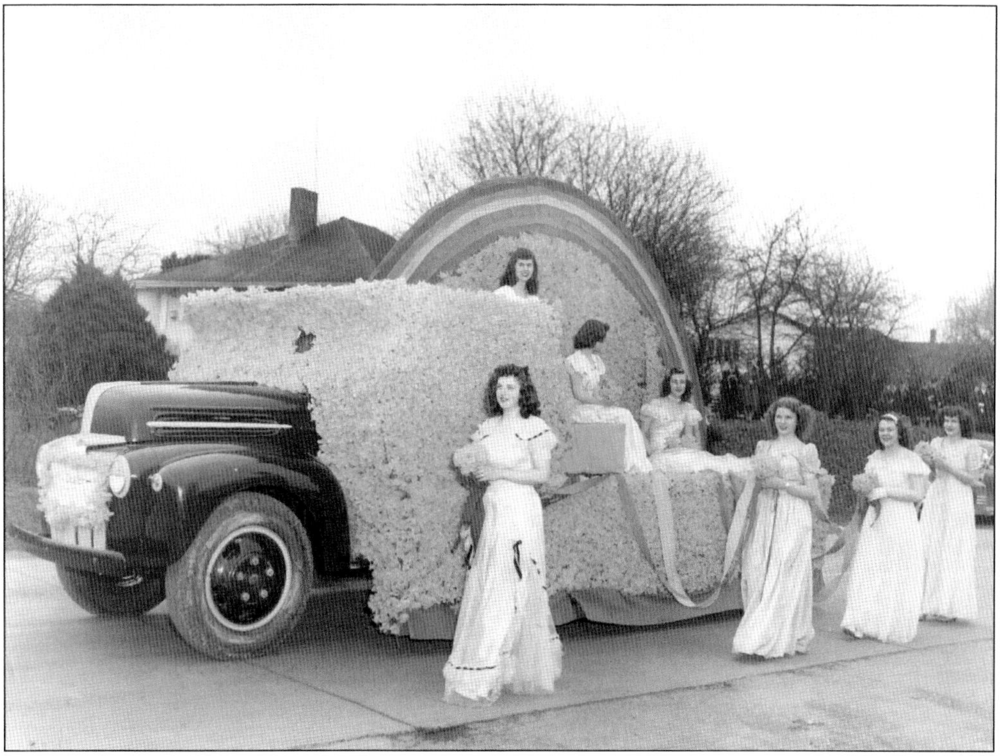

The 1946 Daffodil Parade drew one of the largest crowds to date in parade history. The crowd, estimated at 30,000, viewed this float, covered in daffodils, with Order of Rainbow girls as passengers.

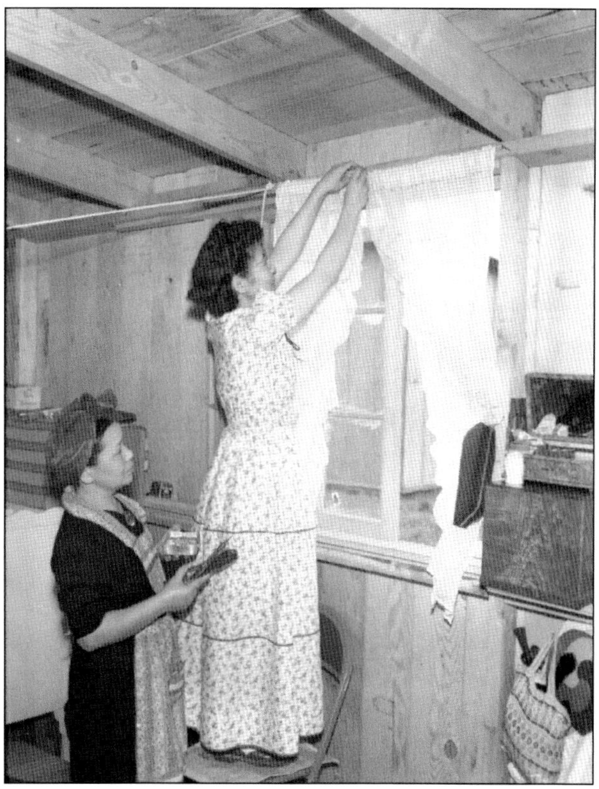

Mrs. Milo Kashiwagi and her mother-in-law, Mrs. Y. Kashiwagi, are decorating a window at Camp Harmony, the internment camp in Puyallup. Nearly 7,000 Japanese Americans lived in these barracks until a more permanent detention center was found for them. In 1942, residents of Japanese ancestry were forcibly rounded up in Western states and sent to internment camps following the bombing of Pearl Harbor on December 7, 1941.

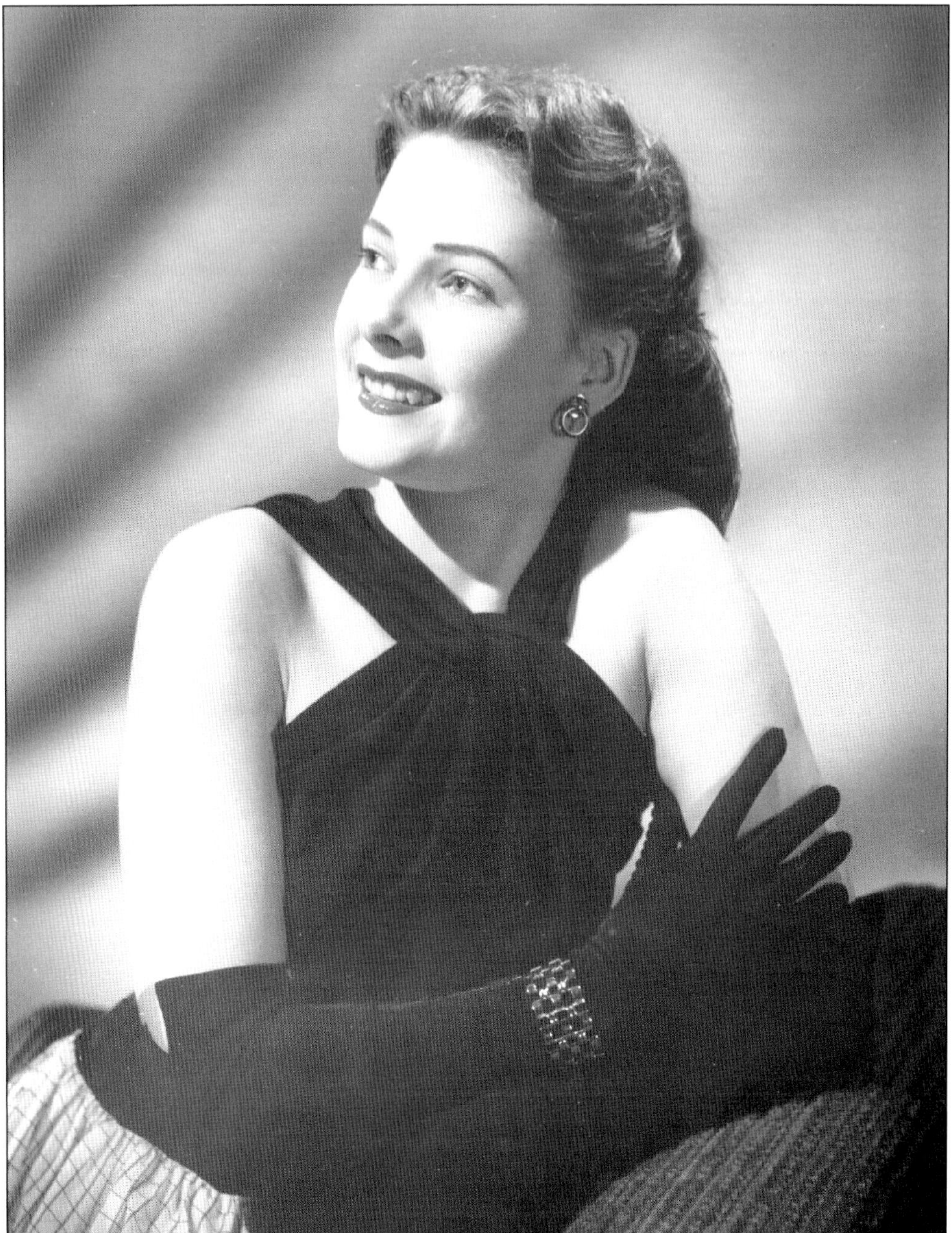

Eileen Larson was Miss Second Division for the grand military ball held on Saturday, May 11, 1946. She was the daughter of Bernie and Inger Larson. The event was officiated by Mayor Harry P. Cain and broadcast live over KMO radio.

The Second Division 23rd Invader Regiment marches through Broadway and Pacific Avenue. The event was the annual Jubilee Parade on June 25, 1946, which drew thousands of spectators.

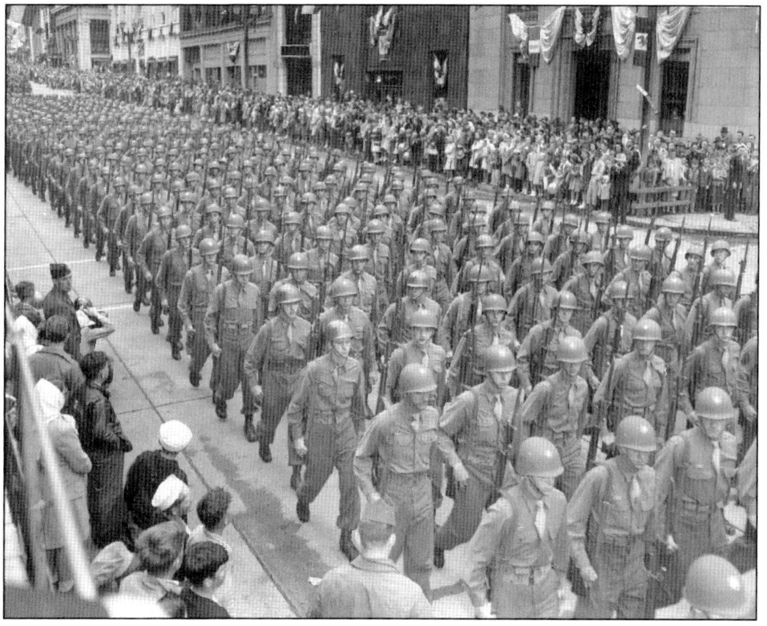

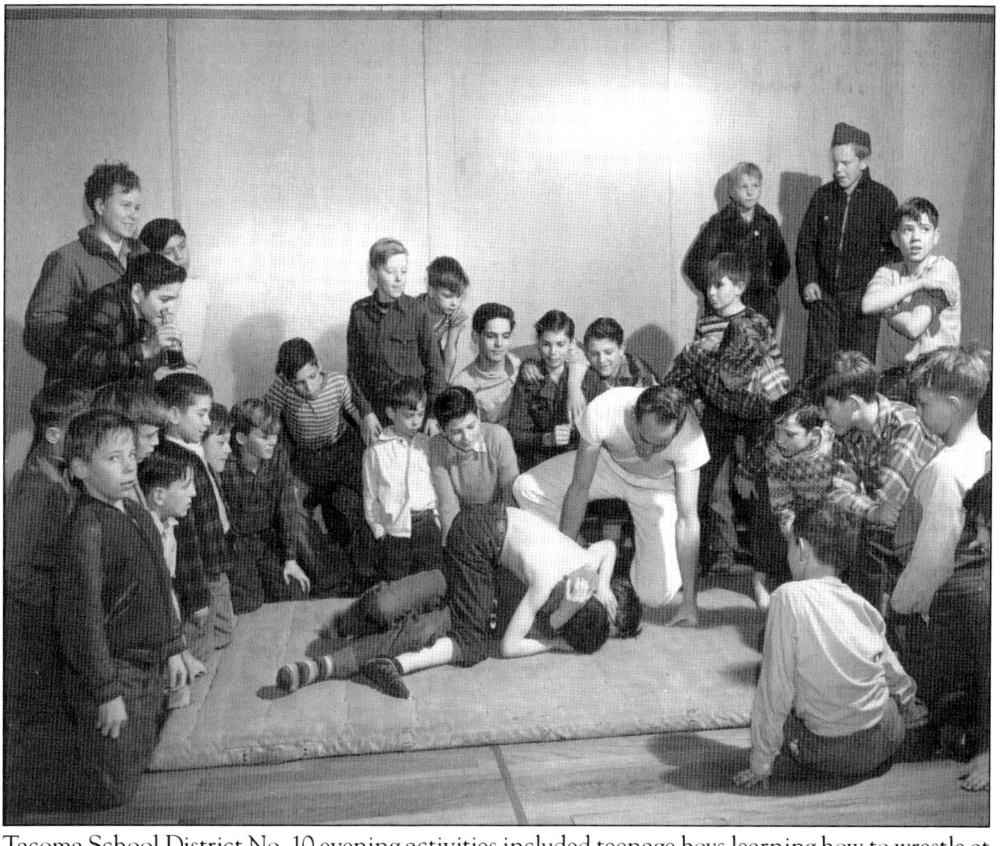

Tacoma School District No. 10 evening activities included teenage boys learning how to wrestle at the Salishan Community Gymnasium. Hollister Gee, majoring in health and physical education at the College of Puget Sound, is overseeing this session.

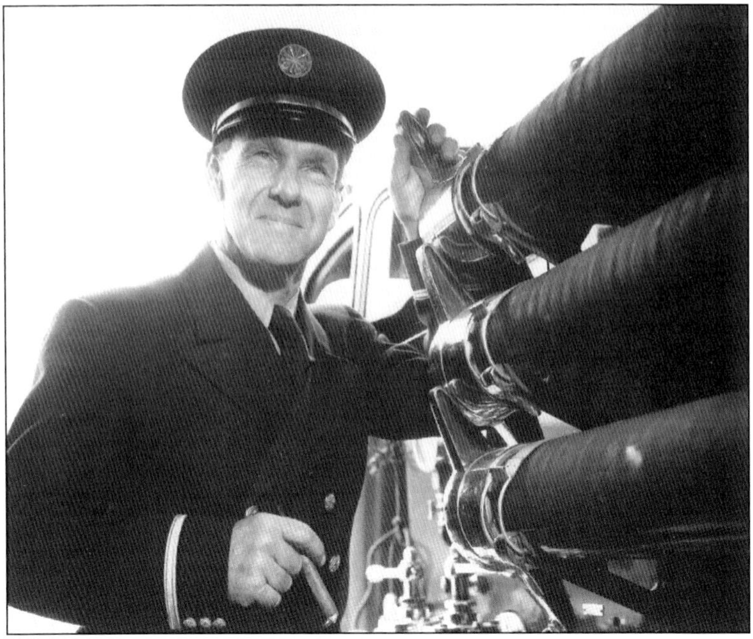

Lesley B. McGaw served as fire chief of the University Place Fire Department from 1941 until his retirement in 1965. He started out as a volunteer chief, and by 1960, University Place had thirty volunteers and three full-time firefighters.

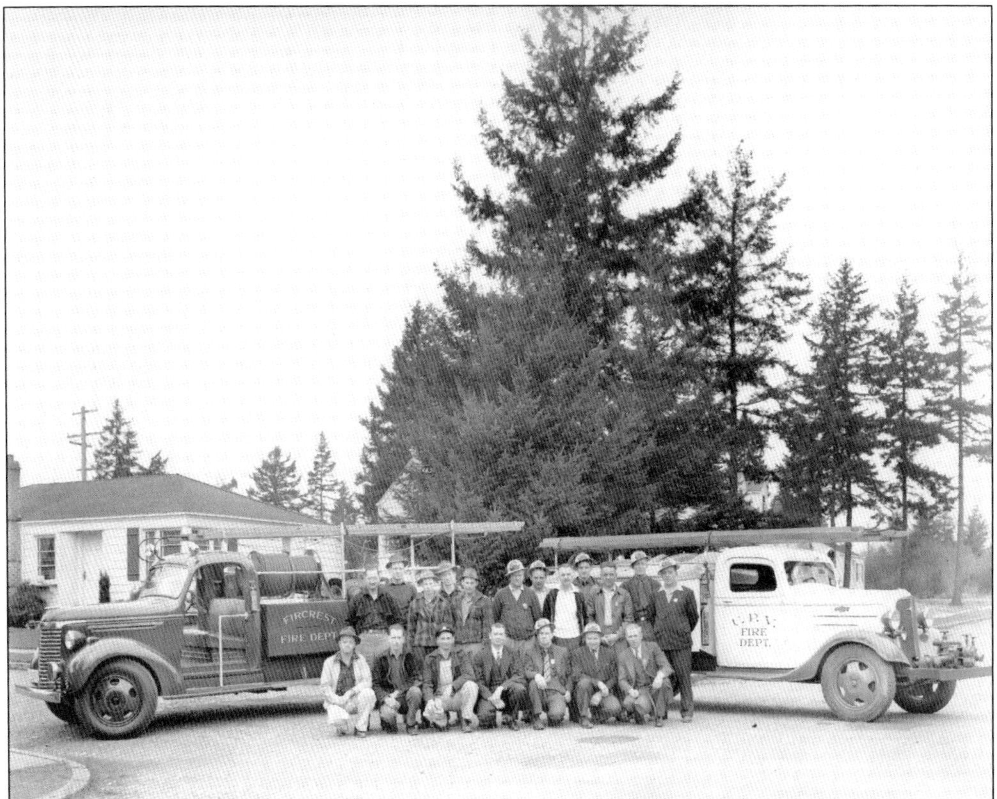

On December 14, 1941, the Fircrest and University Place Fire Departments are shown with ladder trucks for a joint group photograph. Wood Freeman was Fircrest's first fire chief, and the University Place fire chief was Lesley B. McGaw, who served as its chief until he retired in 1965.

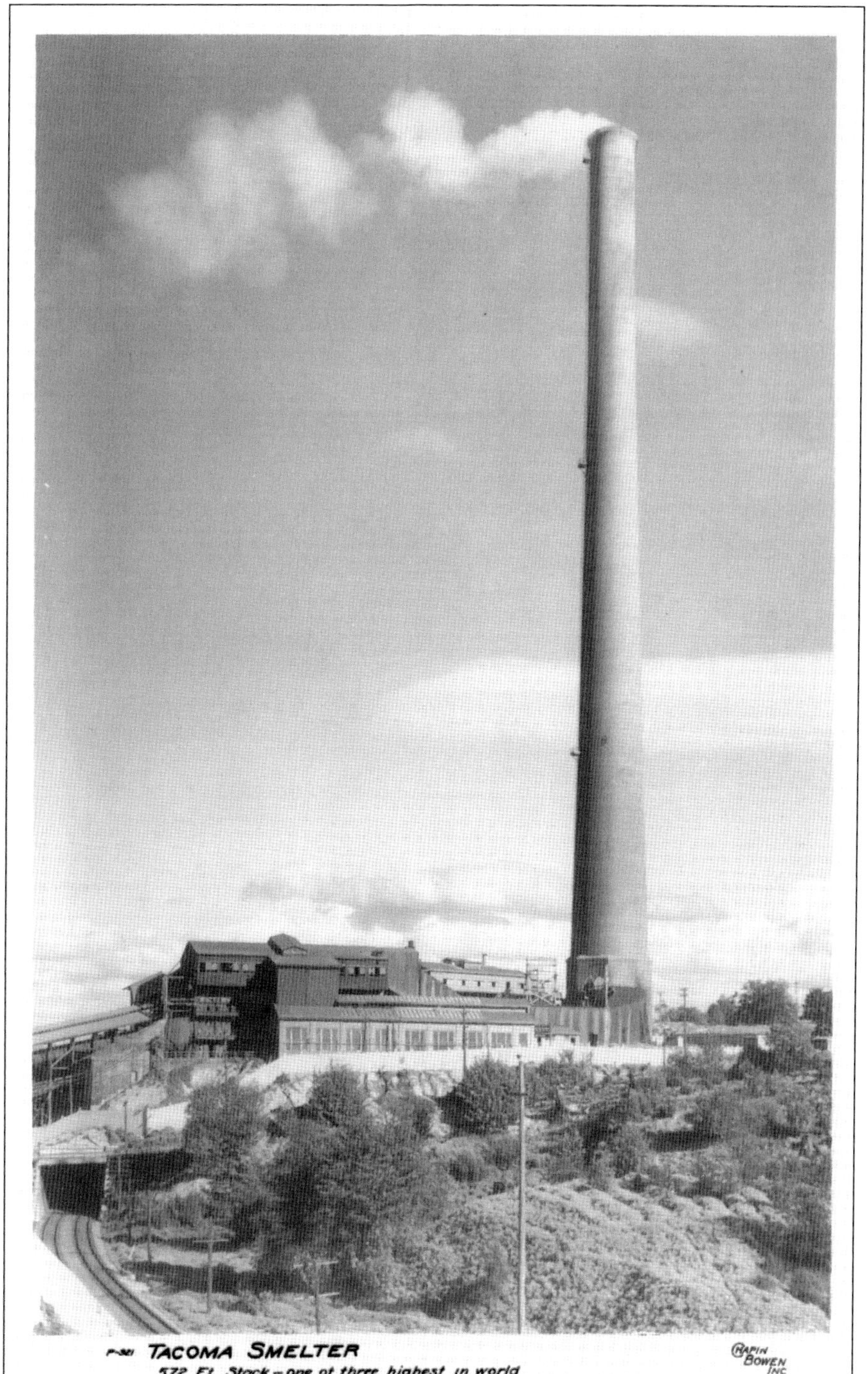

The American Smelting and Refining Company smelter and stack are shown in 1940. The stack was demolished on January 17, 1993, and all traces of the smelter are now removed from the Commencement Bay waterfront. An estimated 100,000 people gathered to witness the demolition of the smokestack.

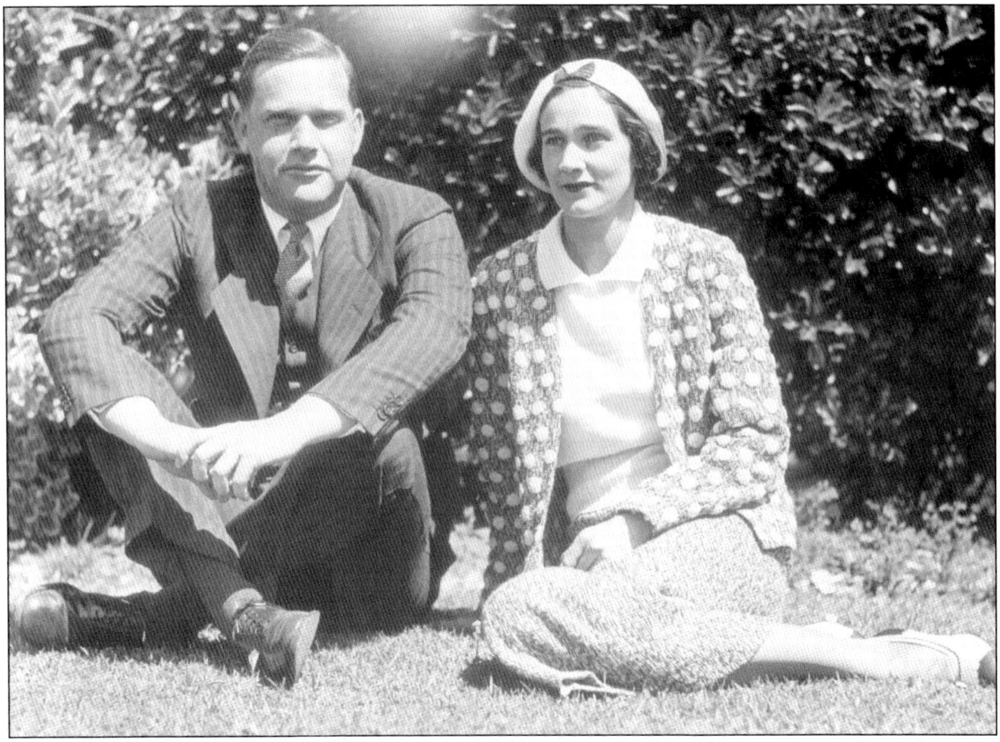

John Philip "Phil" Weyerhaeuser Jr. and his wife, Helen, were the parents of George H. Weyerhaeuser, age nine, who was kidnapped on May 24, 1935. The Weyerhaeusers paid the $200,000 ransom, and their son was returned to them unharmed on June 1. It was at the time the second most-famous kidnapping in the United States, eclipsed only by that of the Lindbergh baby.

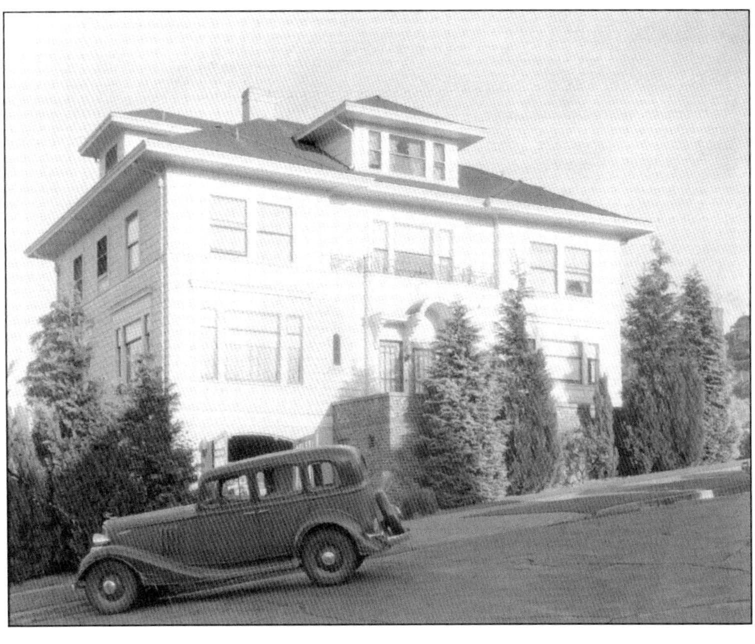

This is the Weyerhaeuser home at 420 N. Fourth Street in Tacoma from which George Weyerhaeuser would begin his walk each day to school at the old Lowell Elementary School before the newer one was built in 1950. George is reported to have continued walking to school after being returned from the kidnapping.

George Weyerhaeuser is seen shortly after his release from kidnappers on June 1, 1935. He was released near Issaquah and sought help to be returned to his parents. He returned to a normal life.

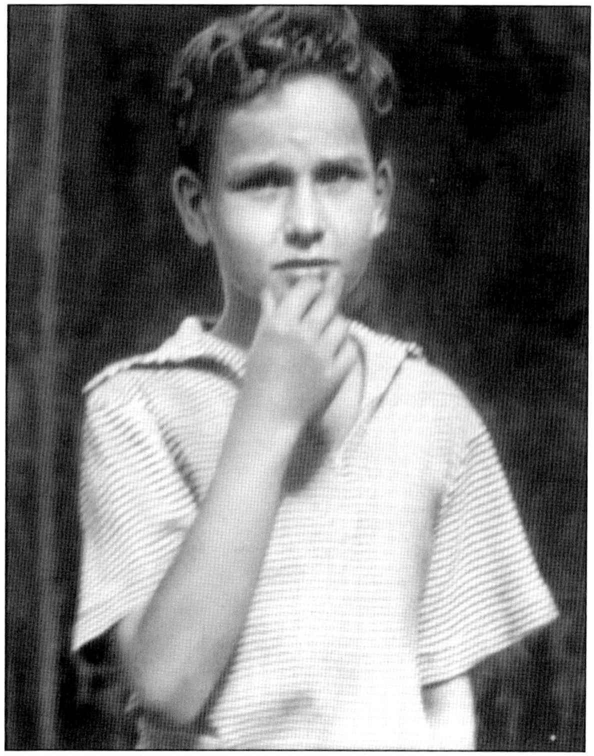

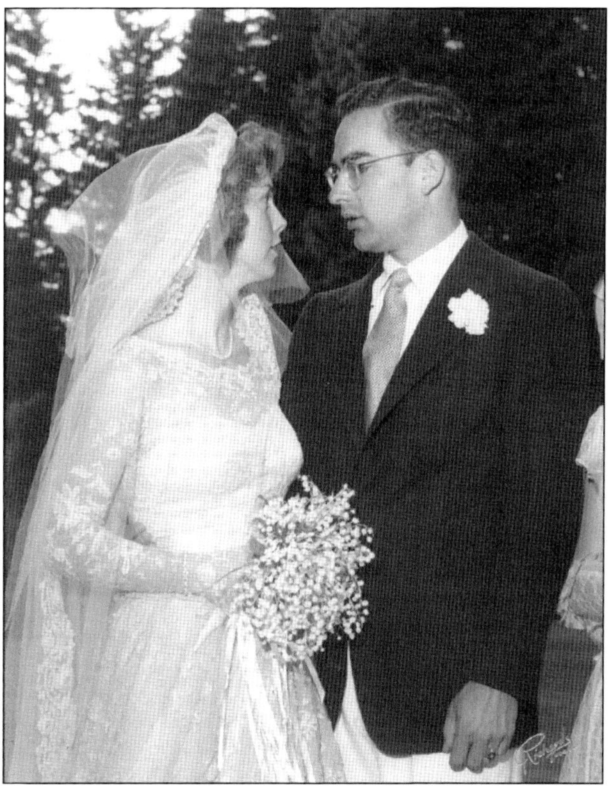

Virginia Lee "Wendy" Wagner was married to George Weyerhaeuser on July 10, 1948, in a ceremony that joined two nationally prominent timber industry families at the Corydon and Eulalie Wagner estate in Lakewood. In 1987, Wagner donated this land to the Friends of Lakewold; it is known as Lakewold Gardens.

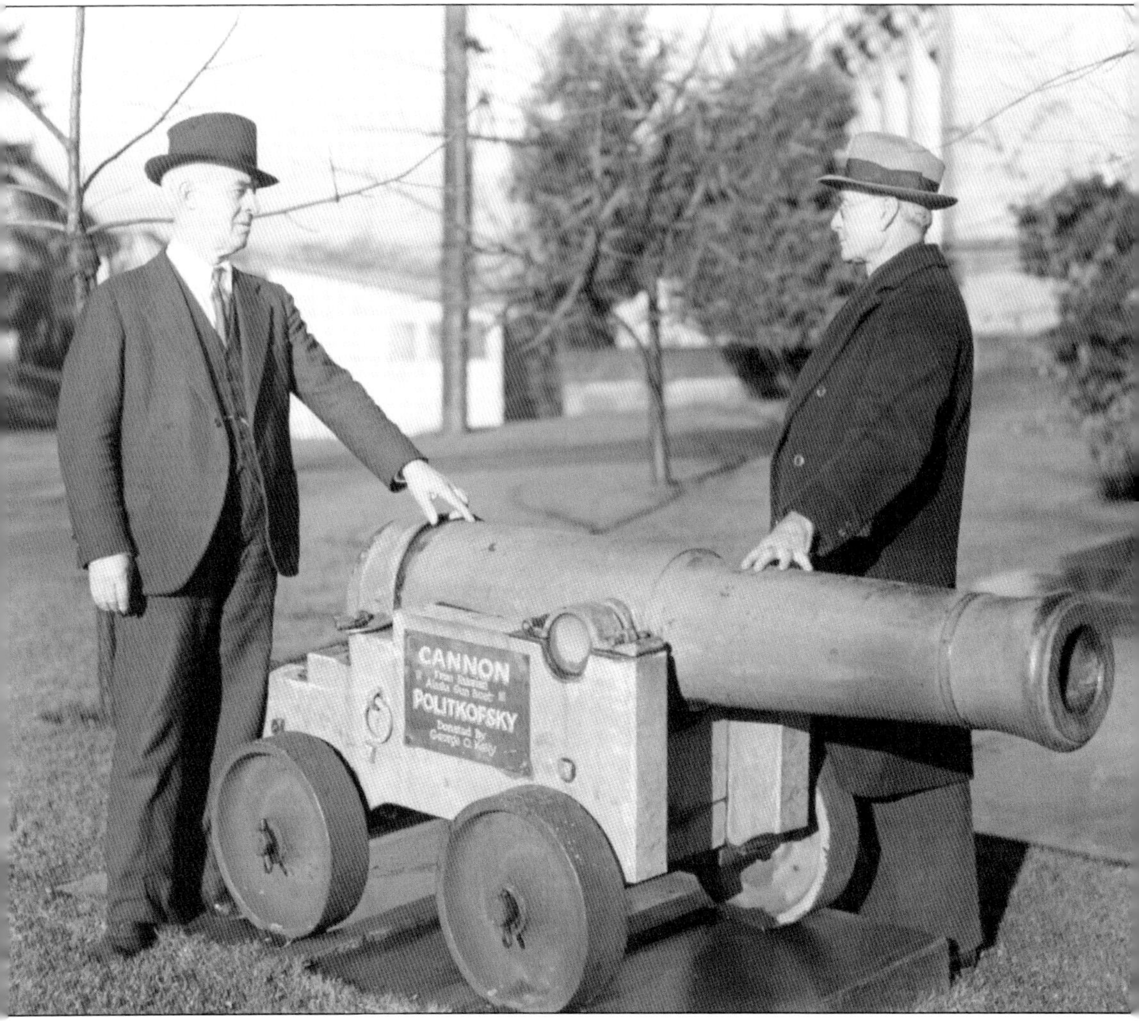

William D. "Billy" Gleason (left) and John McLennan are standing next to a cannon from the Russian steamer *Politkofsky*. On November 11, 1889, when word reached Tacoma that Washington had become a state, this cannon was rolled to Fireman's Park and fired off, once for each state and two or three times for the new state of Washington. The canon was donated to the Washington State Historical Society by George O. Kelly.

On January 1, 1892, Ethel Butler was born to Ethel Alberta Ury and may have been the very first African American child born in Tacoma. She attended old Lincoln Grade School and Central School. She lived her entire life in Tacoma until passing away in February 1970.

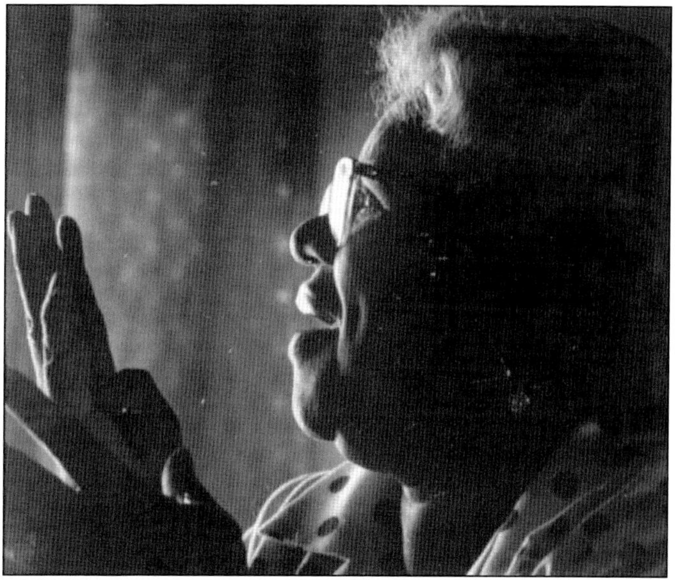

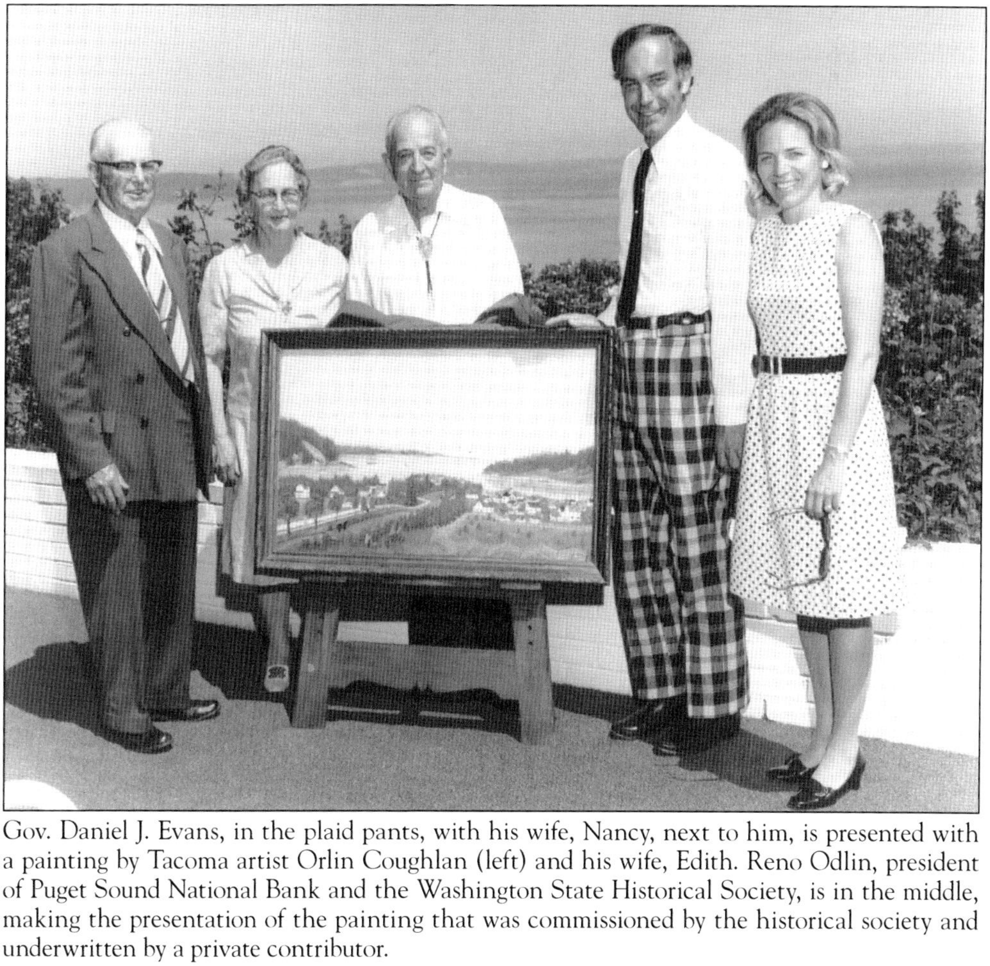

Gov. Daniel J. Evans, in the plaid pants, with his wife, Nancy, next to him, is presented with a painting by Tacoma artist Orlin Coughlan (left) and his wife, Edith. Reno Odlin, president of Puget Sound National Bank and the Washington State Historical Society, is in the middle, making the presentation of the painting that was commissioned by the historical society and underwritten by a private contributor.

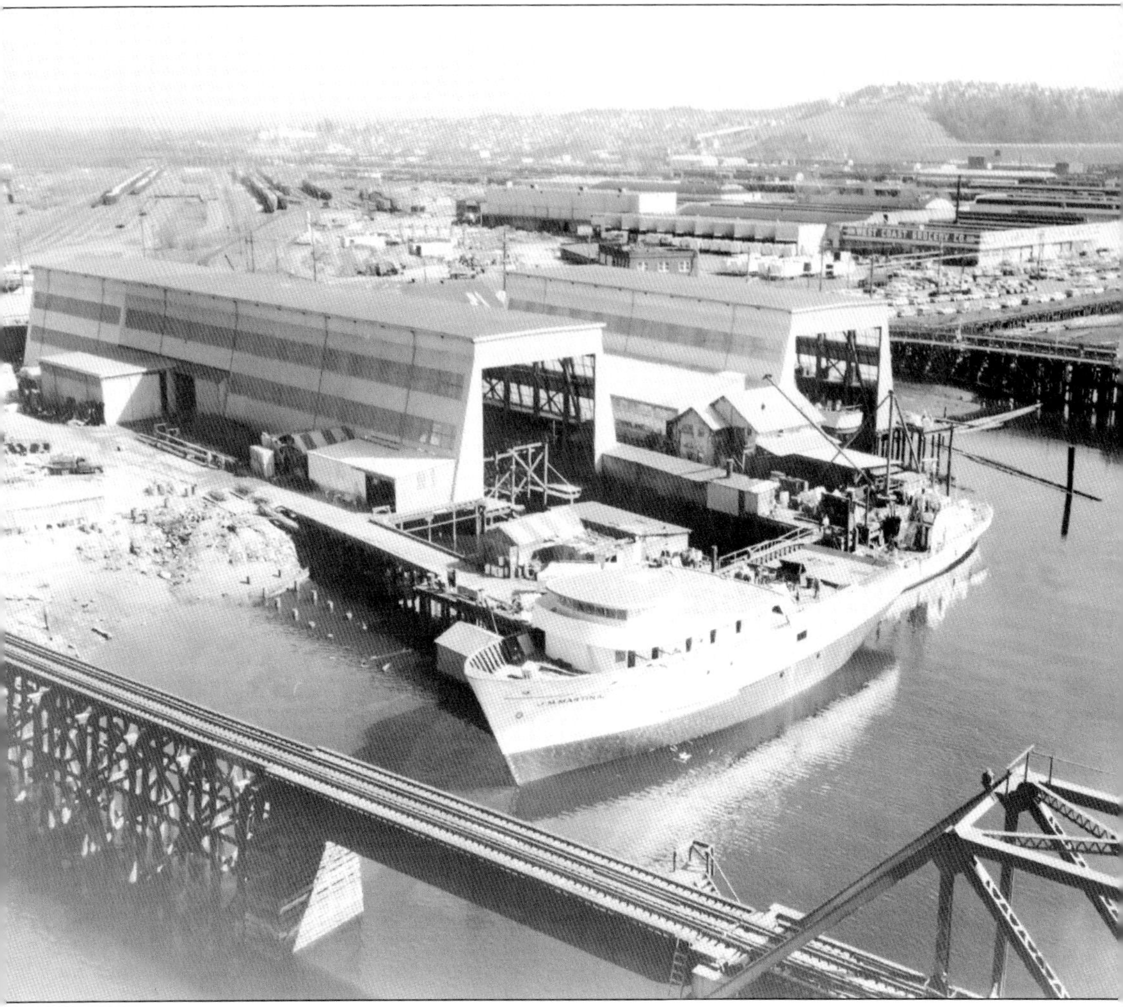

This view of the J.M. Martinac Shipbuilding facility on the Thea Foss Waterway shows a 154-foot tuna boat on April 11, 1967. This was the largest tuna seiner ever built by Martinac Shipbuilding and was named the *J.M. Martinac*. For almost 40 years, the construction of tuna boats was the mainstay of the Martinac business, in addition to pleasure craft and naval vessels.

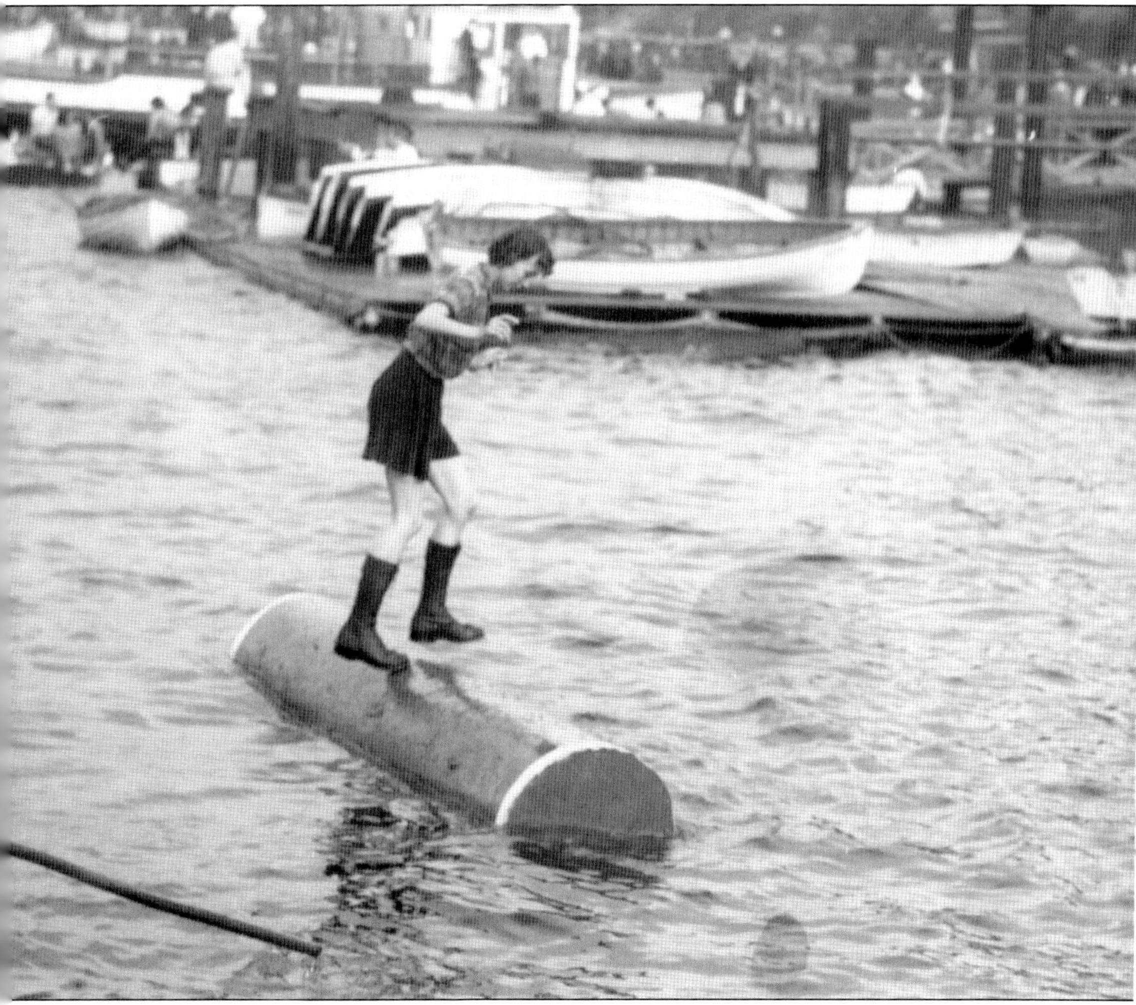

This woman is demonstrating the art and science of birling, more commonly known as log rolling. This event took place on opening day of the Washington State Golden Jubilee celebration in Tacoma on July 16, 1939. The Water Carnival was part of the celebration at Point Defiance Park and attracted 30,000 spectators for the four-hour saltwater spectacle.

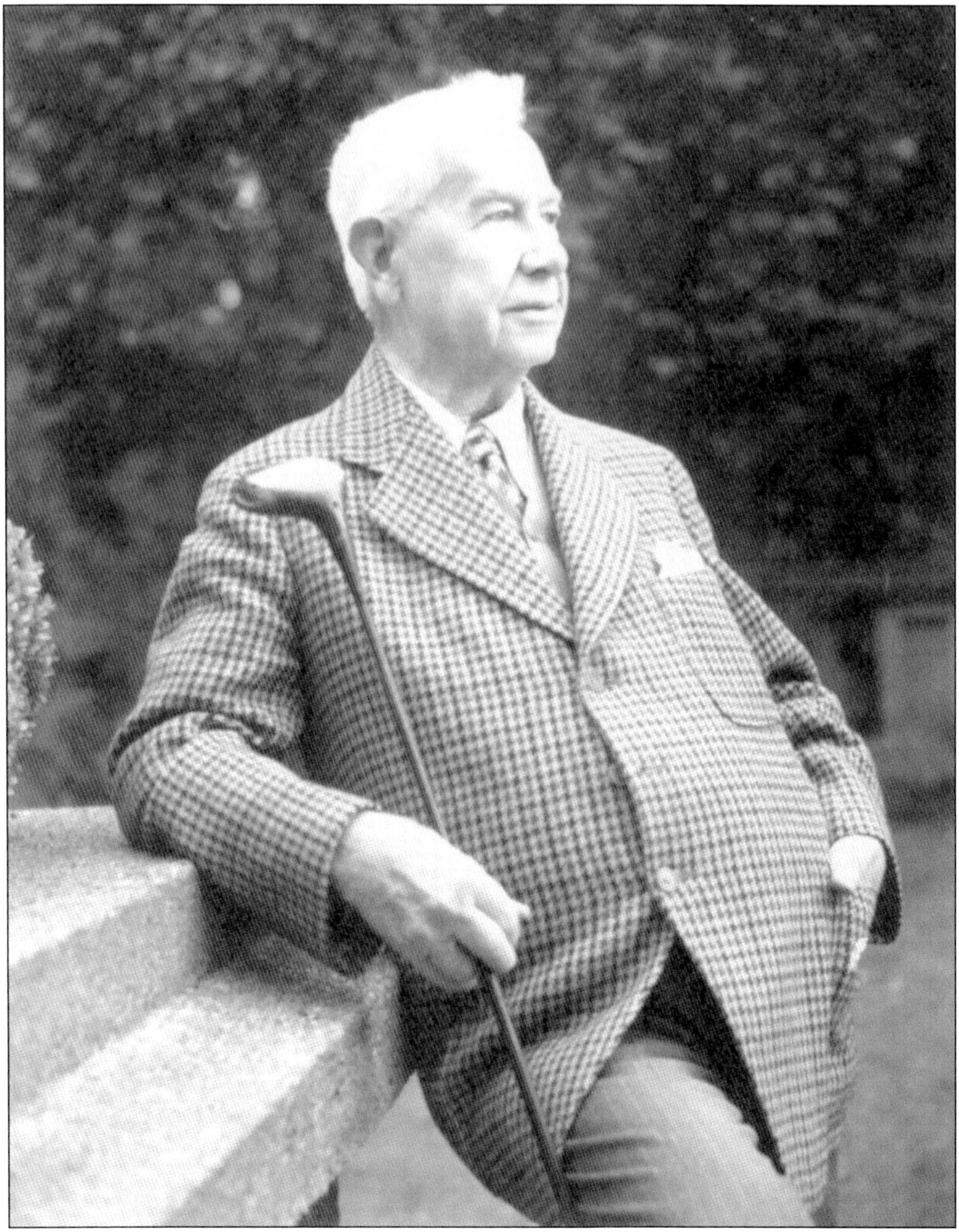

Alexander Baillie was one of the founders of the Tacoma Country & Golf Club, being its first president in 1894. He was the driving force in building the first golf course west of the Mississippi, which was only the fourth one in the United States. He was known as the "father of golf in the West." He was born on September 9, 1859, in Scotland, arrived in Tacoma in 1888, and passed away on September 7, 1949, just two days short of his 90th birthday.

Five

Recent Years

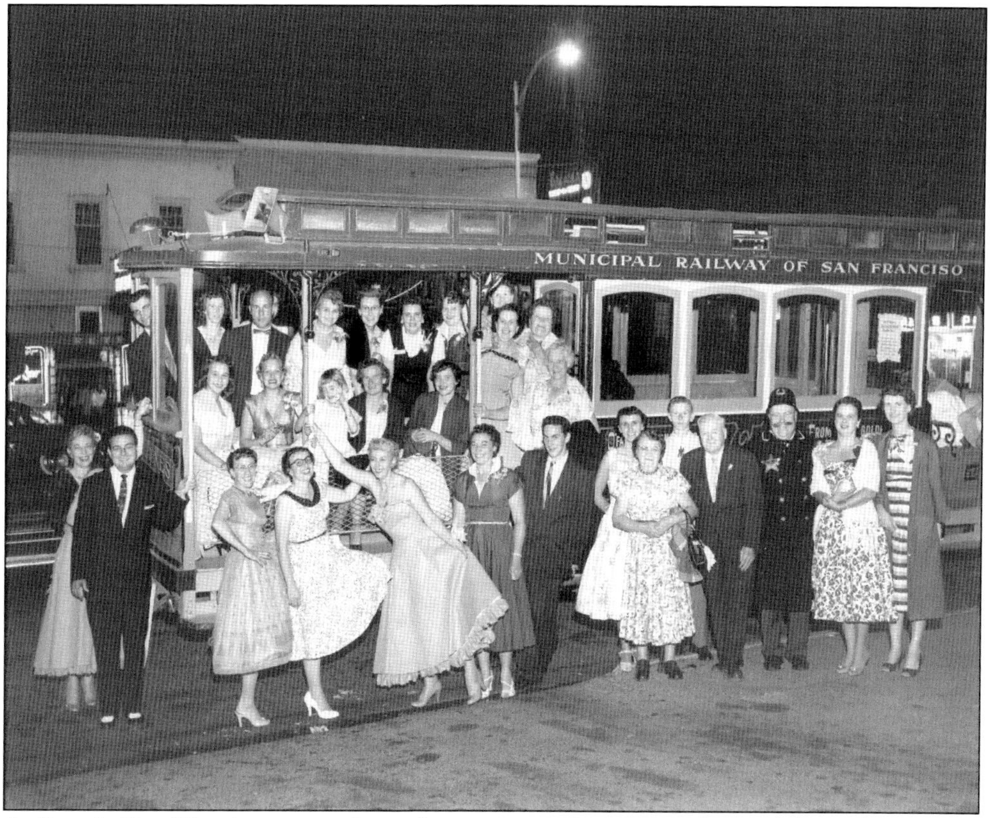

At Steve's Gay 90's, this group of people in evening dress are in front of the authentic San Francisco cable car that was owned by Steve Pease, owner of the restaurant. Steve's was a very popular entertainment spot in Tacoma and a destination for many out-of-town visitors.

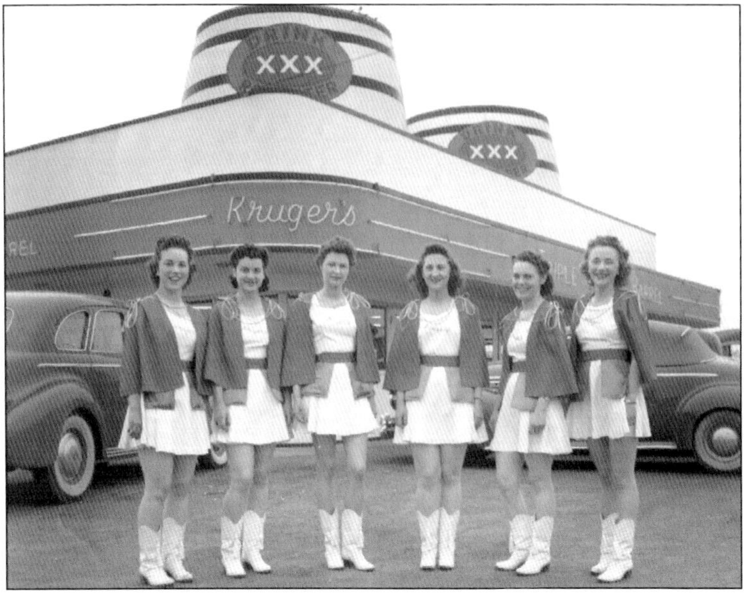

These five carhops lined up in front of Kruger's XXX Root Beer Barrel drive-in restaurant were ready to serve customers in their cars. This drive-in was originally owned by Frank J. Kruger and opened in 1936. In 1943, it was sold to Bill and Thelma Busch and was eventually known as Busch's Drive-In Restaurant.

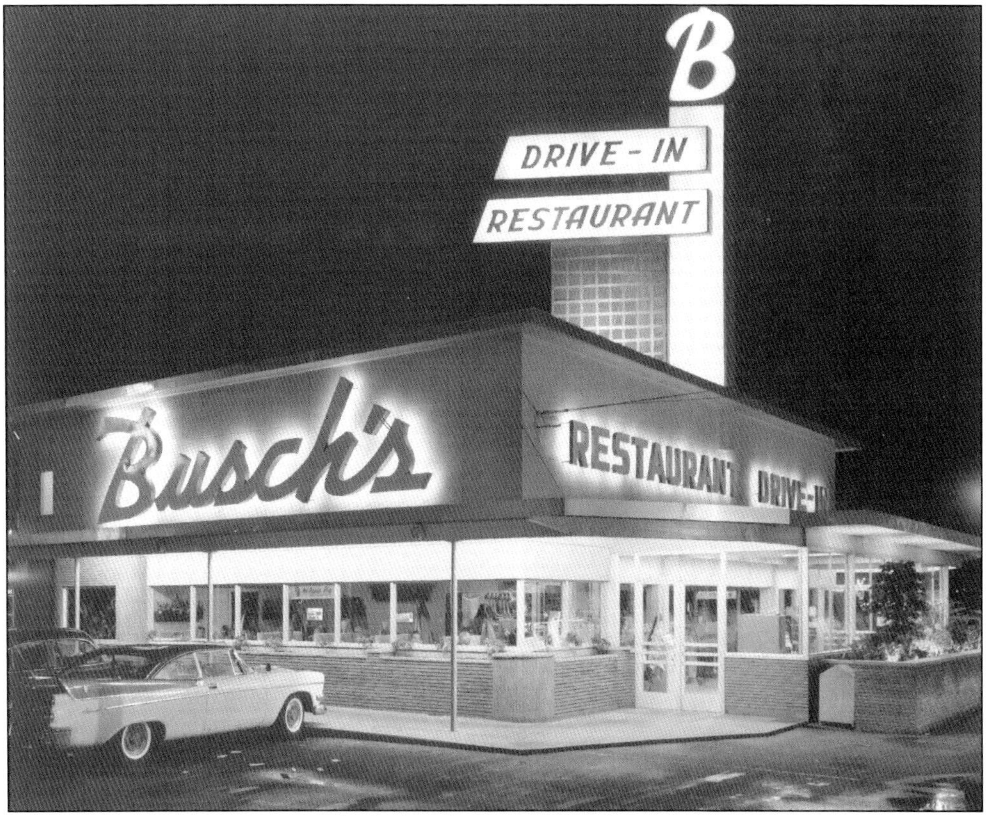

Busch's Drive-In is seen here as it looked in the evenings in the 1950s. At this time, Busch's offered both curbside and inside dining on South Tacoma Way. Originally owned by Bill and Thelma Busch in 1943, it would later be renamed Busch's Round Table Restaurant.

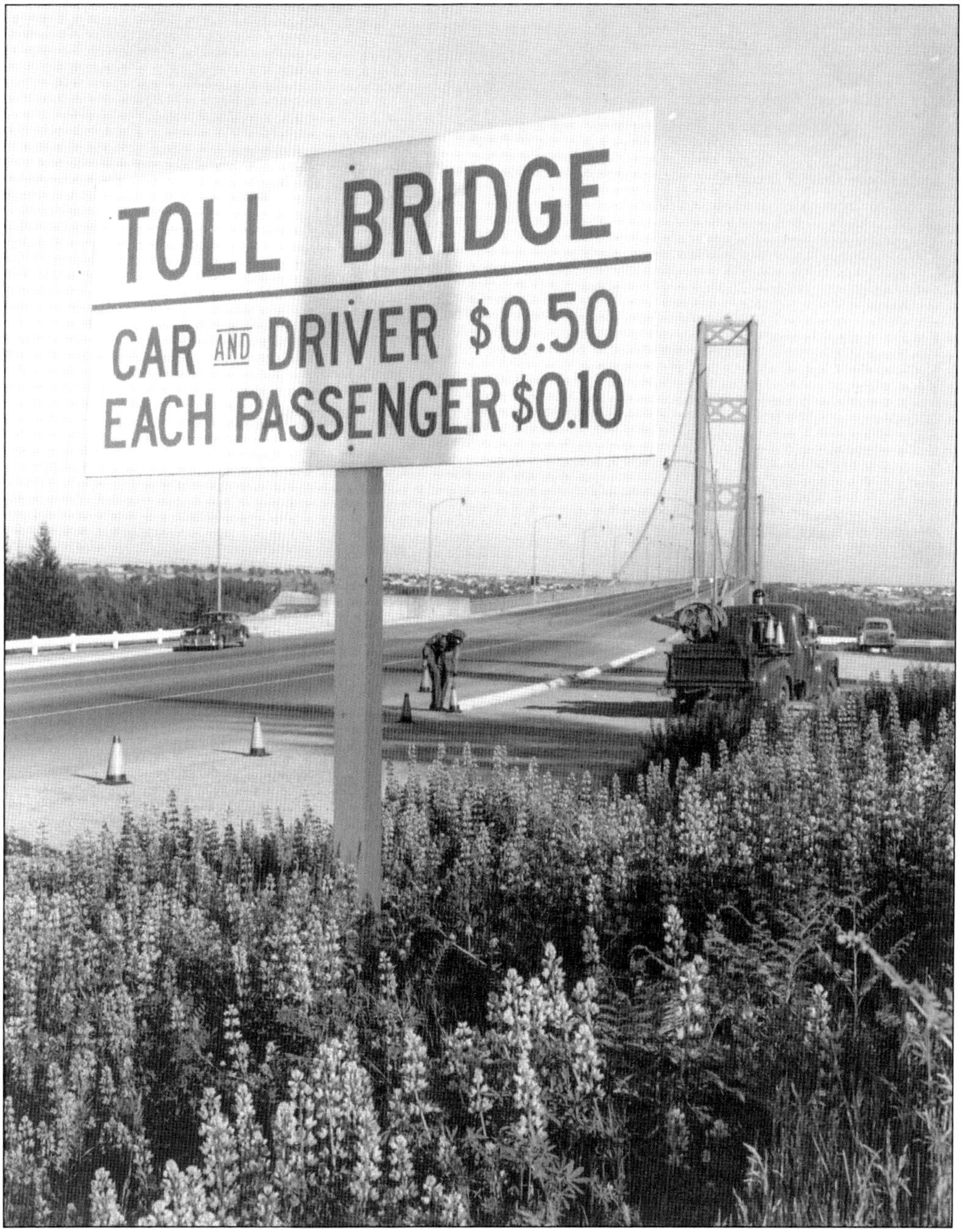

In 1957, this sign was on the Gig Harbor side of the second Narrows Bridge to advise drivers of the tolls. Tolls were charged from the first day the second bridge opened, on October 14, 1950, until they were removed on May 14, 1965.

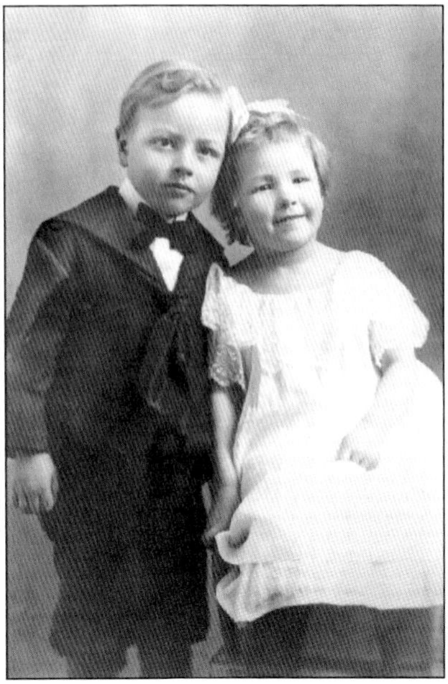

Ben B. Cheney is shown in this 1910 photograph with his sister, Lula, age three. Cheney was born on March 24, 1905, in Lima, Montana, before moving to Tacoma at age 19. In 1936, he started his own mill and came up with a marketing innovation that made him famous in the industry. Cheney began marketing eight-foot-long two-by-four studs. He even came up with the name "studs" instead of the previously used "shorts," hence the name Cheney Studs.

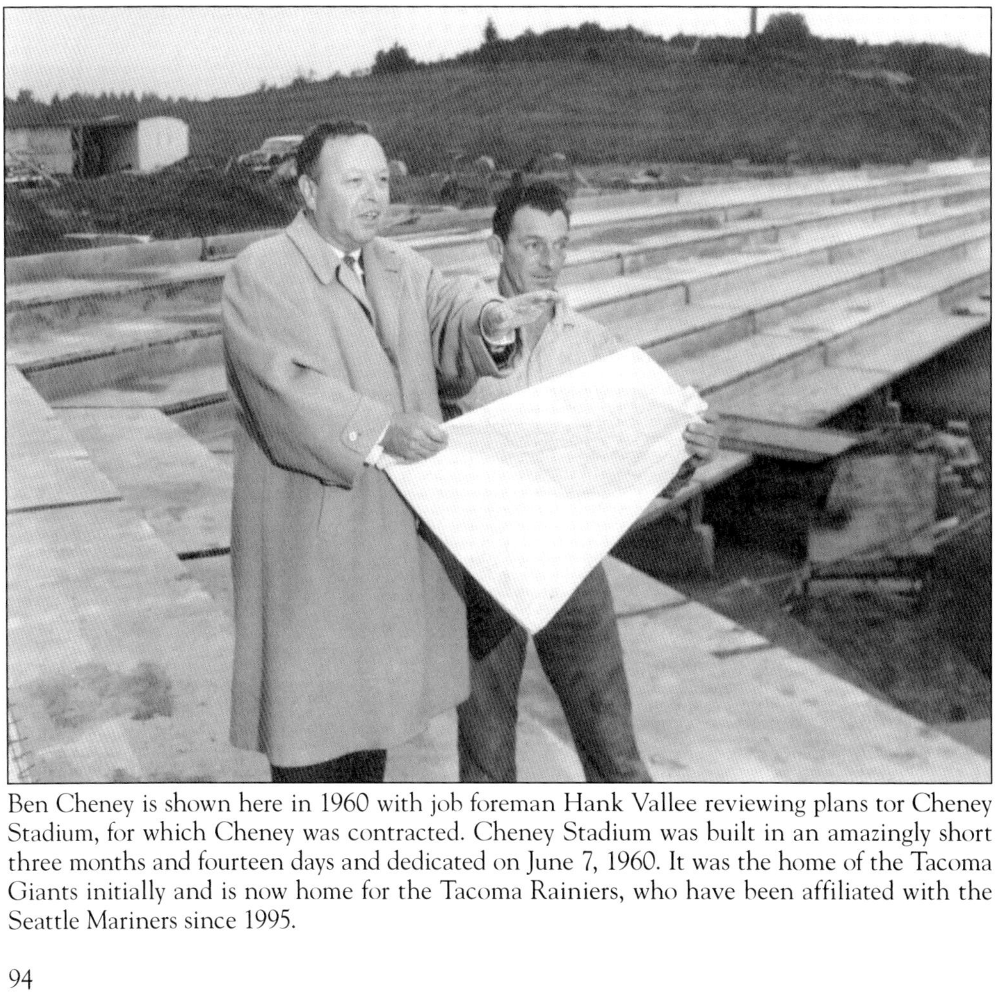

Ben Cheney is shown here in 1960 with job foreman Hank Vallee reviewing plans tor Cheney Stadium, for which Cheney was contracted. Cheney Stadium was built in an amazingly short three months and fourteen days and dedicated on June 7, 1960. It was the home of the Tacoma Giants initially and is now home for the Tacoma Rainiers, who have been affiliated with the Seattle Mariners since 1995.

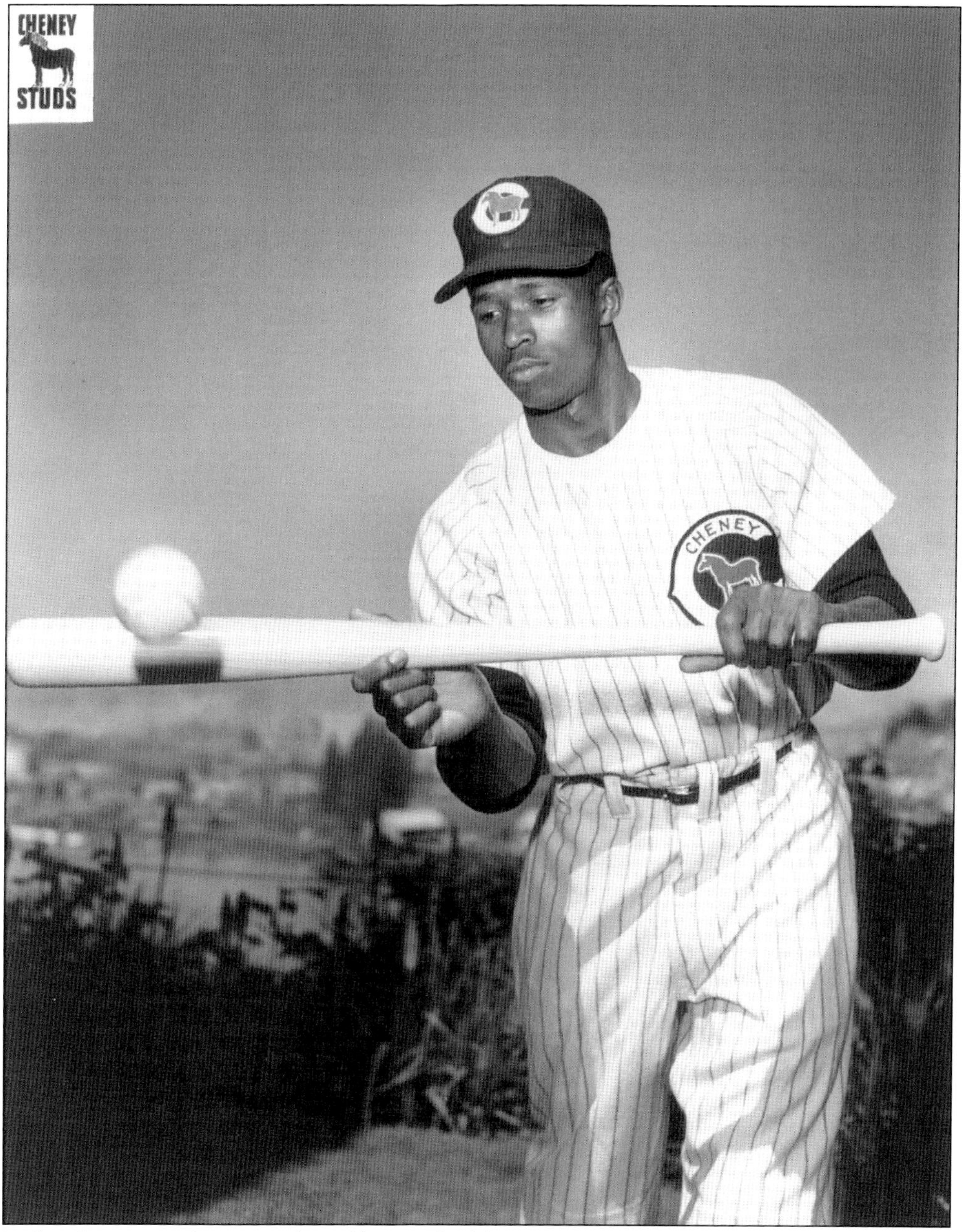

Luther Carr, one of Tacoma's best all-around athletes, is showing his bunting style while playing with the Cheney Studs in 1955, when he batted .399 as an outfielder. He was an outstanding athlete in all sports, including a state record 23-foot, 9.625-inch broad jump. Playing football for Lincoln High School, he made 20 touchdowns in his senior year alone. After playing for and graduating from the University of Washington, he earned a roster spot on the Oakland Raiders of the new American League team. An injury ended his football career before the season began. Following that, Carr had a very successful business and civic career in Seattle.

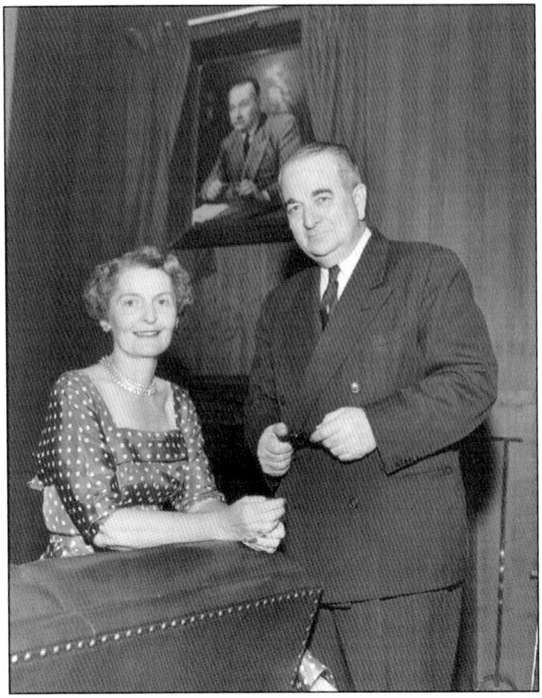

The president of Puget Sound National bank, Reno Odlin, is shown with the artist who painted the portrait hanging behind him, Delia K. Fogg. This portrait was one of several oil paintings made by Fogg of well-known Tacomans. During Odlin's career, he was a former member of the Federal Reserve Board, president of the American Bankers Association, commander of the Washington State American Legion, and president of the Washington State Historical Society.

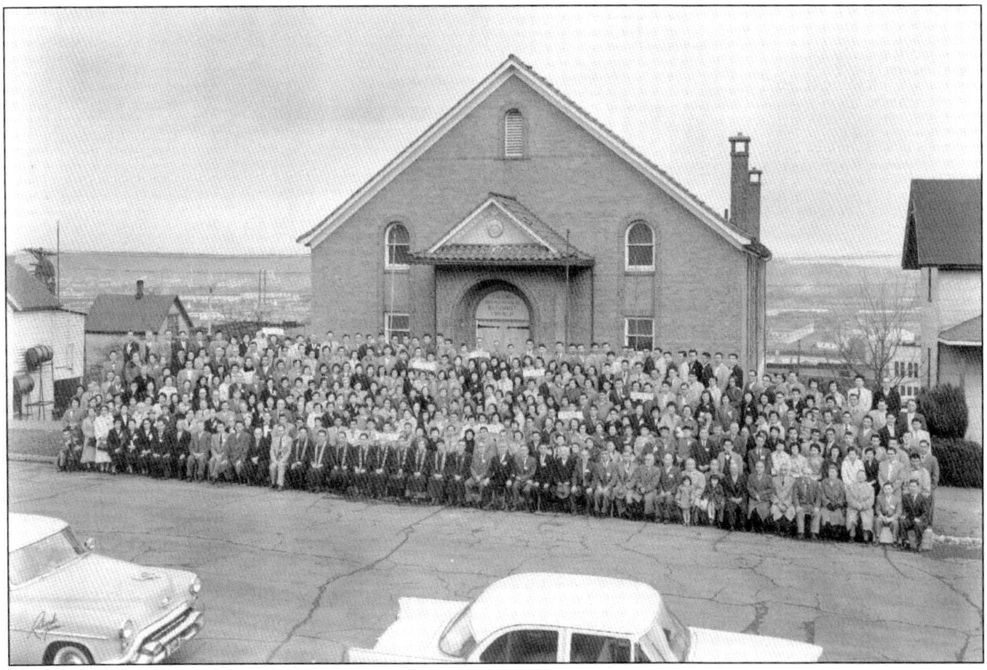

The Tacoma Hongwanji Buddhist Church at 1717 Fawcett Avenue was host to 300 participants in the ninth annual Northwest Young Buddhist League convention on February 19, 1956. This three-day convention featured nine Buddhist ministers including Sunya Pratt, the first ordained woman Buddhist minister in the United States. This church was established in 1915, and the temple, which was built in 1930, is still in operation today and is on the Tacoma Register of Historic Places.

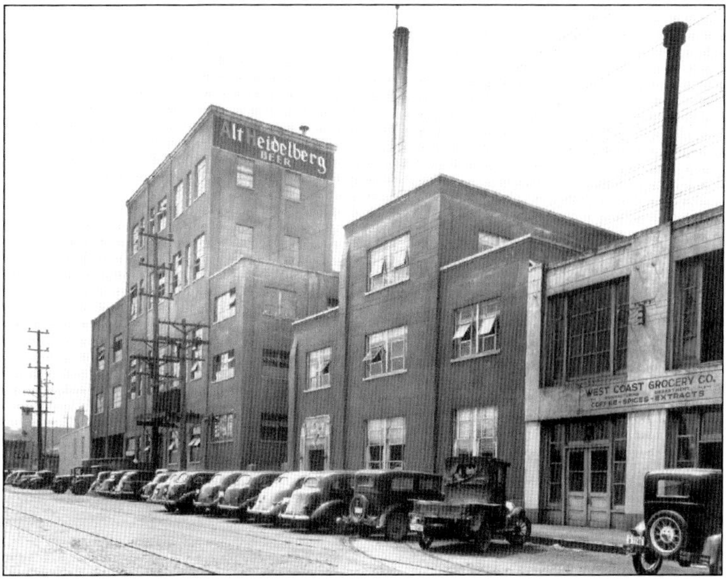

The Columbia Brewing Company plant, which brewed Heidelberg Beer, is shown in June 1938, next to the West Coast Grocery Company warehouse on the right. Columbia was the first Tacoma brewery to offer public legal beer on April 7, 1933, in over 17 years, following Prohibition. Their flagship brand of beer, Alt Heidelberg, was changed to just Heidelberg on July 15, 1953.

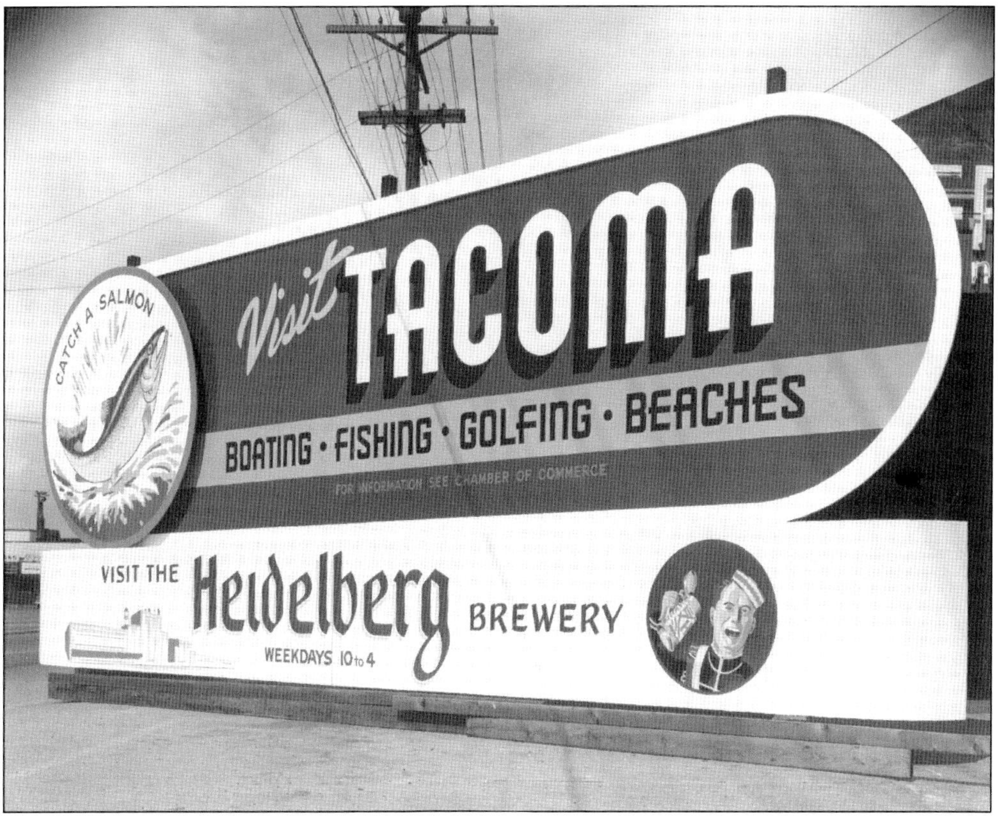

This 30-foot sign advertises reasons to visit Tacoma in the 1950s. There were a number of these signs made by the Douglas Fir Plywood Association and placed around the state highways. This one featured Heidelberg Brewery. Others included Mt. Rainier, the Narrows Bridge, Point Defiance, Fort Nisqually, and the Washington State Historical Society.

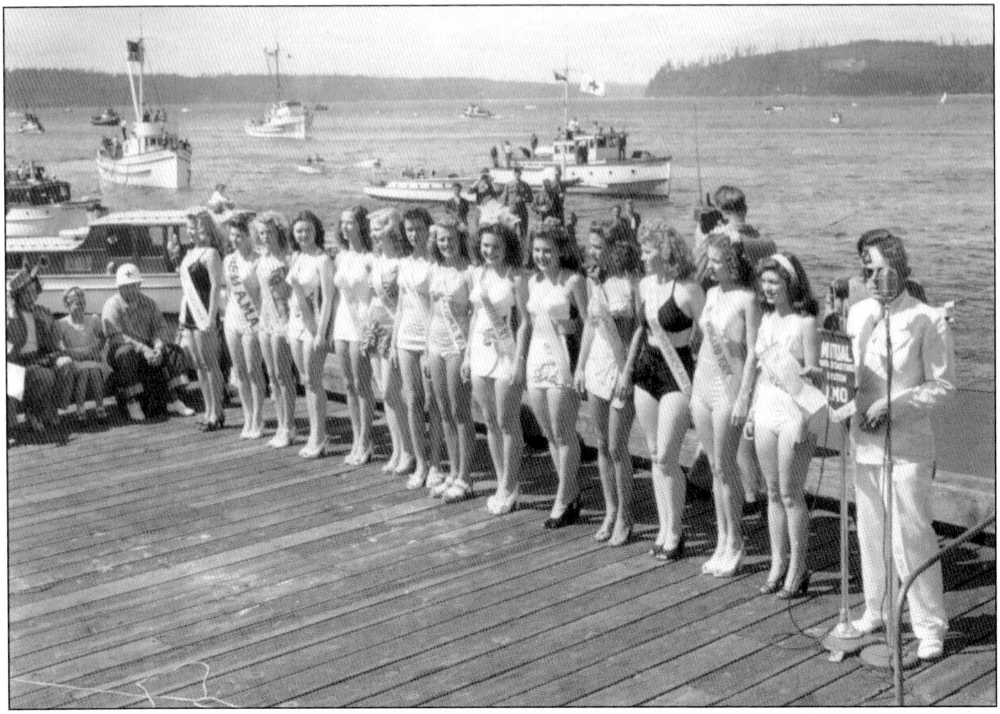

A radio announcer from KMO is ready to announce the winner of the 1946 Jubilee Regatta Queen contest over the air. The annual Jubilee Regatta had many Water Carnival events, such as boat races, a fireboat display, a water-skiing show, and a lawn bowling tournament.

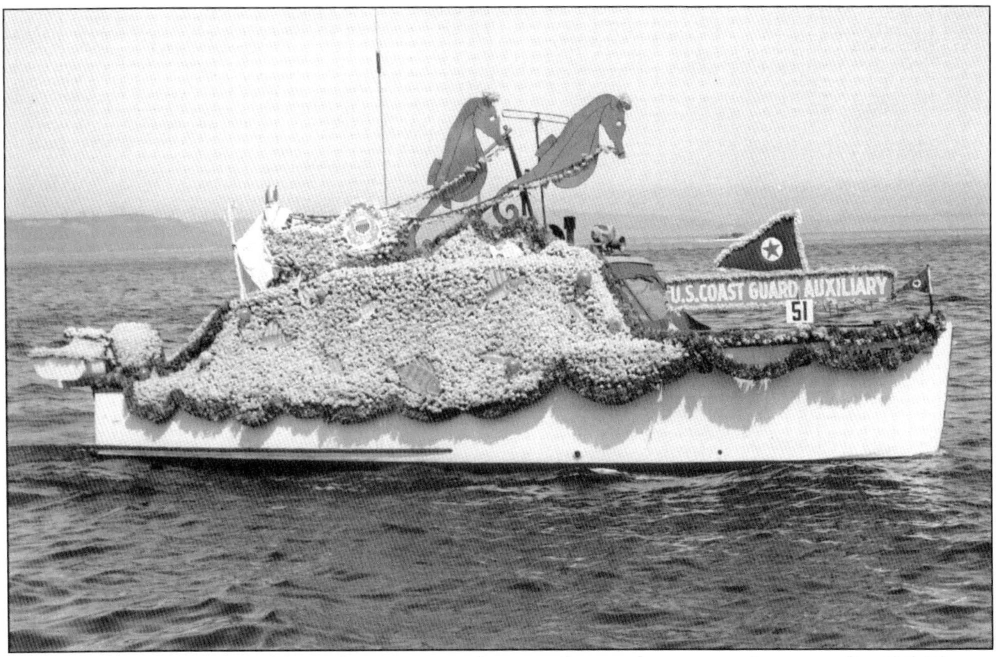

Chester Gibson, owner of the *Hilma III*, won the grand prize for visiting boats in the 1954 Puget Sound Daffodil Regatta. His entry, shown here, depicted Neptune and a chariot of seahorses and was from the Queen City Yacht Club of Seattle. It was decorated extensively with daffodils.

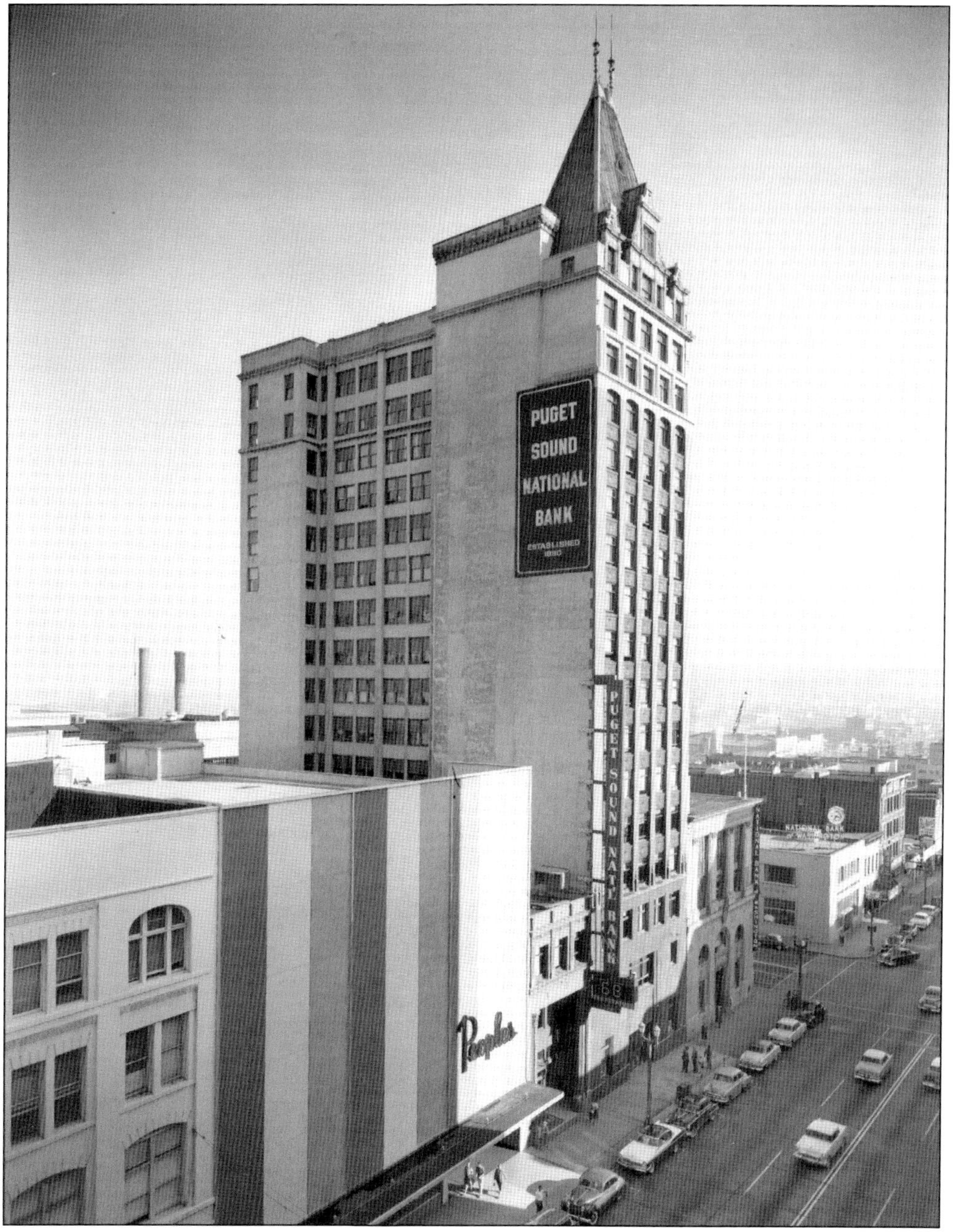

Puget Sound National Bank was established in 1890. This 16-story headquarters was the tallest building west of the Mississippi when completed in 1911, until it was surpassed by Seattle's Smith Tower in 1914. It is presently called the Key Bank Center and is the fifth tallest building in Tacoma, after Wells Fargo Plaza, Hotel Murano, Washington Building, and the Tacoma Municipal Building.

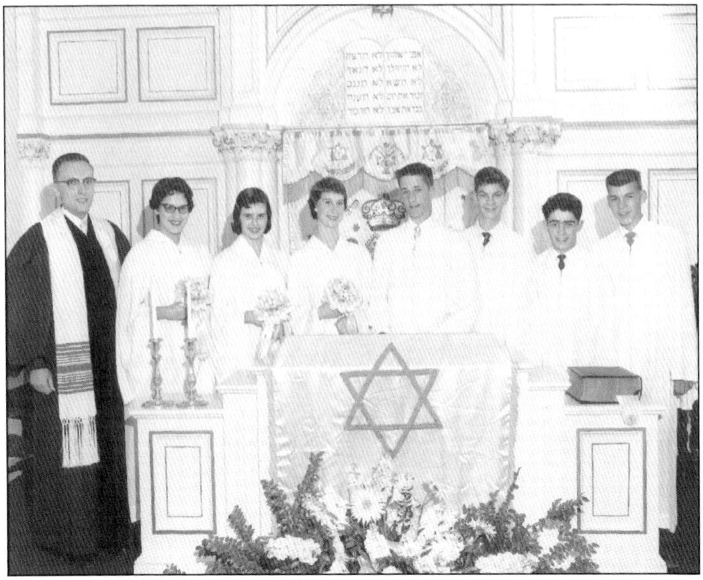

The Temple Beth Israel congregation held this confirmation class of seven young people on May 18, 1956. From left to right are Rabbi Allan H. Schwartzmann, Melvin M. Almo, Arlen Lloyd Brotman, Janis Rita Callin, Jeraldine Beth Fingold, Kerry Frederick Klegman, Norman David Schwartz, and Elsa Beth Warnick. Participants ranged from 16 to 18 years of age.

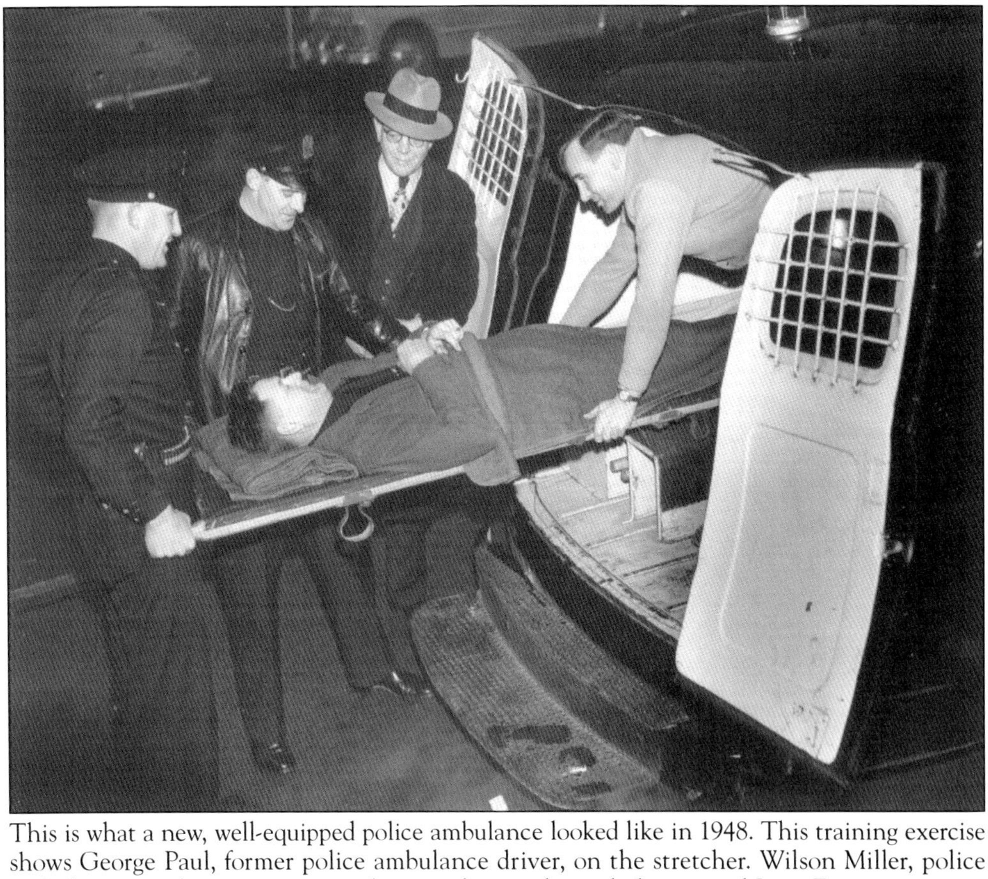

This is what a new, well-equipped police ambulance looked like in 1948. This training exercise shows George Paul, former police ambulance driver, on the stretcher. Wilson Miller, police ambulance conductor, is putting the stretcher in the ambulance, and Jesse Eastman, garage keeper for the police garage, is in the ambulance. Looking on are R.V. Larson (left) and Arthur Gilbo, ambulance drivers.

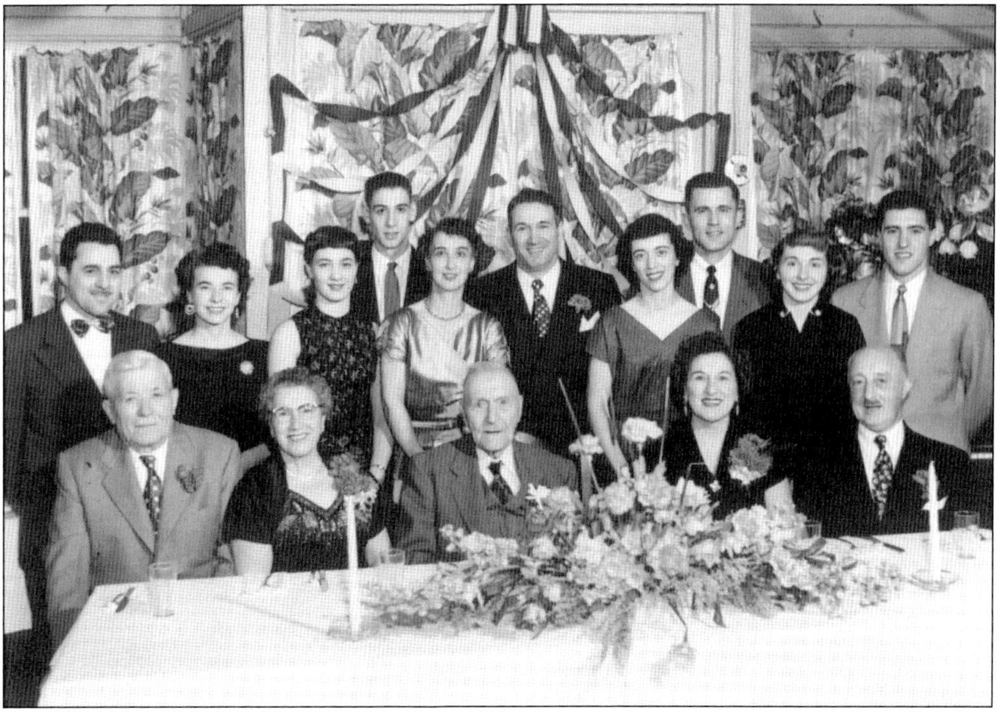

Andrew Guich was a founding member of the Slavonian-American Benevolent Society of Tacoma in 1901. He is shown celebrating his 100th birthday on February 20, 1954, at the Slavonian Hall with family members. Guich helped establish the Slavonian Hall in 1906 and was president of the society for 12 years. He is seated at center, flanked by his two surviving sisters, Katherine Borovich and Ruth Muylle, and surrounded by other family members. The Slavonian Hall is listed in the National Register of Historic Places and located in Old Town Tacoma.

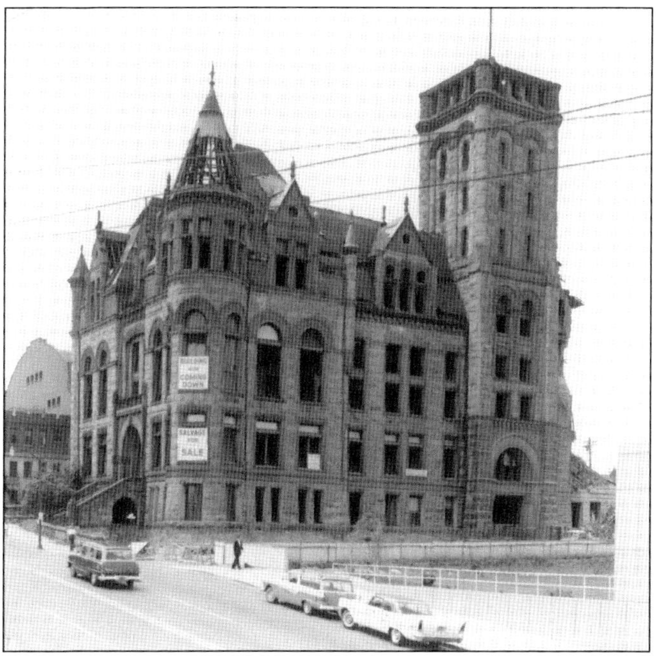

The old Pierce County Courthouse at 1012 South G Street is shown in July 1959 with large signs stating, "This building is coming down," and "Salvage for sale." The building was originally built in 1892 and was in a serious state of deterioration at this time. It was demolished when the current courthouse was completed that year and became a parking lot.

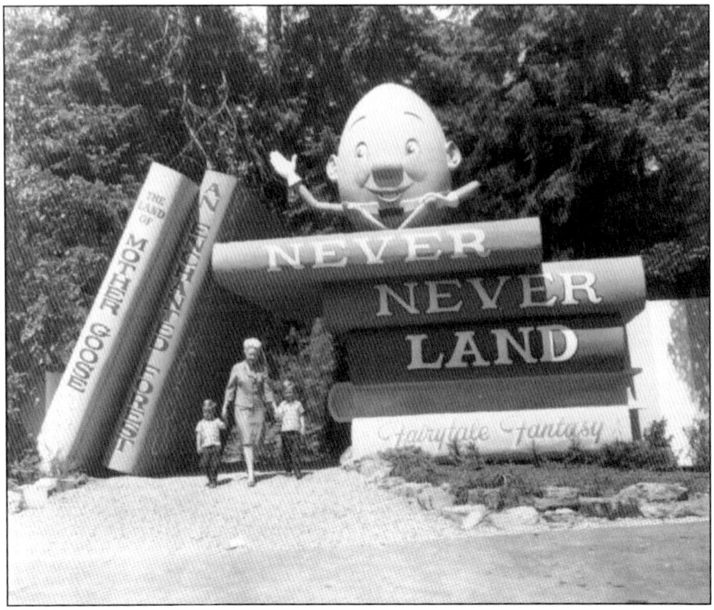

Never Never Land was a very popular attraction in Point Defiance Park from 1964 until 2010, when all elements had to be removed due to deterioration and vandalism. Metro Parks Tacoma has a couple of the old statues, which could possibly be refurbished to their original luster someday.

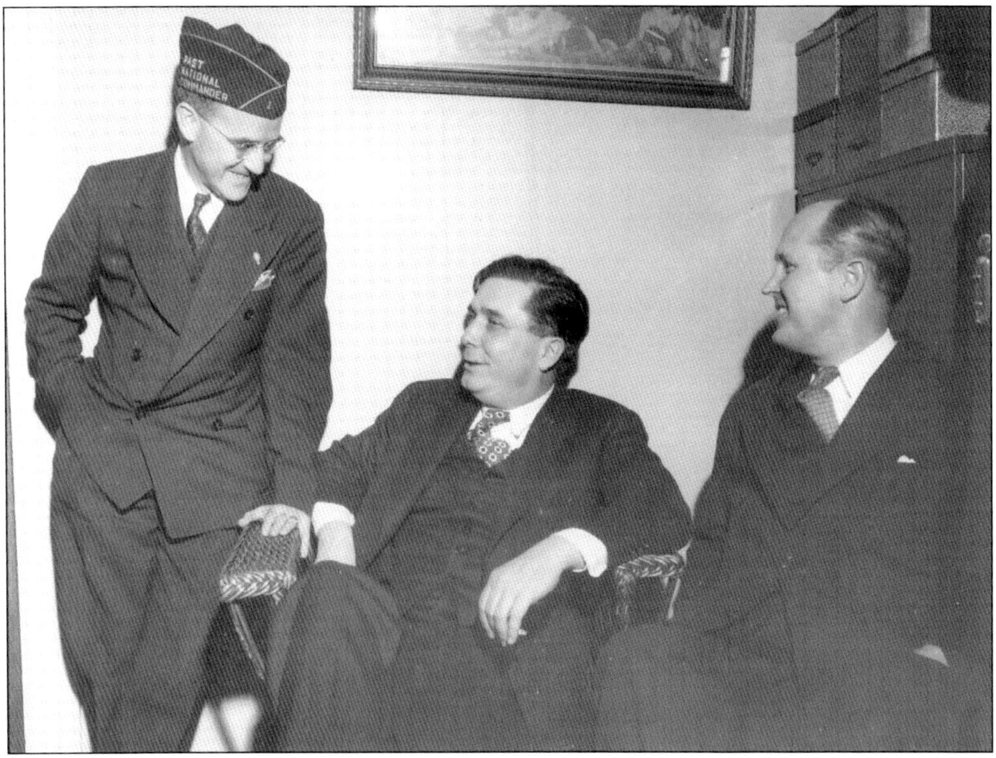

Gov. Arthur Langlie (far right) is shown on February 11, 1944, with past national commander of the American Legion Warren H. Atherton (left) during a campaign visit to Tacoma by the 1940 Republican presidential nominee Wendell Willkie (center). Willkie was a guest of honor at the Lincoln Day banquet sponsored by the Pierce County Republican Club, and following that, he was escorted by the Edward B. Rhodes Post No. 2 drum and bugle corps to address the Legionnaires at the Rhodes Post.

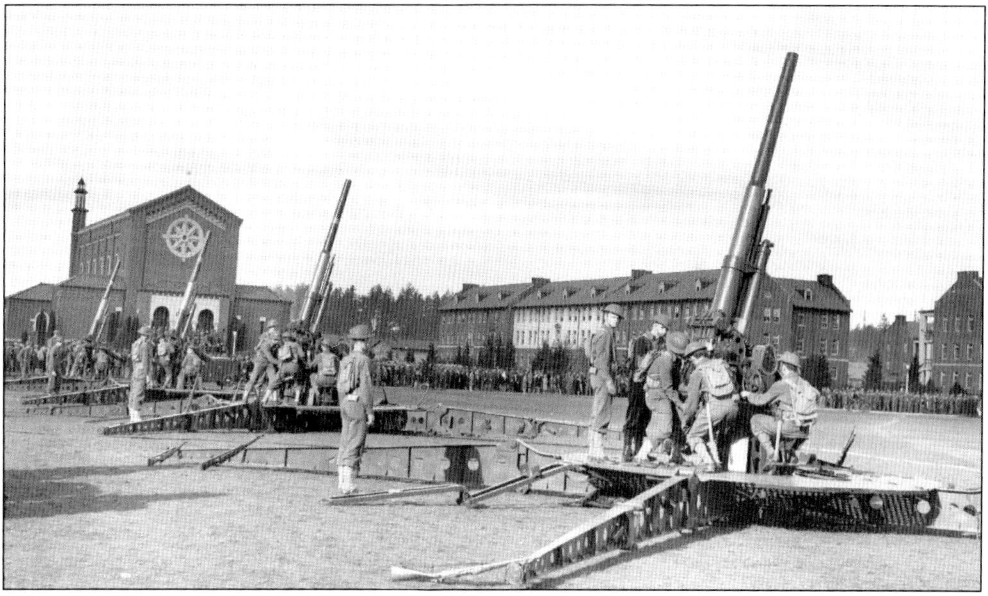

Fort Lewis soldiers are practicing artillery techniques on the parade grounds in this 1941 photograph. The citizens of Pierce County donated the land for this military base to the government in 1917, which was named for Meriwether Lewis of the Lewis and Clark Expedition. The Fort Lewis Chapel is in the background.

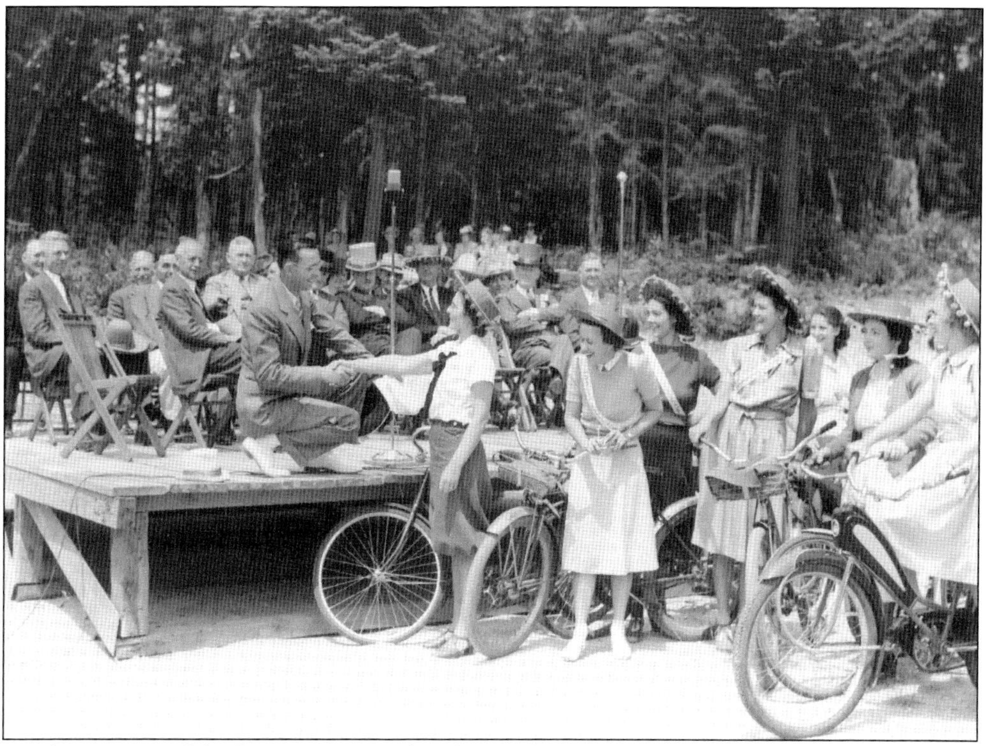

For the opening of the first Narrows Bridge, these Lakewood Community Club ladies are waiting on the west side of the bridge to ride their bicycles across once the bridge was open to traffic. Their ride was to begin at 12:00 p.m. on July 1, 1940.

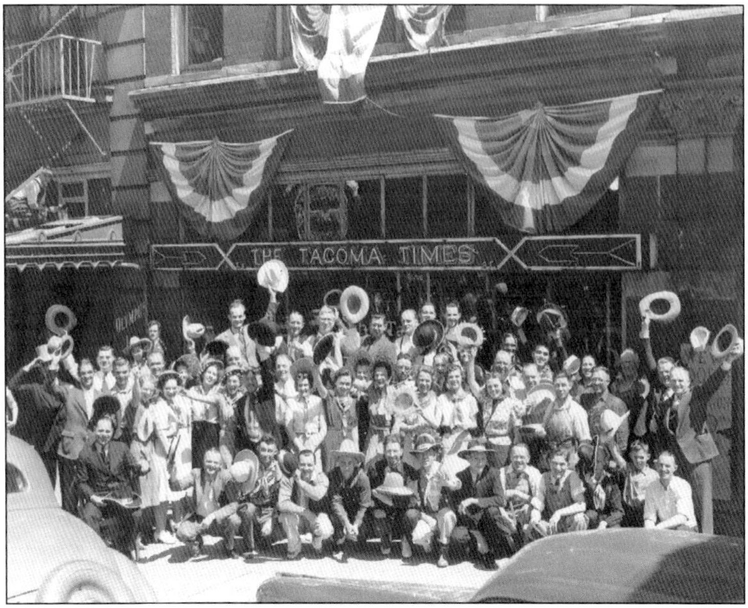

On July 29, 1939, the staff of the *Tacoma Times* appears in front of the newspaper's office with their Jubilee hats to celebrate Washington's 50th year as a state. The *Tacoma Times* was published from 1903 to 1949. The office shown was used until February 10, 1940.

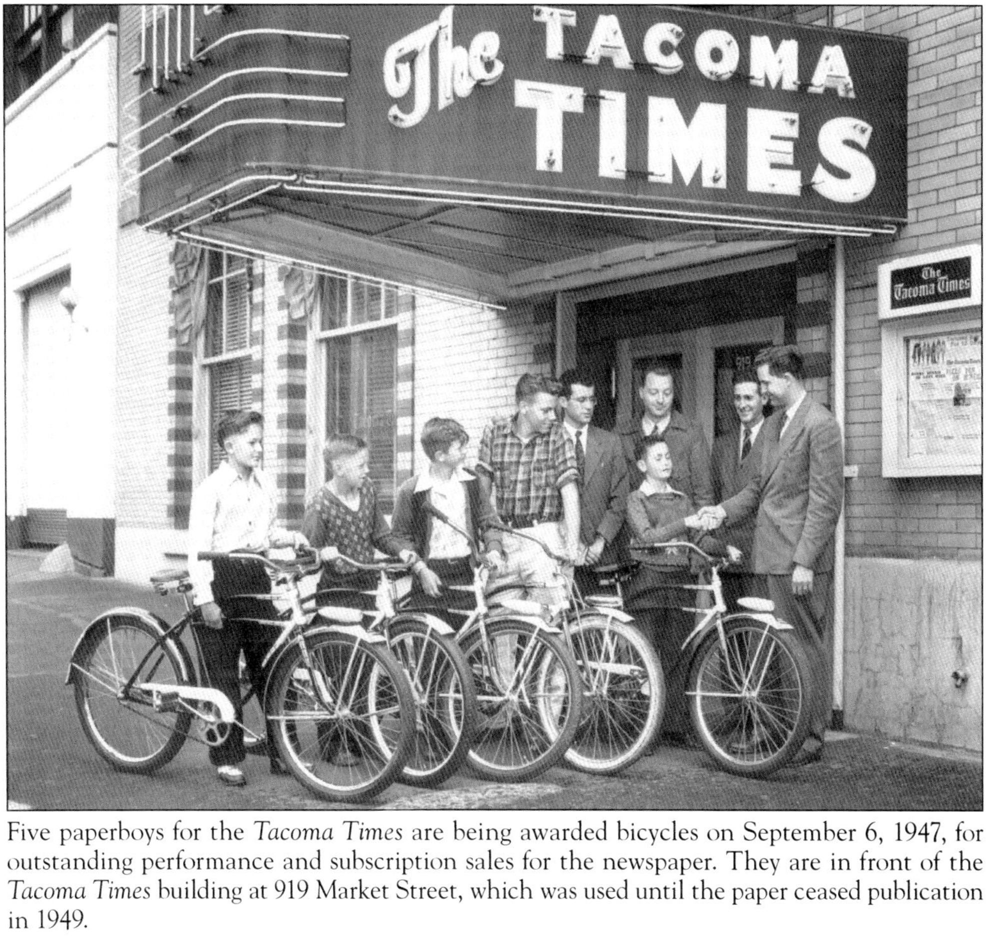

Five paperboys for the *Tacoma Times* are being awarded bicycles on September 6, 1947, for outstanding performance and subscription sales for the newspaper. They are in front of the *Tacoma Times* building at 919 Market Street, which was used until the paper ceased publication in 1949.

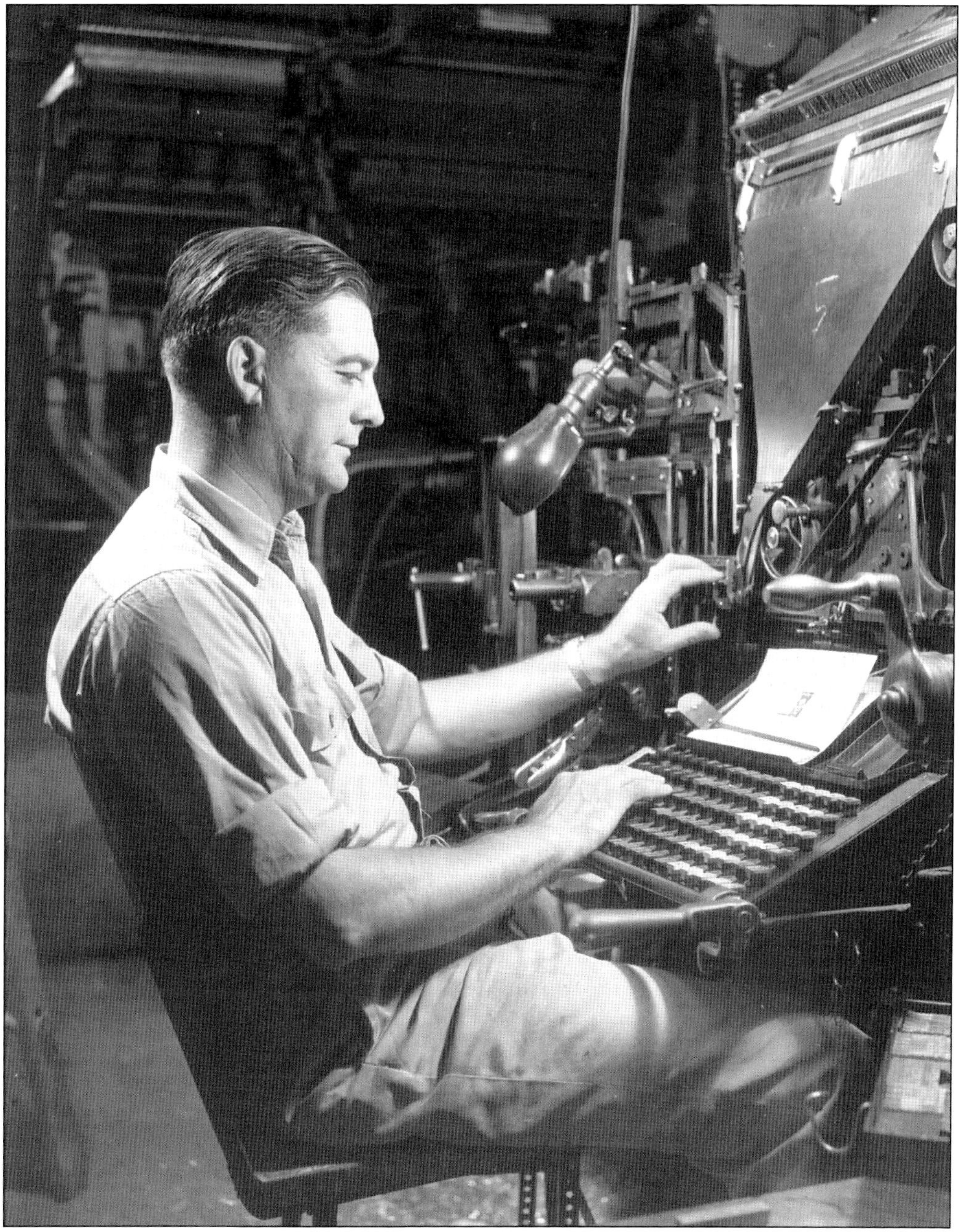

Bill Pettyjohn, a linotype setter for the *Tacoma Times*, is shown on July 21, 1949, shortly before the paper ceased publication. Linotype was one of the methods to set type for newspapers from the late 19th century to the 1980s. It has been largely replaced by phototypesetting, lithography printing, and computer typesetting today.

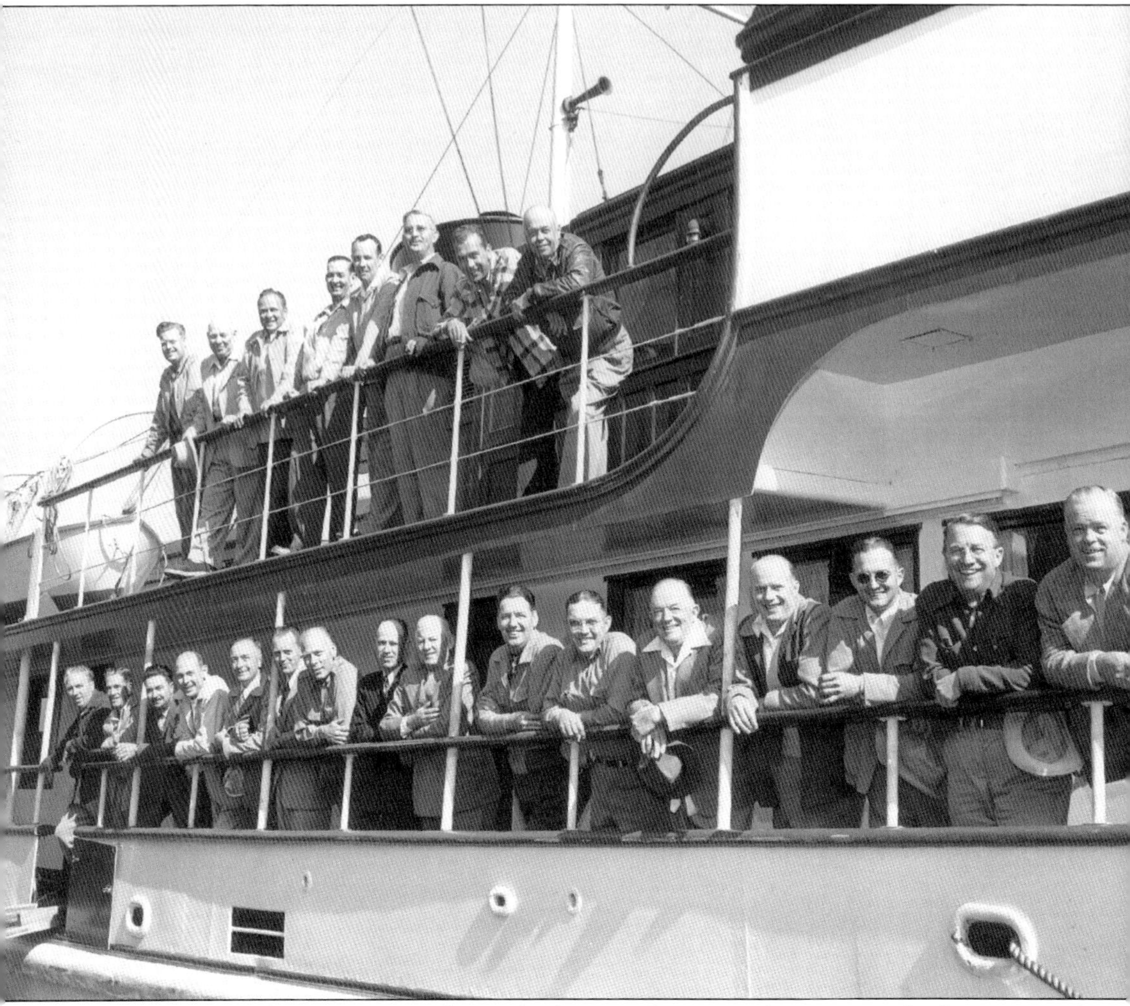

Many Tacoma businessmen and civic leaders are shown on the *Acania*, which was recently refurbished by the J.M. Martinac Shipbuilding Corporation. This vessel was a charter ship owned by Fred Borovich, captain; Ted Ultsch, chief engineer; and Joseph S. Martinac.

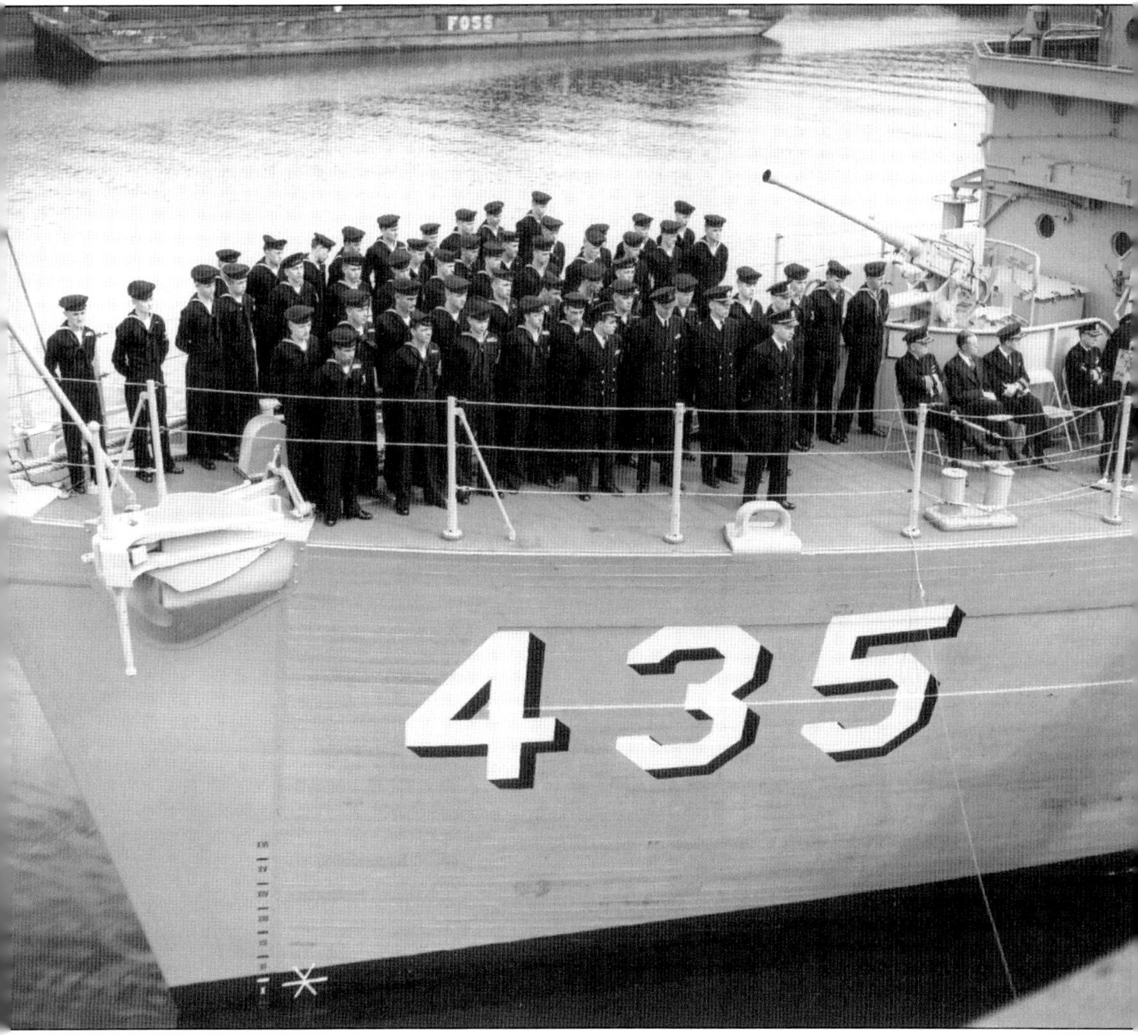

On March 20, 1954, the crew of the USS *Endurance* was preparing for its commissioning ceremony in Tacoma. This ship was built by J.M. Martinac Shipbuilding Corporation and was the first of nine 171-foot minesweepers of this class to be built in Tacoma.

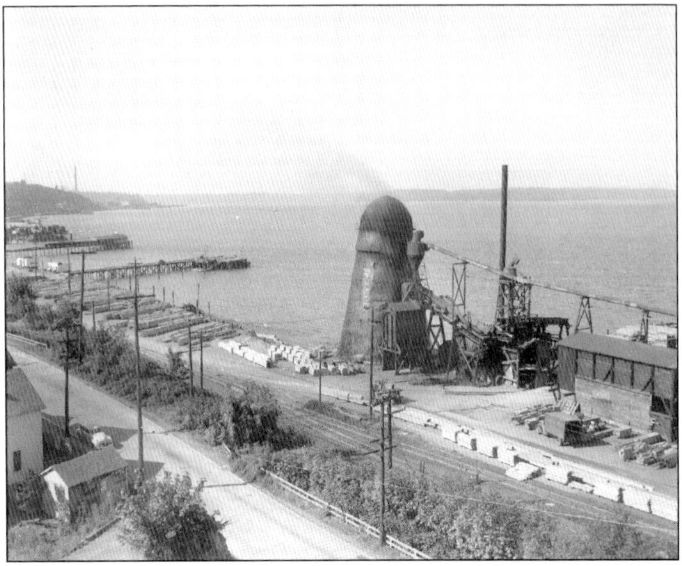

This Henry Mill & Timber Company plant, originally a sawmill, was built in 1924. It was on Ruston Way, next to Commencement Bay, for almost 20 years. This plant built many caisson panels for the first Narrows Bridge. The company won many prefabrication contracts during World War II, after which it was taken over by the Tacoma Fabricating Company, which closed the facility in 1950.

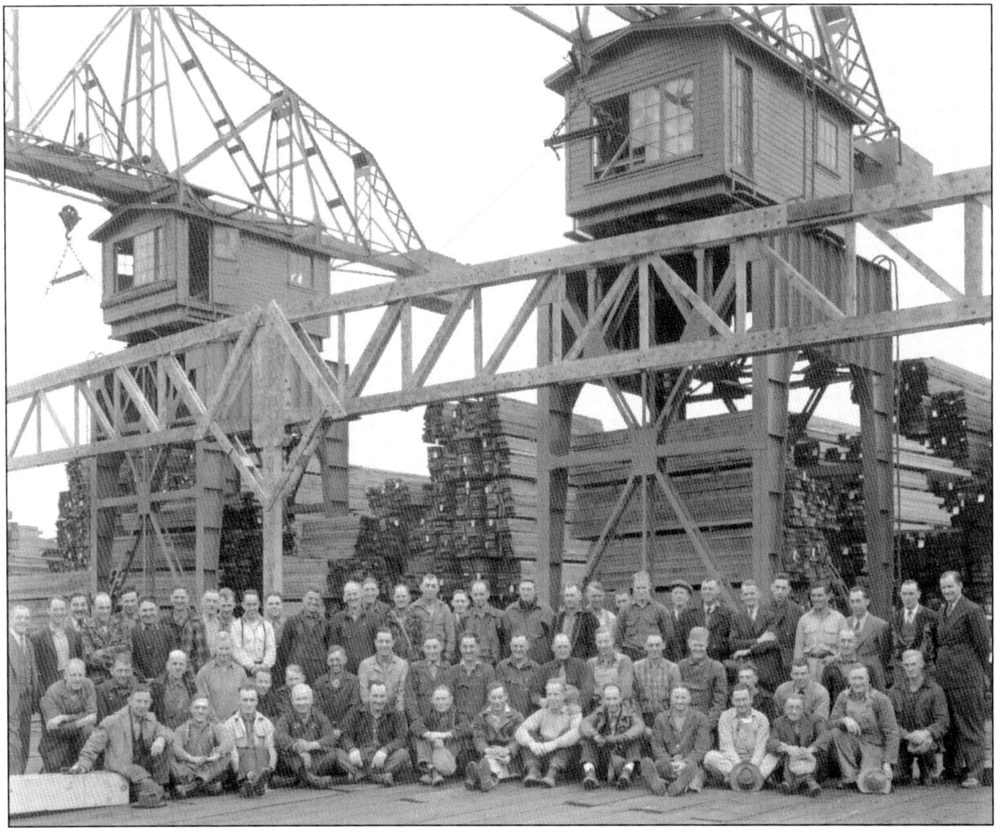

These Henry Mill & Timber Company employees are shown in front of two large cranes that were used to unload timber and load finished products onto ships or railroad cars. Most items were precut, trimmed, bored, grooved, and even finished before they were sent to the building site. There were many Army and Navy contracts for shipyards, storehouses, and cantonments for World War II.

Tacoma rock group the Ventures are shown here on April 26, 1960; from left to right are Nole F. "Nokie" Edwards, Bob Bogle, Howie Johnson, and Tacoma native Don Wilson. This group originated in Tacoma in 1959, and during 1961–1966, they sold one million albums each year. They are best known for their hits "Walk Don't Run" and "Hawaii 5-0." In 2008, they were inducted into the Rock and Roll Hall of Fame. Nokie Edwards passed away on March 12, 2018.

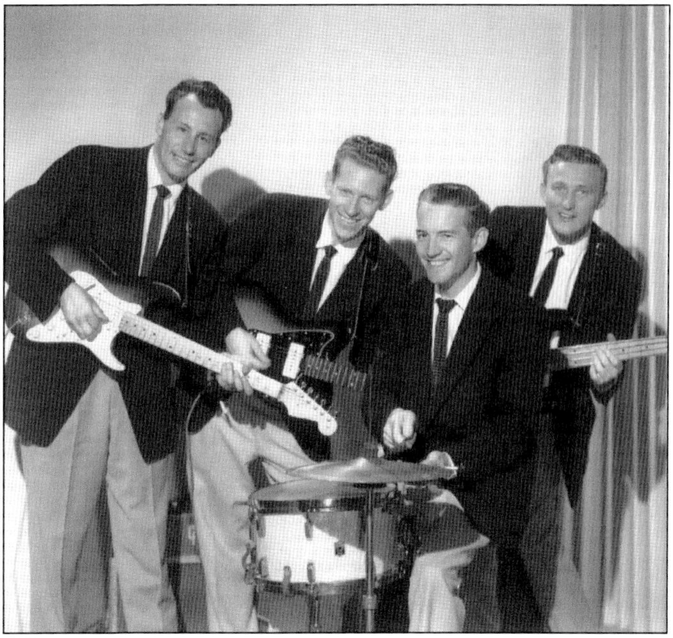

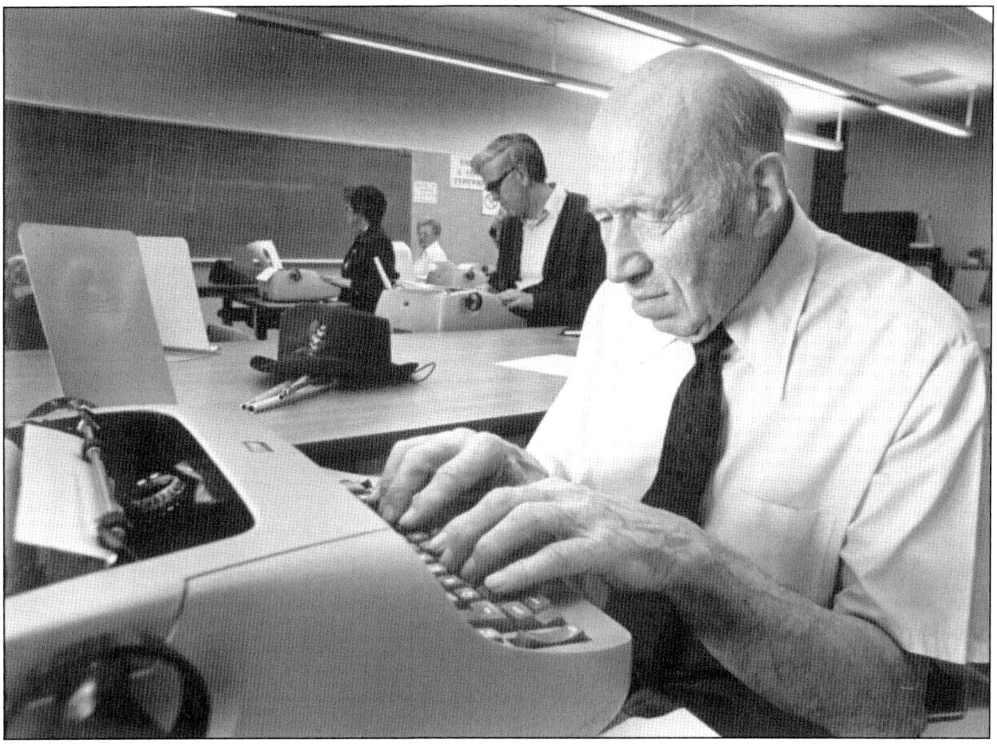

Burgon Mesler is shown on May 7, 1978, at the age of 88, while taking a typing class at Tacoma Community College. Even though he was blind, he wanted to take the course so that he could leave his memoirs to his 52 grandchildren and many great-grandchildren. He became blind in later life, in about 1973, after he had served in the Navy and been a machinist in the Puget Sound Naval Shipyard, a contractor, and even a mountain climber.

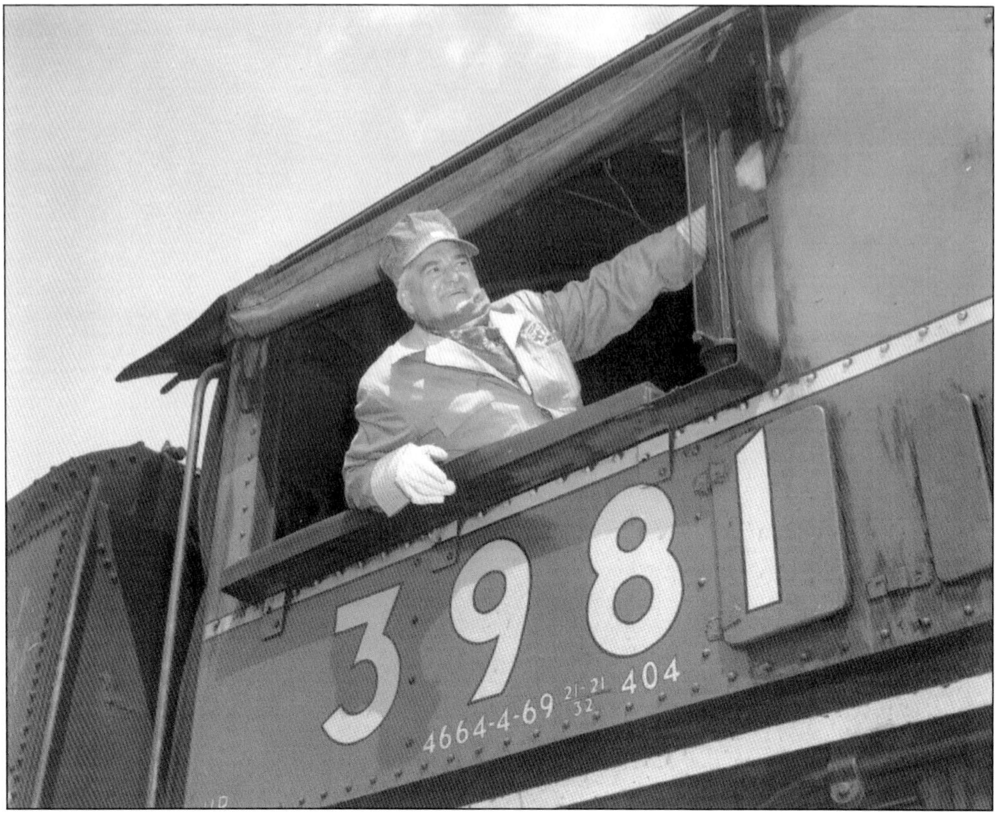

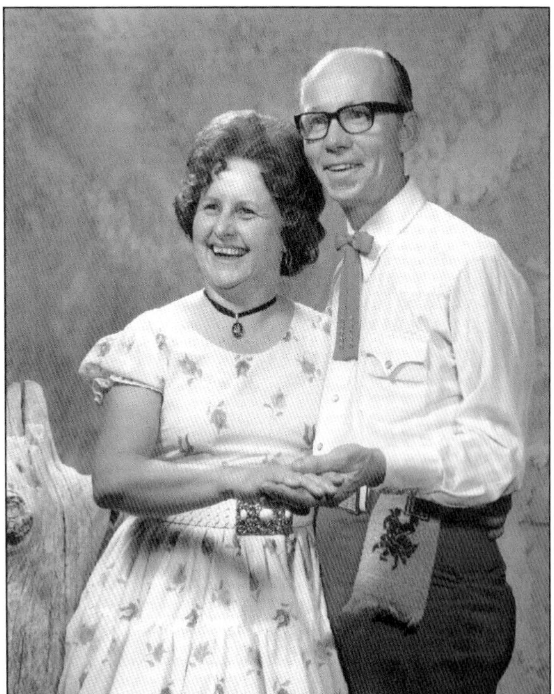

Leon Titus, president of Titus Motor Company, is shown dressed as a train engineer fulfilling a longtime dream on May 7, 1948, to ride in the cab of Union Pacific locomotive No. 3981. This engine was used on the Seattle-Tacoma-Portland run. At 122 feet long, it was the largest engine in the Pacific Northwest.

Otto and Margaret Bodenhorn were the chairs for the Fall Festival of the Rainier Council of the Washington State Federation of Square and Folk Dancers held in Tacoma in November 1974 at the state armory. Dances for this festival were called by the Rainier Teachers & Callers Association. (Photograph by Leroy Seeley.)

Robert G. Anderson is shown shortly before his retirement as head of the Tacoma Public Works Department. He spent 30 years in the department following experience with the state highway department and Army Corps of Engineers and a term as president of the Washington state chapter of the American Public Works Association.

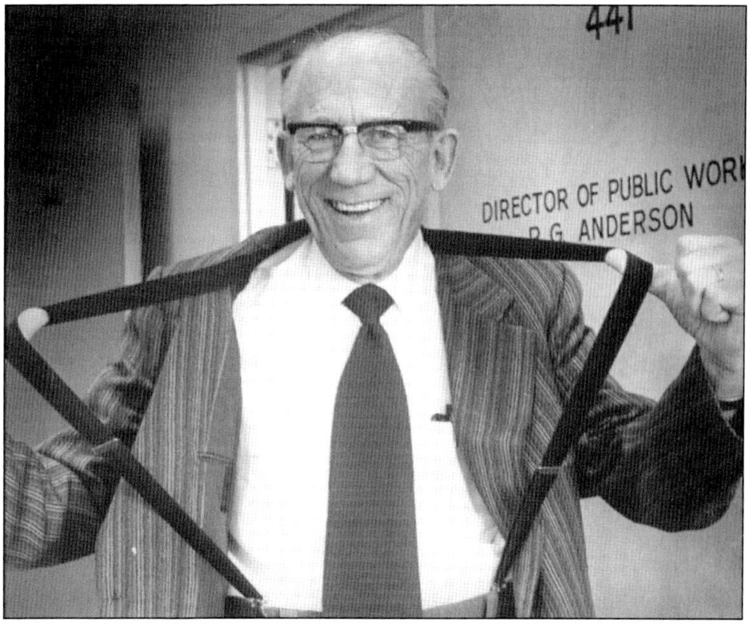

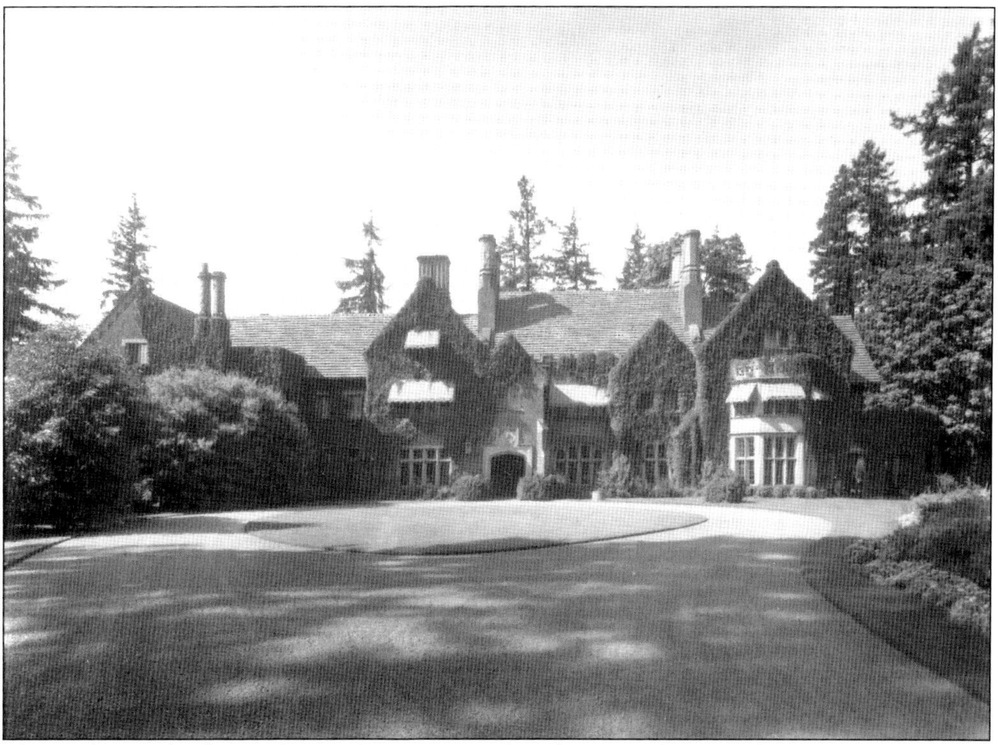

This Tudor Gothic house designed in 1910 was the Chester and Anna Thorne estate known as Thornewood. It is located on the shore of American Lake, 12 miles south of Tacoma. Chester Thorne is known as the father of the Port of Tacoma and was very active in much of Tacoma's early development. He was born in 1863, graduated from Yale with a degree in engineering, was president of National Bank of Commerce for 34 years, and passed away on October 16, 1927. The house is now the Thornewood Castle Bed and Breakfast.

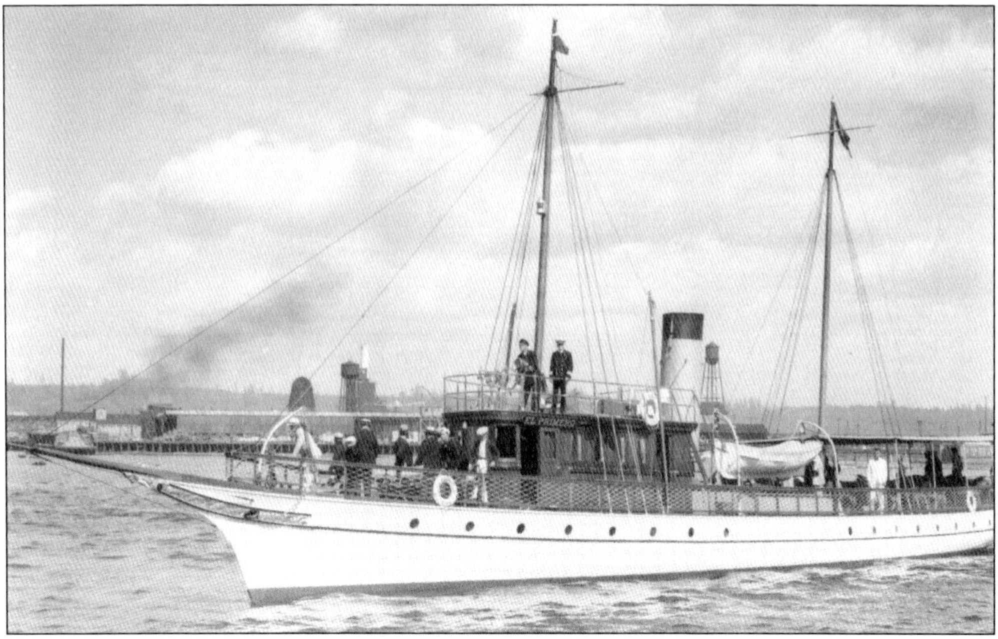

The SS *El Primero* is seen in 1934 while it was owned by S.A. "Sam" Perkins, publisher of the *Tacoma Daily Ledger and News*. The yacht was built at Union Iron Works in San Francisco in 1893 after being purchased by Tacoma banker Chester Thorne. It became Perkins's vessel in 1911, and following that, it was used as a World War II naval patrol vessel and returned to Perkins after the war. At this writing, it is for sale in Bremerton, Washington.

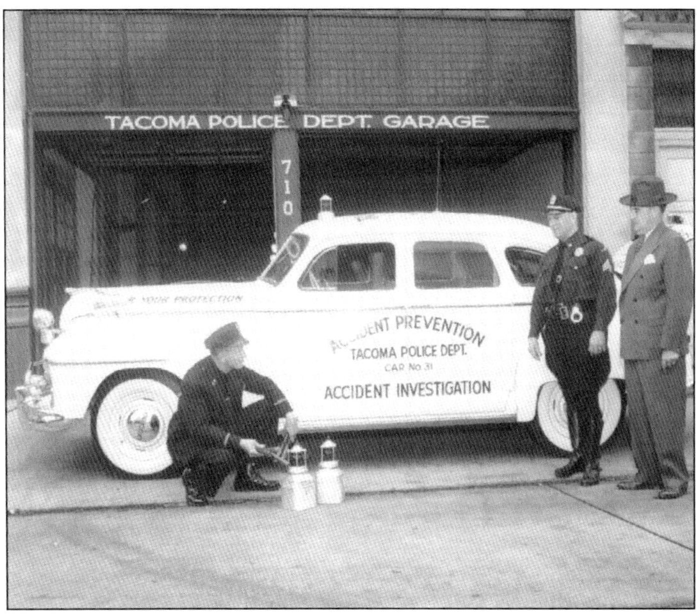

The Tacoma Police Department used to have "crash cars" that were used as accident investigation tools. These vehicles would show up with the investigating officer at an accident scene during the detailed investigation. This is a new vehicle the police department received in September 1947. From left to right are patrolman Emil Smith, Sgt. Bob Marshall, and safety commissioner Robert S. Temme.

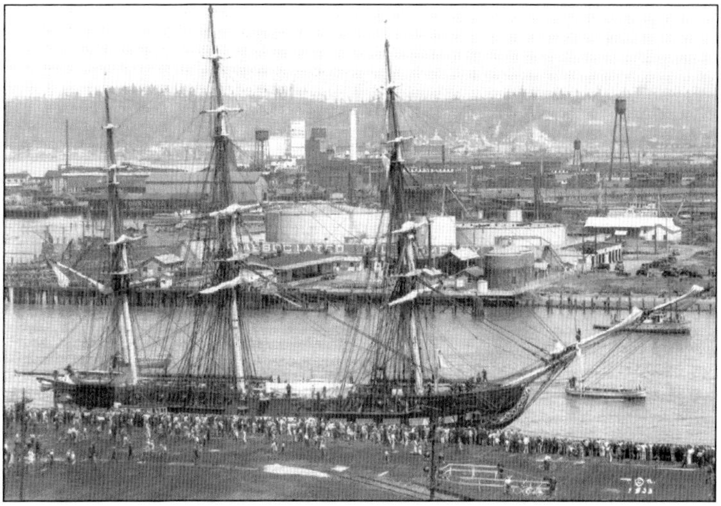

The oldest commissioned warship in the world, USS *Constitution*, "Old Ironsides," visited Tacoma in June 1933, and over 84,000 people toured her. She was launched on October 21, 1797, after an act signed by Pres. George Washington created the US Navy. She is still in commission and is docked at Boston Naval Historical Park.

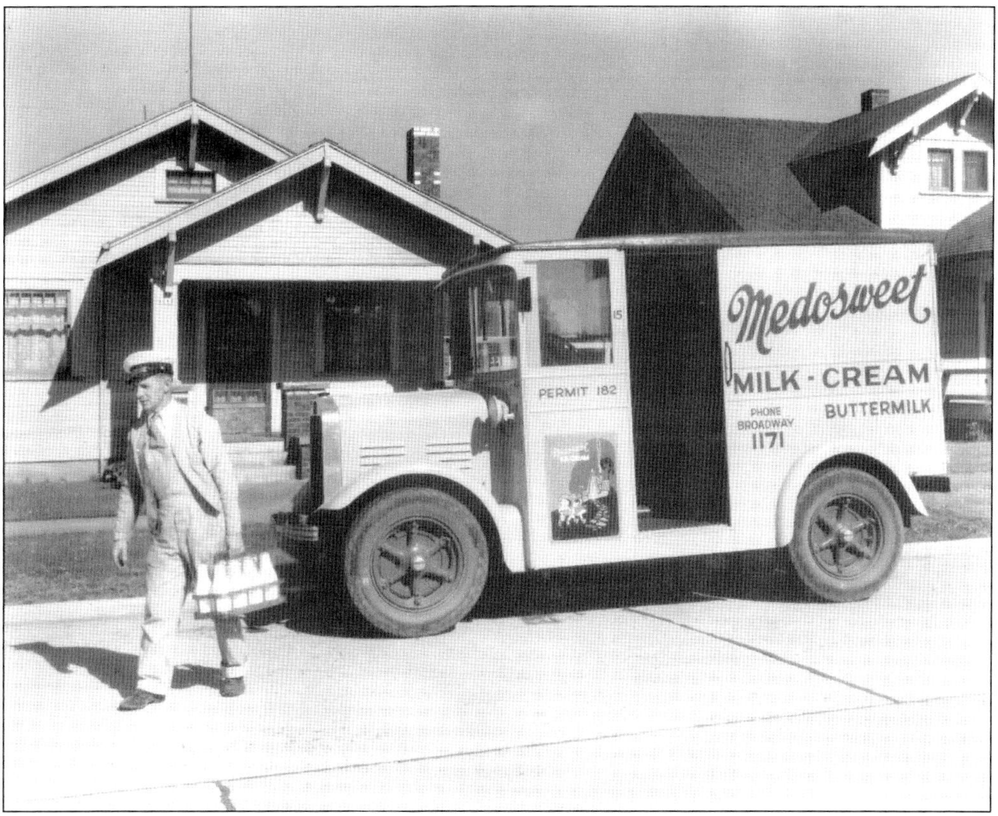

The delivery of milk was almost a daily occurrence in Tacoma by the Medosweet Dairies in the 1930s. The dairy had a laboratory to guarantee high quality milk, cream, and buttermilk for its customers. Milk was delivered to grocers and residential clients the day it was brought in by the company's approved producers to make sure the product was fresh when received.

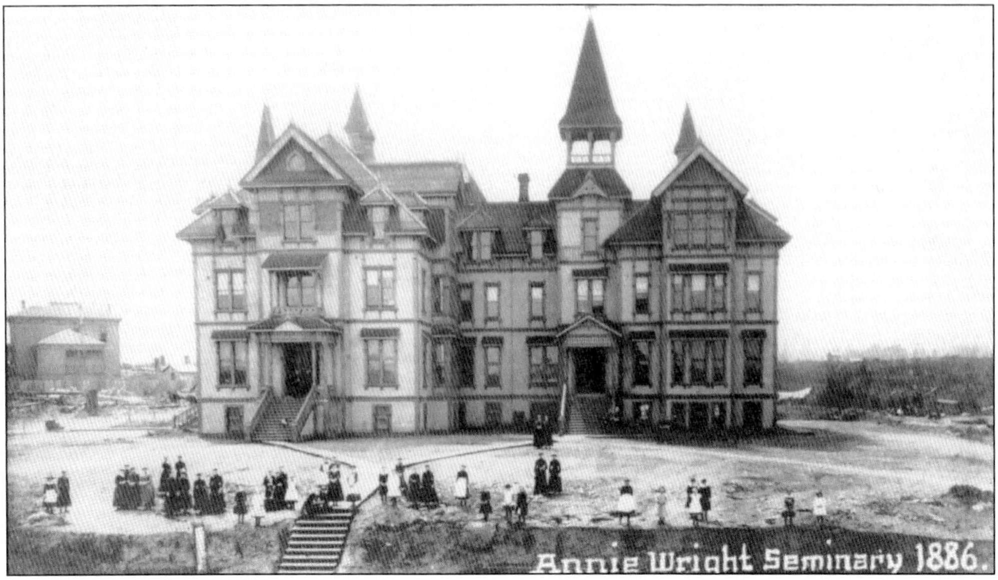

Annie Wright Seminary is seen here in 1886 at 611 Division Avenue. This was a private school for girls that opened in September 1884 and remained at this location until this building was demolished in 1924 and the school moved to its current location at 827 Tacoma Avenue North.

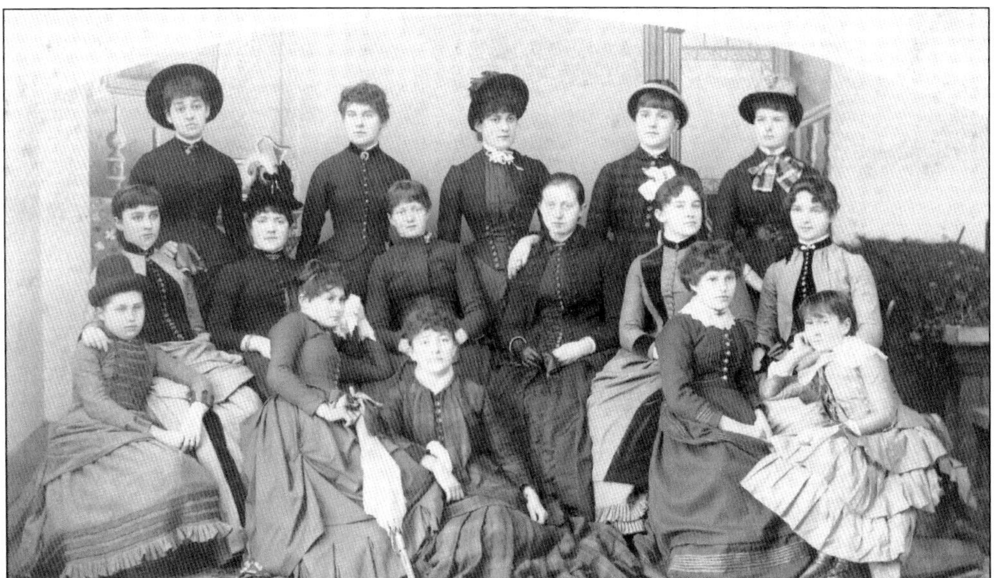
This group of Annie Wright Seminary students shows what the fashions were like when the above photograph was taken. The seminary opened while Washington was still a territory, with 46 students and a faculty of 10. The school was named for the daughter of Charles Wright, who was a director and later president of the Northern Pacific Railroad, responsible for getting the railroad completed to Puget Sound.

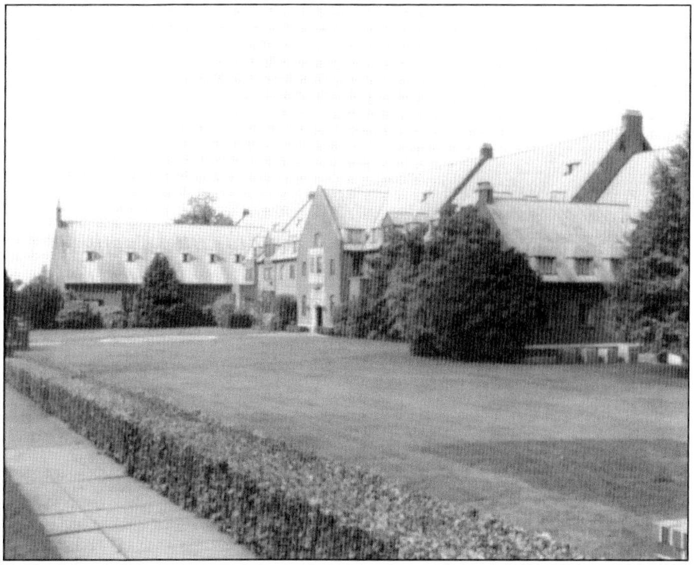

This photograph of Annie Wright Seminary was taken in 1971, long after the school had moved from its original location and shortly after it was renamed Annie Wright School. In 2011, the name was again changed to Annie Wright Schools to highlight the institution's distinct combination of both coed and single-gender programs. The first group of middle school boys graduated in 1990, and the first program for high school boys started in 2017.

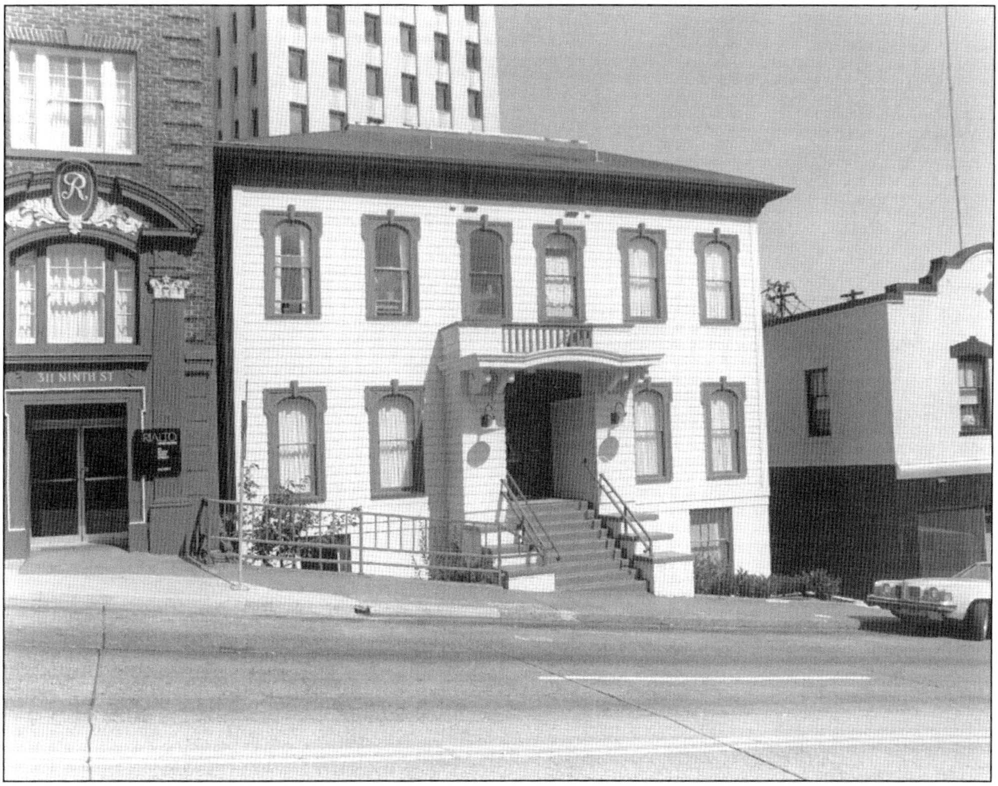

The Hosmer House, located at 309 S. Ninth Street, was built originally to be the home of Theodore Hosmer, New Tacoma's first mayor and manager of the Tacoma Land Company. It was first built in 1875, is one of the oldest known residences in Tacoma, and was relocated from its original site of 748–750 St. Helens Avenue in 1904. After a few renovations and upgrades through the years, Pioneer Human Services currently owns and maintains this building as the Exley Apartments. The building was added to the Tacoma Register of Historic Places on July 19, 2016.

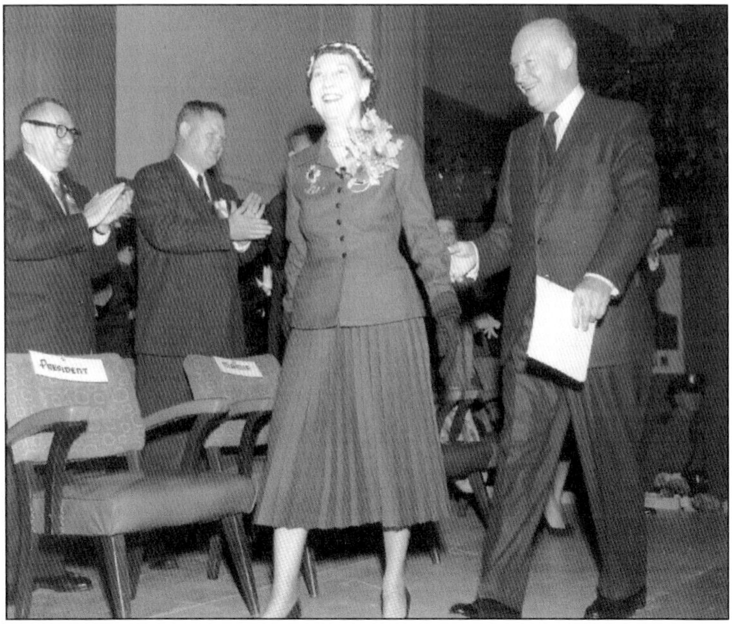

Four days after his 66th birthday, Pres. Dwight D. Eisenhower, shown with his wife, Mamie, is heading into the College of Puget Sound fieldhouse to address about 8,000 Tacomans prior to the November elections. Tacoma mayor John Anderson is shown to the left of Mamie.

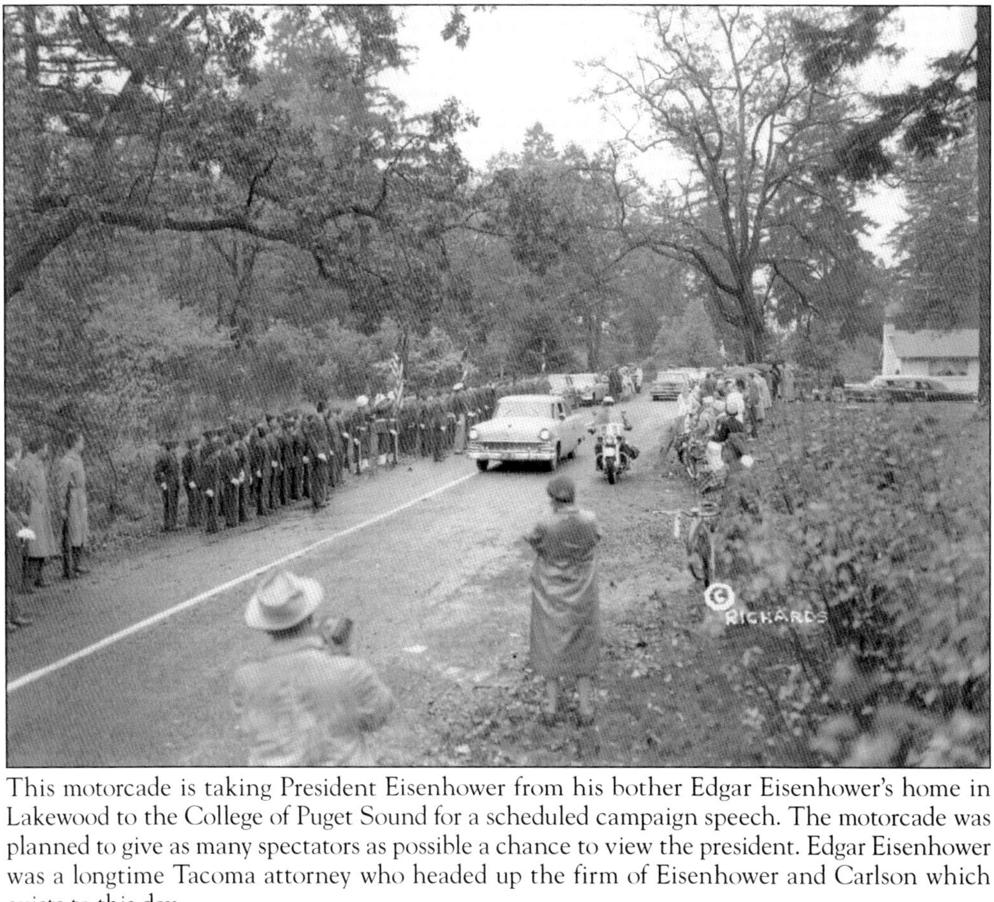

This motorcade is taking President Eisenhower from his bother Edgar Eisenhower's home in Lakewood to the College of Puget Sound for a scheduled campaign speech. The motorcade was planned to give as many spectators as possible a chance to view the president. Edgar Eisenhower was a longtime Tacoma attorney who headed up the firm of Eisenhower and Carlson which exists to this day.

Six

Then and Now

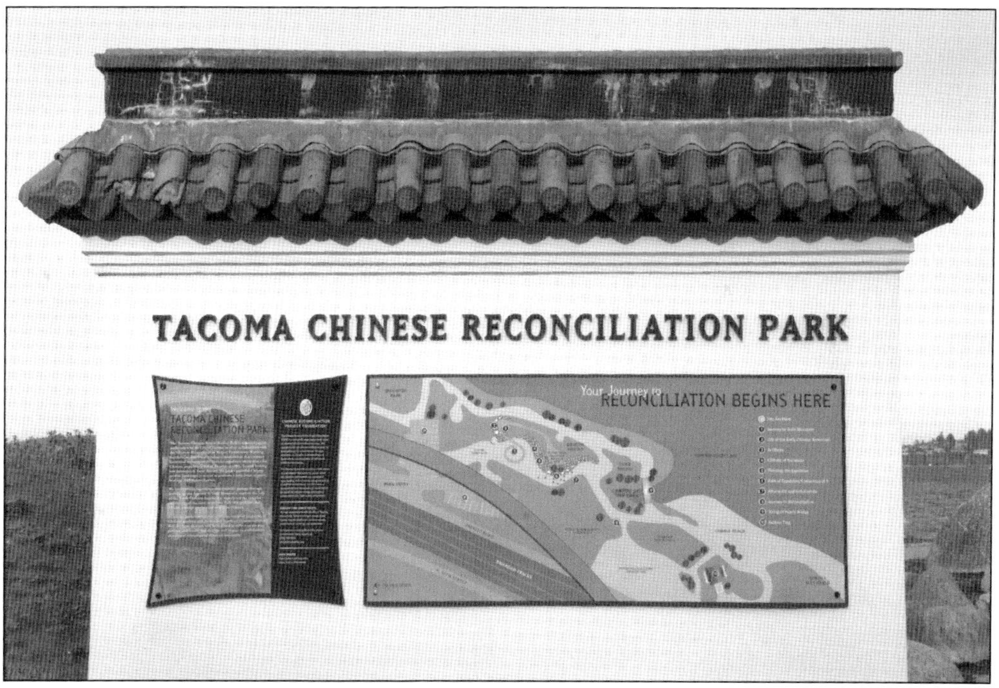

City of Tacoma Resolution No. 32415 was adopted by the Tacoma City Council on November 30, 1993, as a way to reconcile the expulsion of the Chinese community in 1885. The Chinese Reconciliation Project Citizens Committee had since September 1992 sought a way to reconcile the expulsion of the Chinese community and recommended a "living memorial which will be an educational tool to prevent the recurrence of similar events and to promote a peaceful, multicultural community." Because of the actions of the committee and city council, Tacoma has a Chinese Reconciliation Park on Ruston Way. (Photograph by author.)

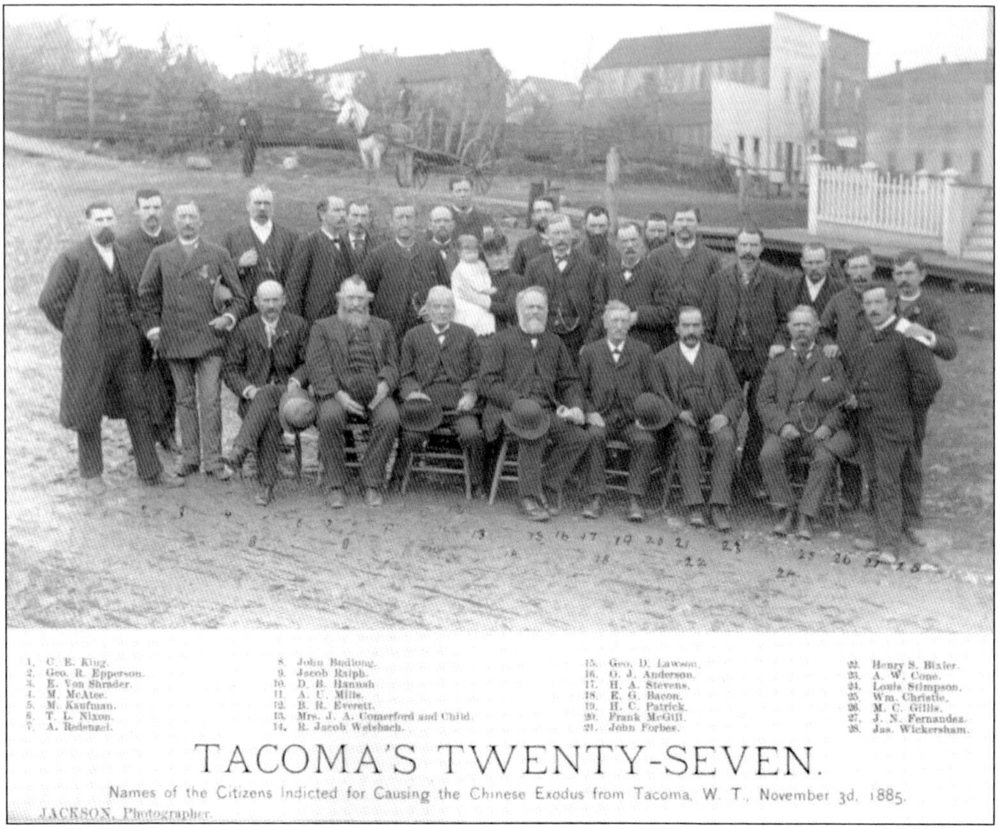

On November 3, 1885, a group of prominent Tacoma leaders marched Chinese residents to the train station and forced them aboard a train to Portland. In the following days, many structures in the Chinese community were burned. This became known as the "Tacoma Method" of dealing with what was perceived as a Chinese problem at the time. On November 7, Mayor Weisbach, the fire chief, and 25 others who were involved with the expulsion were indicted on felony conspiracy charges. This group became known as the Tacoma 27. After many procedural delays and appeals, all the indictments were dropped in 1887.

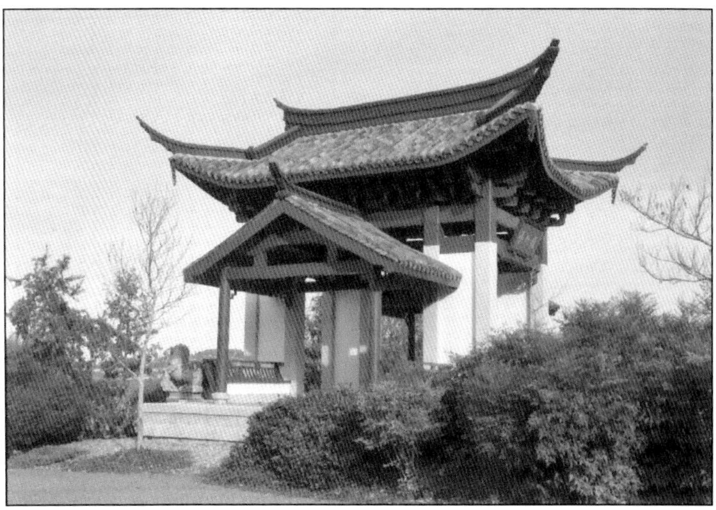

The Chinese Reconciliation Park is a four-acre park at the southern end of Ruston Way waterfront along Commencement Bay, in the area of the early Chinese settlement that was burned down during the expulsion. (Photograph by author.)

The Tacoma Elks Temple at 565 Broadway was built in 1915 and actively used until 1965, when the Elks moved to another location near Allenmore. This lodge remained empty and neglected until purchased by McMenamins in 2009. The building was listed in the National Register of Historic Places on December 23, 1977. McMenamins plans to open it as an entirely new and refurbished facility in 2019.

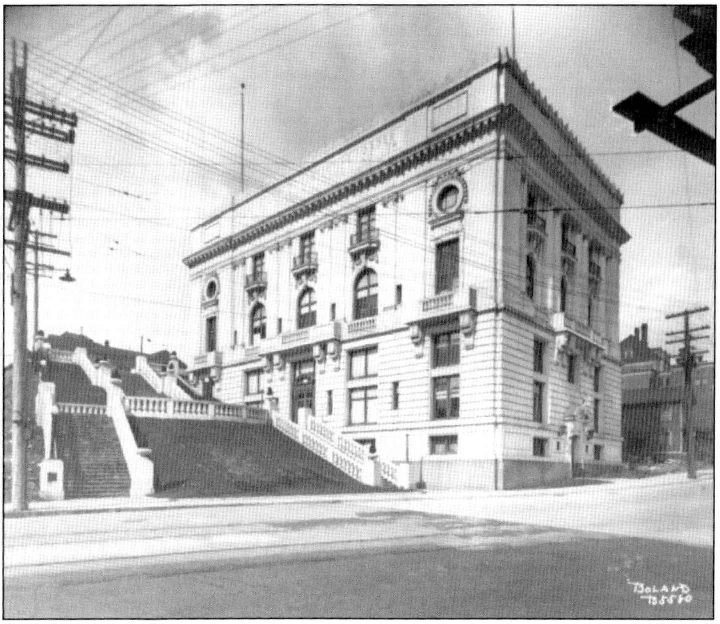

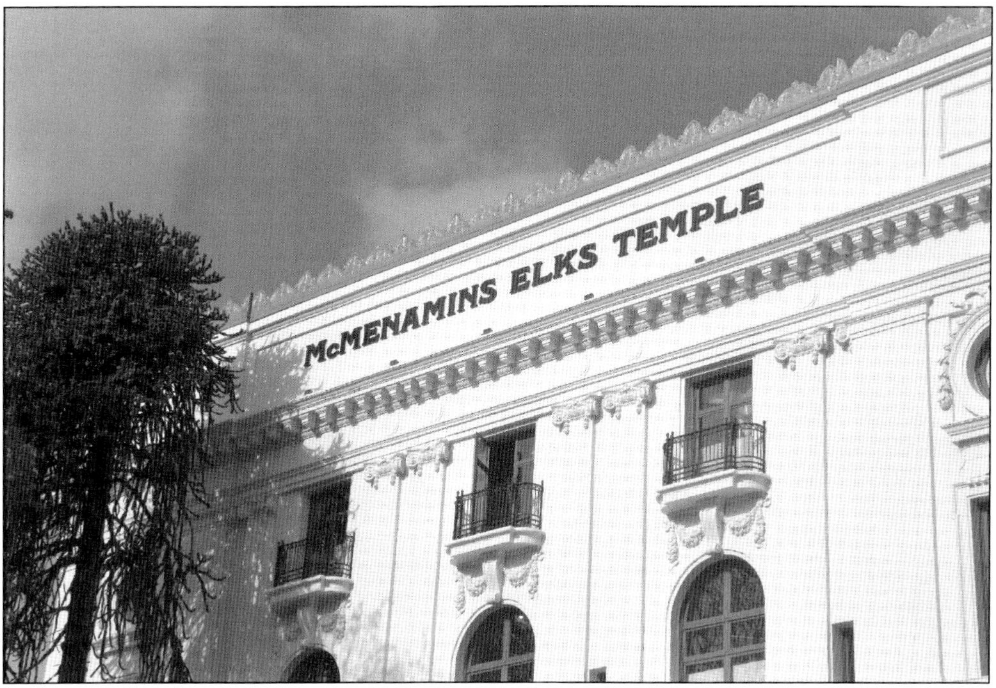

The remodeled Elks Temple is to have six levels with a mix of 45 hotel rooms with private baths. There also will be conference rooms, three restaurants, a brewery, a game room, and a music venue. An outdoor cafe and patio along the Spanish Steps eventually will offer outdoor acoustic music. The planned opening date is spring 2019. (Photograph by author.)

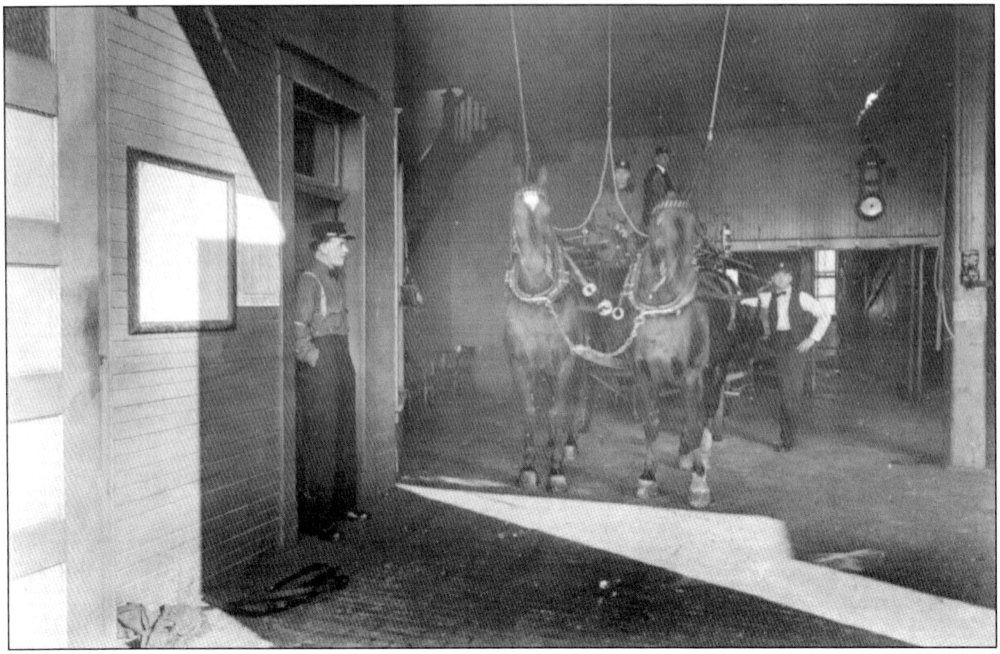

Earl G. Jones looks over three firefighters and two horses inside Engine House No. 9 before the turn of the 20th century. The "new" Engine House No. 9 was built from brick in 1907. This fire station is located at 611 North Pine Street.

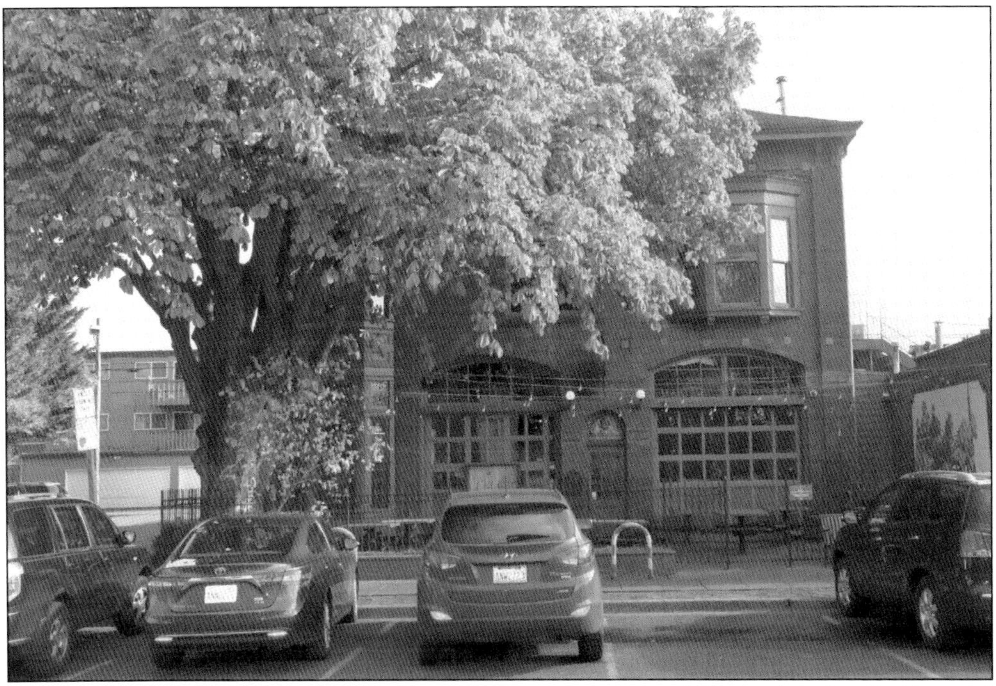

Engine House No. 9 is now a tavern and brewery serving customers daily. It is listed in the National Register of Historic Places. (Photograph by author.)

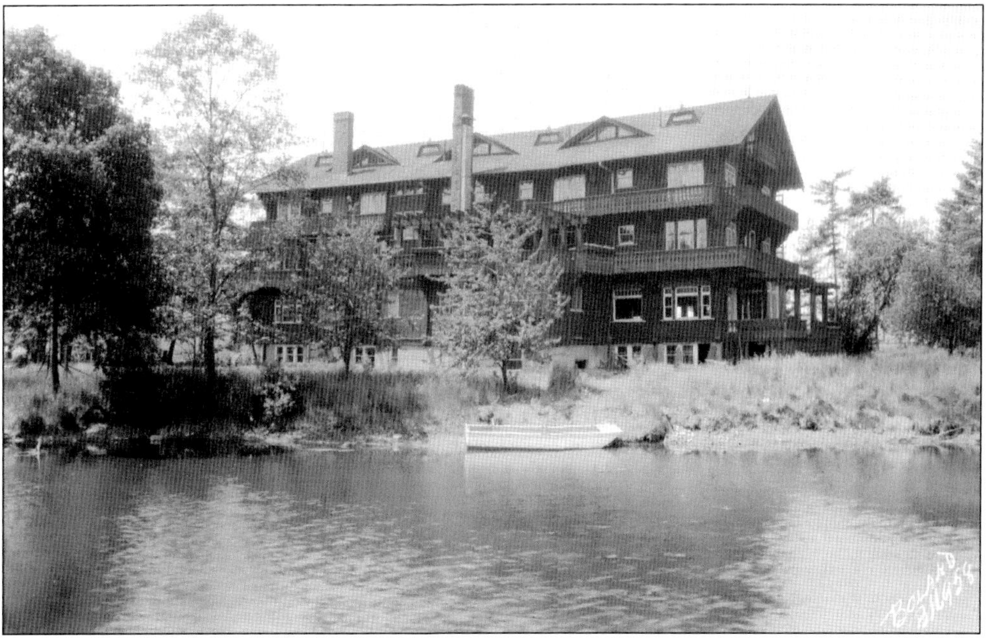

This is the Hotel Hesperides as it looked in June 1927, shortly after it was acquired by Tacoma's Metropolitan Park District. Aaron R. Titlow created this resort hotel on the 200 acres he owned on what is now called Titlow Beach. The hotel had 30 rooms within the three-and-a-half-story structure. The grand opening was in 1911, and it was a tourist destination until Titlow passed away in 1923. (Courtesy Washington State Historical Society)

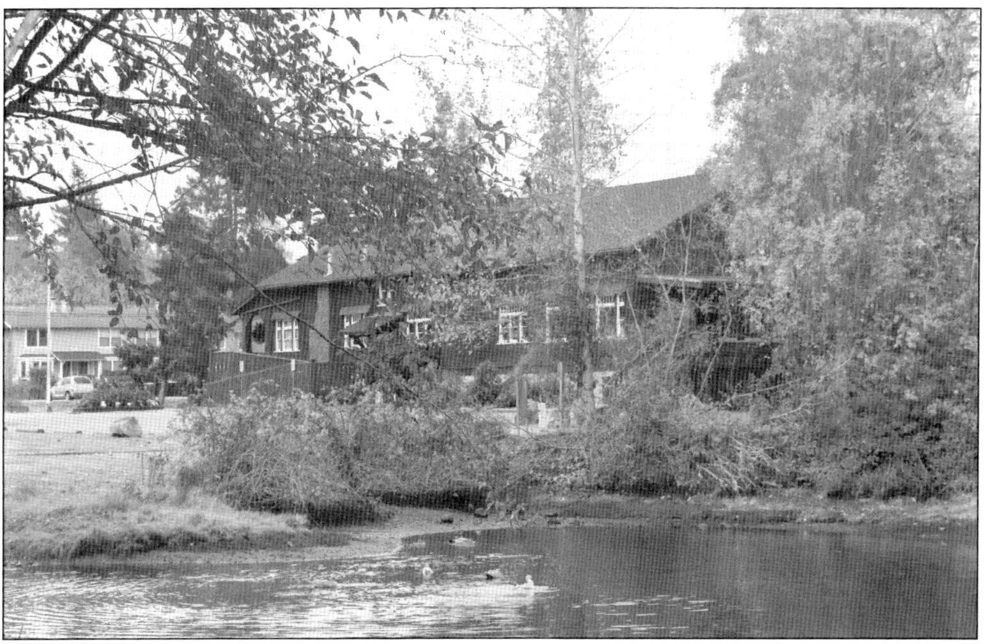

In 1928, the Tacoma Metropolitan Park District opened Titlow Lodge. During a Works Progress Administration park improvement project in 1937–1941, the top two stories were removed. The Titlow Lodge/Hotel Hesperides was placed on the Tacoma Register of Historic Places on April 3, 2018. (Photograph by author.)

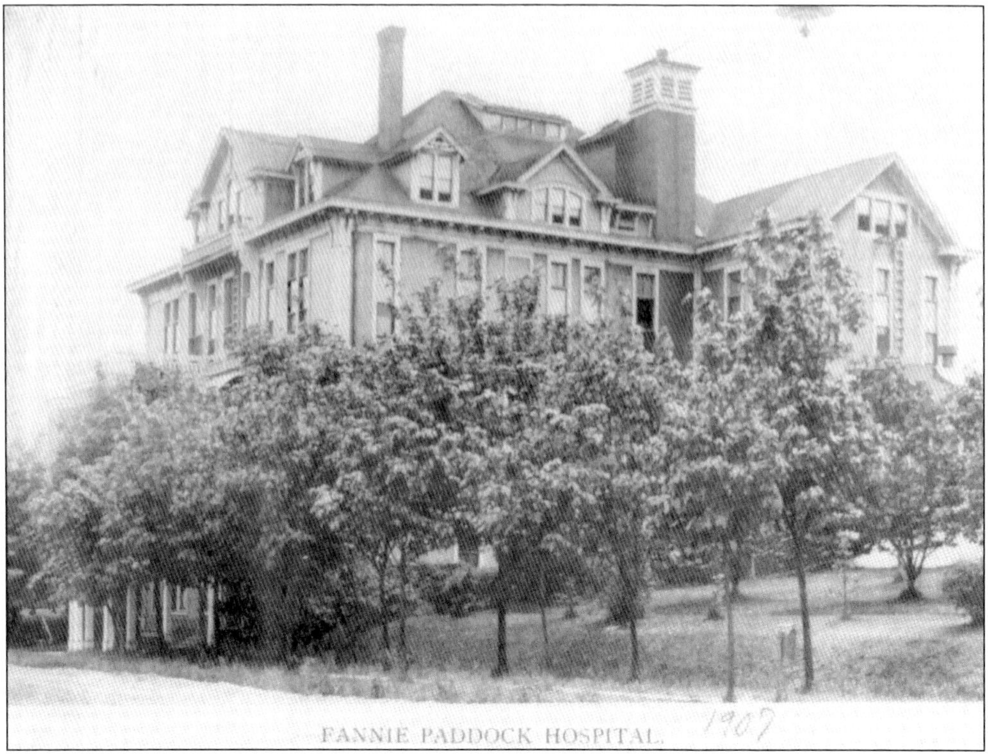

Fannie C. Paddock Memorial Hospital was dedicated on April 29, 1882, at 2511 N. Starr Street. MultiCare Health System's roots date to the founding of this hospital. Bishop John A. Paddock established the hospital and named it for his wife, who had passed away only a year earlier.

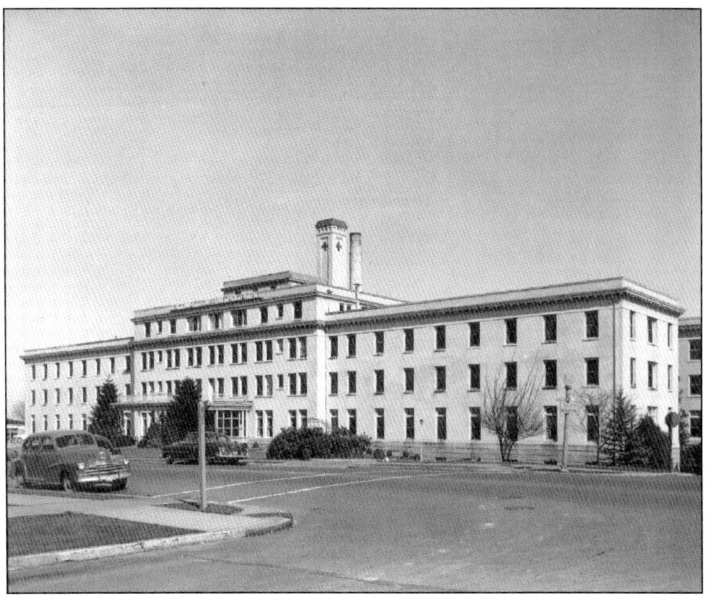

Tacoma General Hospital is seen here in 1954 as a comparison to what the Fannie C. Paddock Memorial Hospital looked like before the turn of the 20th century. Today, Tacoma General Hospital is a state-of-the-art level II trauma center with 437 beds. Adjacent to it is a 72-bed level II trauma center for children, named Mary Bridge Children's Hospital and Health Center.

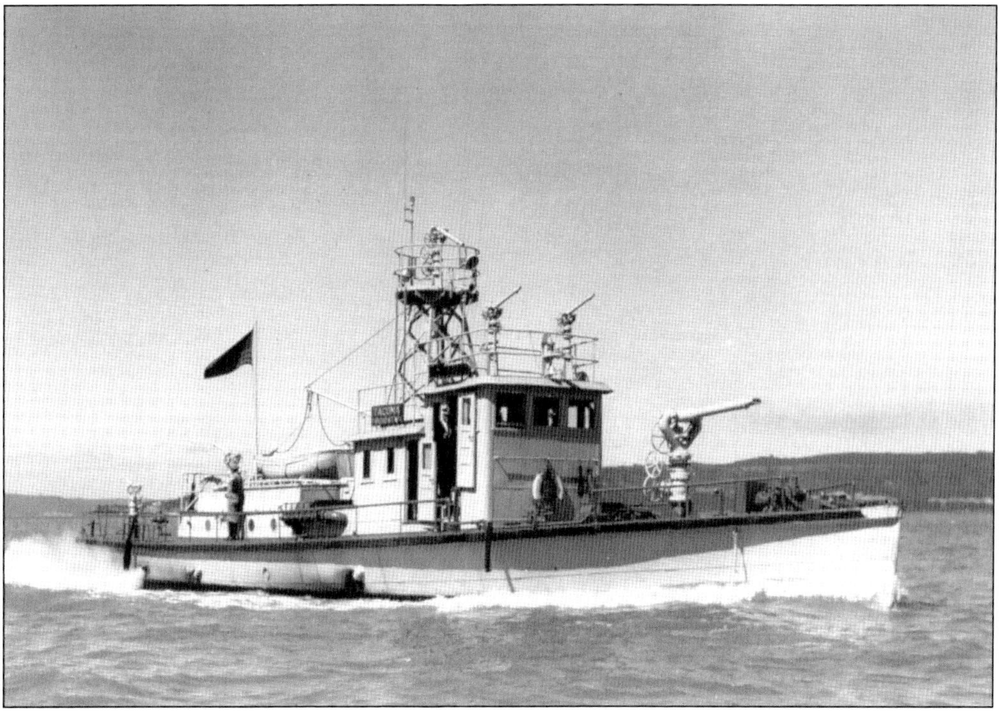

Tacoma fireboat No. 1, Tacoma's first fireboat, is seen here. She was launched in 1929 and served 36 miles of marine shoreline for over 53 years before being retired in 1982.

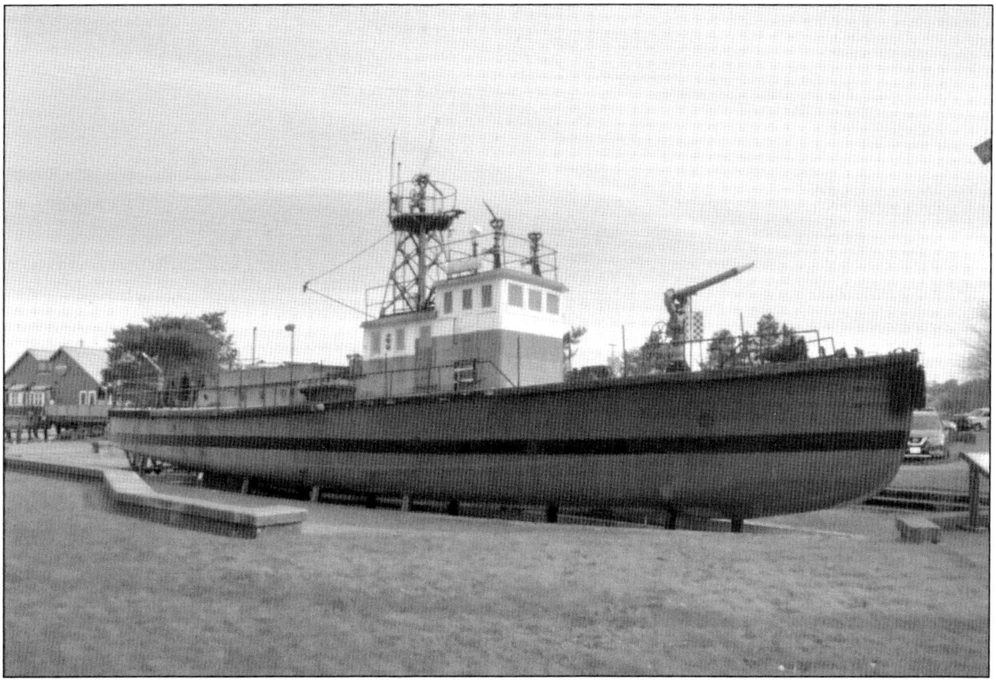

Fireboat No. 1 is seen here as she appears today on Ruston Way. In 1989, she was designated one of only five fireboats listed as a National Historic Landmark and remains on display on Ruston Way. (Photograph by author.)

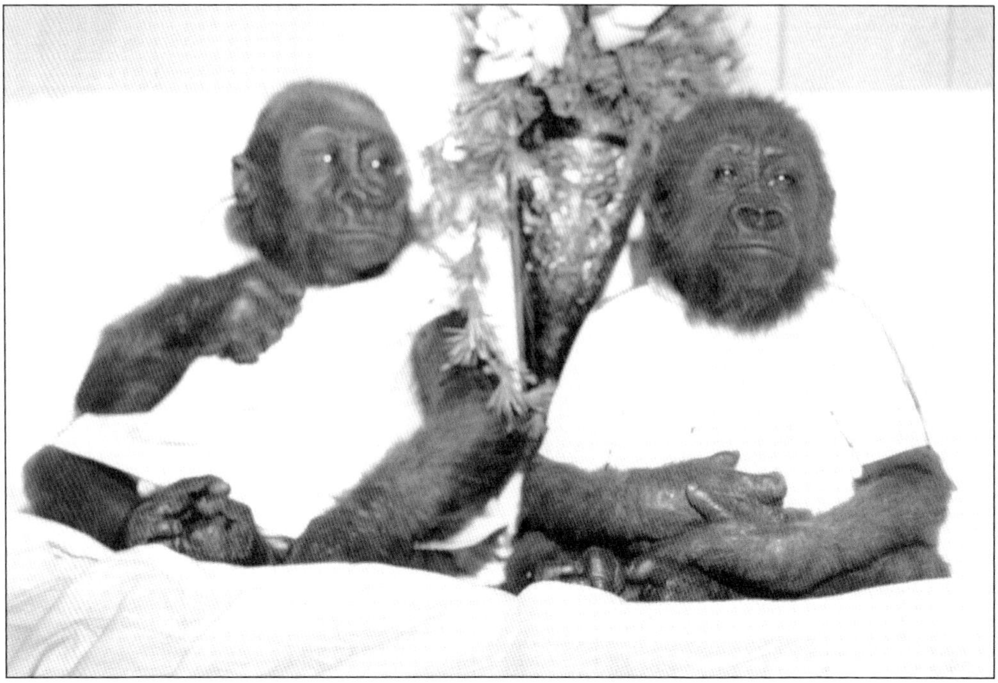

The owner of the B&I Circus Store on South Tacoma Way, E.L. Irwin, purchased these two gorillas, Burma and Ivan, in August 1964. Burma passed away shortly after arriving from the Congo, but Ivan continued to live off and on at the Irwin home until he was moved permanently to the little gorilla house at the B&I store in 1967, where he continued to live for nearly 30 years before being transferred to Woodland Park Zoo in Seattle for a short time before being eventually moved to the Atlanta Zoo, where he passed away on August 20, 2012.

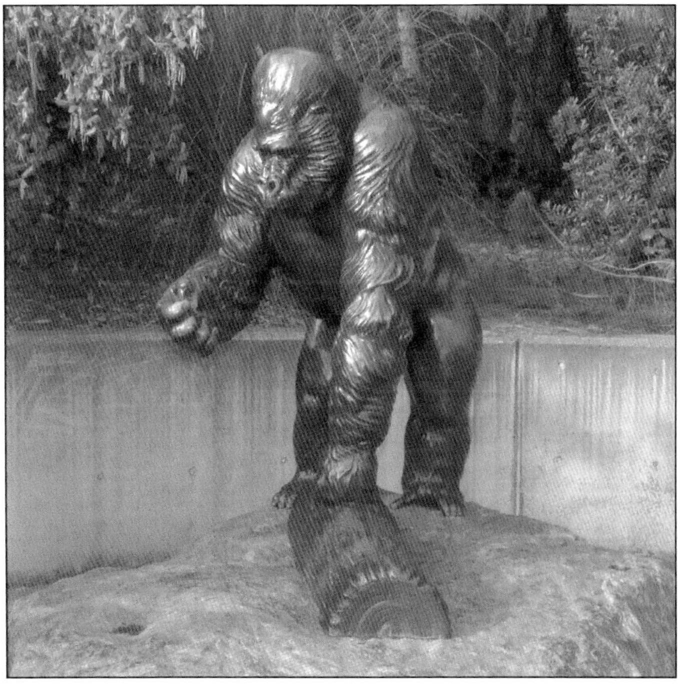

Ivan is now a 600-pound bronze sculpture near the entrance of Point Defiance Zoo & Aquarium in Tacoma. He now enjoys fresh air, sweeping views of Commencement Bay, and visits from admirers from all over the world. He is now in nature, surrounded by trees and wildlife within one of the largest urban parks in the United States. His ashes have been mixed within the bronze of this sculpture. Presently, there are no captive gorillas at Point Defiance Zoo. (Photograph by author.)

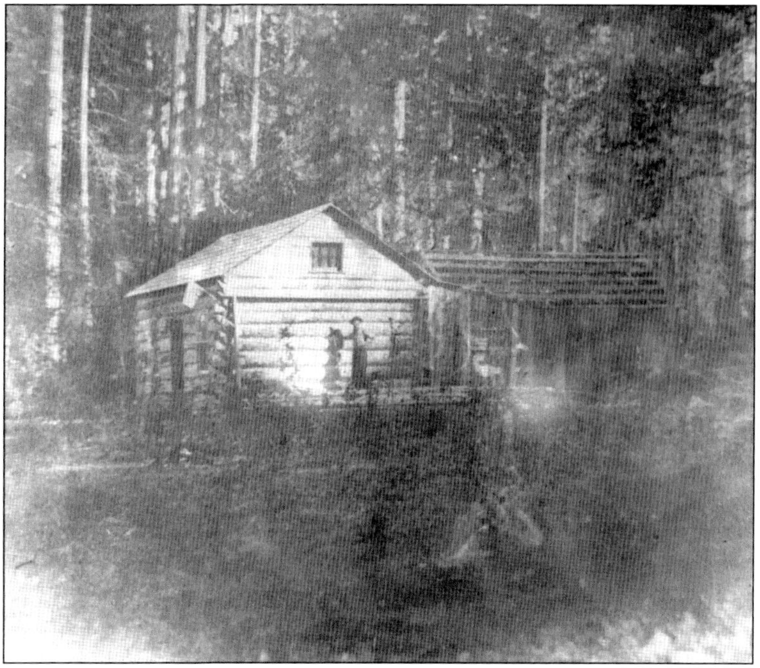

Job Carr was Tacoma's first permanent settler, and this is the log cabin he built near the beach in Old Town in 1865. By 1869, this cabin became the first post office and first polling place in what is now called Old Town. Job Carr was considered Tacoma's first mayor before formal incorporation took place in 1875.

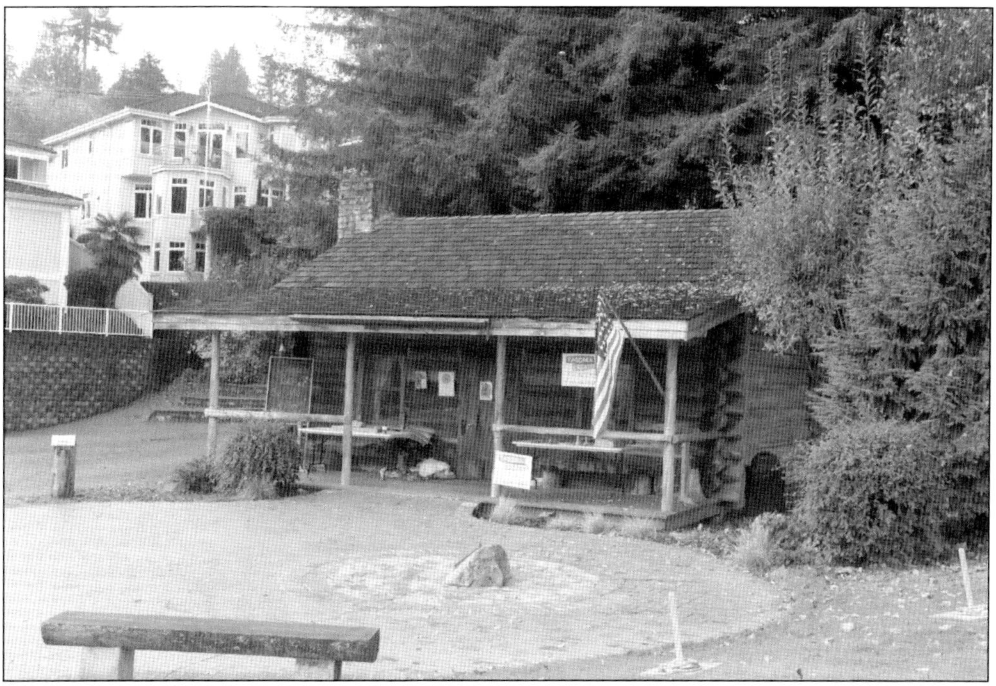

The Job Carr Cabin Museum is a replica of Tacoma's first permanent non-Native residence. It was built in 2000, about a block away from the original site of Job's frontier home. The museum is open year-round and staffed and financed by volunteer sponsors and donors in the community. Many educational programs and activities are put on for schools and groups upon request. (Photograph by author.)

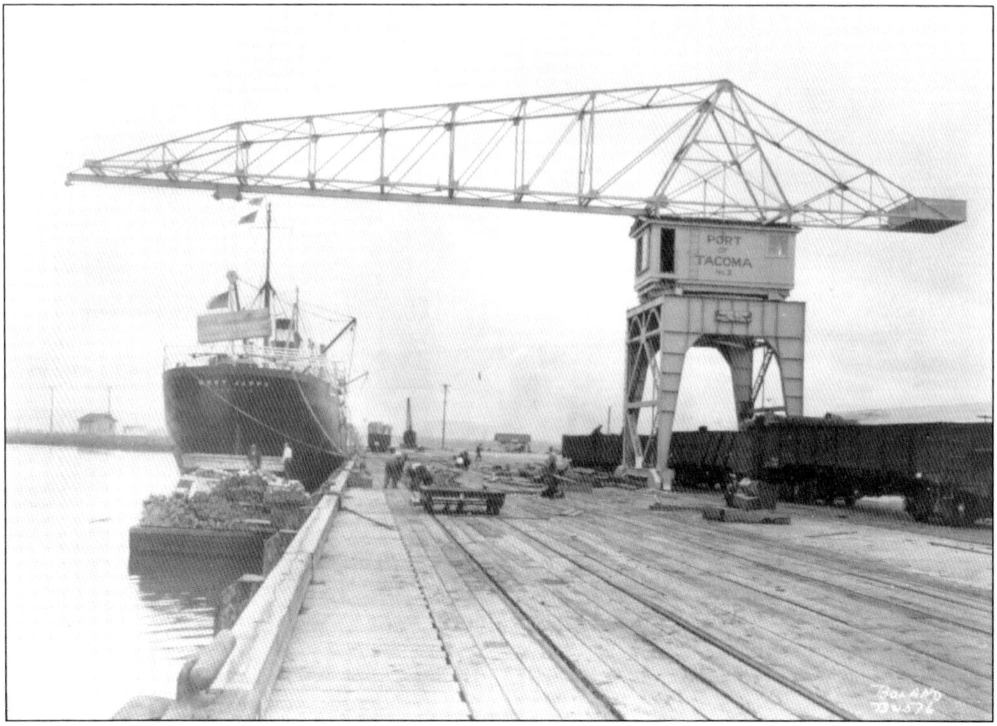

This crane was used on the wide dock at the Port of Tacoma in 1921. It was tall enough that a freight train could pass through its legs. The cargo ship *West Jappa* is shown to the left. The port was created by a vote of Pierce County citizens on November 5, 1918.

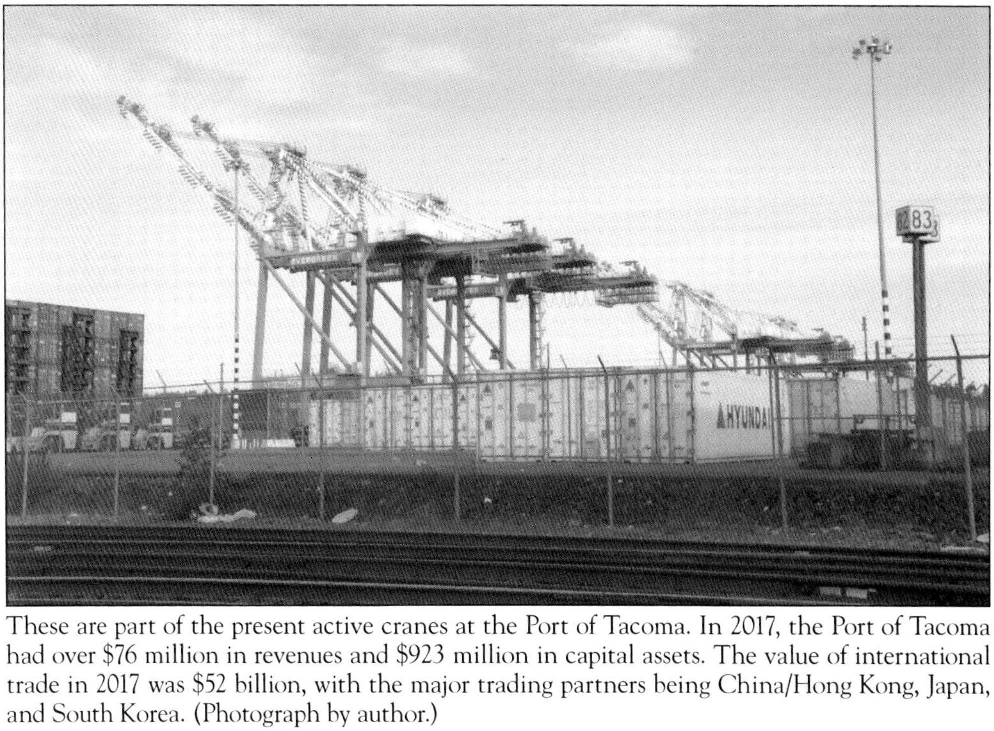

These are part of the present active cranes at the Port of Tacoma. In 2017, the Port of Tacoma had over $76 million in revenues and $923 million in capital assets. The value of international trade in 2017 was $52 billion, with the major trading partners being China/Hong Kong, Japan, and South Korea. (Photograph by author.)

Bibliography

Bancroft, Hubert Howe. *History of Washington, Idaho, and Montana 1845–1889*. San Francisco, CA: the History Company, 1890.

Harvey, Paul W. *Tacoma Headlines: an Account of Tacoma News and Newspapers from 1873 to 1962*. Tacoma, WA: *Tacoma News Tribune*, 1962.

Hawthorne, Julian. *History of Washington the Evergreen State*. New York, NY: American Historical Publishing Co., 1893.

Hunt, Herbert. *Tacoma, Its History and Its Builders*. Chicago, IL: S.J. Clarke Publishing Company, 1916.

Hunt, Herbert and Floyd C. Kaylor. *Washington West of the Cascades*. Chicago, IL: S.J. Clarke Publishing Company, 1917.

Jepsen, David J. and David J. Norberg. *Contested Boundaries*. Hoboken, NJ: Wiley Blackwell, 2017.

MacGougan, Denny. *Tacoma*. Fox Island, WA: Baker/Anderson Enterprises, 2003.

Peters, Nick. *Historic Photos of Tacoma*. Nashville, TN: Turner Publishing Company, 2007.

Pierce County. *Survey & Inventory of Historic Properties*. Tacoma, WA: Artifacts Architectural Consulting, 2010.

Pierce County Pioneer Association. *Commemorative Celebration at Sequalitchew Lake, Pierce County Washington, July 5, 1906*. Tacoma, WA: Vaughan and Morrill Printing, 1906.

Prosch, Thomas W. *McCarver and Tacoma*. Seattle, WA: Lowman & Hanford Stationery and Printing Company, 1906.

Discover Thousands of Local History Books Featuring Millions of Vintage Images

Arcadia Publishing, the leading local history publisher in the United States, is committed to making history accessible and meaningful through publishing books that celebrate and preserve the heritage of America's people and places.

Find more books like this at
www.arcadiapublishing.com

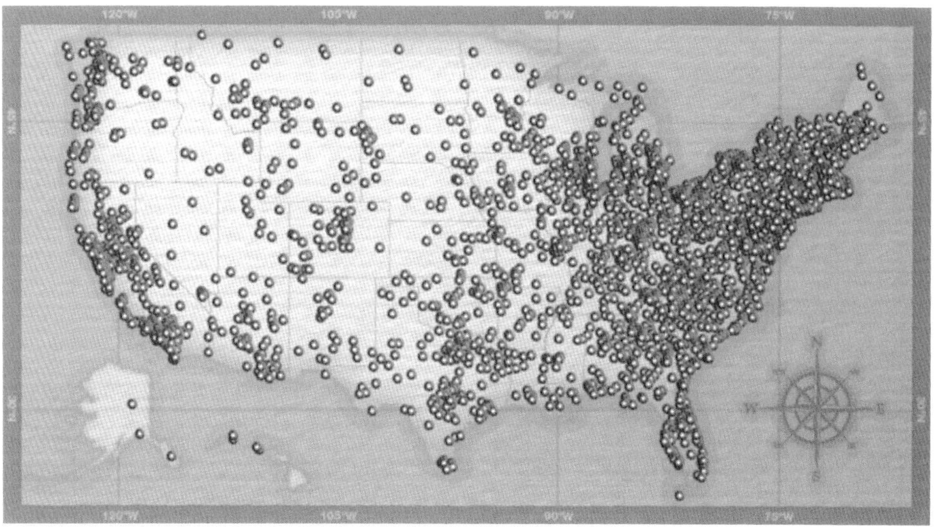

Search for your hometown history, your old stomping grounds, and even your favorite sports team.

Consistent with our mission to preserve history on a local level, this book was printed in South Carolina on American-made paper and manufactured entirely in the United States. Products carrying the accredited Forest Stewardship Council (FSC) label are printed on 100 percent FSC-certified paper.

MADE IN THE USA